Inter-agency
Network for Education
in Emergencies

Minimum Standards for Education:

Preparedness, Response, Recovery

Humanitarian
Standards
Partnership

2024 Edition

The Inter-agency Network for Education in Emergencies (INEE) is an open, global network of members working together within a humanitarian and development framework to ensure that all individuals have the right to a quality, safe, relevant, and equitable education.

INEE's work is founded on the fundamental right to education.

inee.org

© 2024 Inter-agency Network for Education in Emergencies (INEE)

1st edition 2004
2nd edition: 2010
3rd edition: 2024

A catalogue record for this book is available from the British Library.

ISBN: 978-1-78853-443-7 Paperback

ISBN: 978-1-78853-444-4 PDF

DOI: http://doi.org/10.3362/9781788534444

Suggested Citation:

Inter-agency Network for Education in Emergencies (INEE). (2024). *Minimum Standards for Education: Preparedness, Response, Recovery*. INEE. https://inee.org/minimum-standards

License:

The Inter-agency Network for Education in Emergencies wishes to thank the many individuals and organizations who collaborated on the INEE MS, 2024 Edition. For a complete list of acknowledgments, visit the INEE website.

To give feedback or suggestions for the improvement of this publication, please contact minimum.standards@inee.org.

Practical Action Publishing Ltd

www.practicalactionpublishing.com

Since 1974, Practical Action Publishing has published and disseminated books and information in support of international development work throughout the world. Practical Action Publishing is a trading name of Practical Action Publishing Ltd (Company Reg. No. 1159018), the wholly owned publishing company of Practical Action. Practical Action Publishing trades only in support of its parent charity objectives and any profits are covenanted back to Practical Action (Charity Reg. No.247257, Group VAT Registration No. 880 9924 76).

The views and opinions in this publication are those of the editors and do not represent those of Practical Action Publishing Ltd or its parent charity Practical Action. Reasonable efforts have been made to publish reliable data and information, but the editors and publisher cannot assume responsibility for the validity of all materials or for the consequences of their use.

The manufacturer's authorised representative in the EU for product safety is Lightning Source France, 1 Av. Johannes Gutenberg, 78310 Maurepas, France.
compliance@lightningsource.fr

TABLE OF CONTENTS

FOREWORD

Today, hundreds of millions of learners worldwide are affected by crises, which threaten their access to the transformative effects of inclusive and equitable quality education. Tens of millions are out of school altogether, and thus denied their right to education.

Yet, evidence shows that quality education provides physical, psychosocial, and cognitive protection during emergencies. The commitment enshrined in Sustainable Development Goal 4—to achieve quality education for all—reaffirms education as one of the most powerful and proven vehicles to rise above the impacts of crises and support sustainable development.

Since 2004, the INEE Minimum Standards have provided a framework for quality education in emergencies. They have been a key tool for convening education stakeholders around common standards and outcomes. As part of the Humanitarian Standards Partnership, they have further articulated the belief that people affected by crises have a right to live life with dignity and that humanitarian actors must take all possible steps to alleviate the human suffering that arises out of calamity and conflict.

Since the INEE MS were updated in 2010, the field of education in emergencies has changed significantly. Through sustained advocacy, the fundamental human right to quality education for those affected by crises has become firmly established as a core part of the global education agenda and of humanitarian response. The life-saving and life-sustaining role of education is now more widely accepted, due to the efforts of those working to advance education in emergencies across the globe.

This right is now reflected in global policy commitments and national practice, most notably Sustainable Development Goal 4 and the Education 2030: Incheon Declaration and Framework for Action. Additionally, the INEE Minimum Standards are also expressly recognized in the Incheon Declaration and Framework for Action (Section 26) and the United Nations General Assembly Resolution on the Right to Education in Emergency Situations (Section 5) as the principal guide for education in emergencies planning and response. In 2016, Education Cannot Wait, the first global fund dedicated to education in emergencies and protracted crises, was founded to generate a greater shared political, operational, and financial commitment to meet the educational needs of millions affected by crises. Global convenings such as the 2019 and 2023 Global Refugee Forum and the 2022 Transforming Education Summit have also helped mobilize political will and action around education in emergencies. Through pledges made at the 2019 Global Refugee Forum, both the Initiative for Strengthening Education in Emergencies Coordination and the Geneva Global Hub for Education in Emergencies were established. Additionally, the global commitments outlined during the 2022 Transforming Education Summit resulted in more than 40 countries and over 100 partners outlining plans and commitments that uphold the right to education, including in emergency situations.

However, at the same time, new challenges have arisen to which the field of education in emergencies must respond. Beginning in 2020, the COVID-19 pandemic caused widespread school closures, imperiling the hard-earned gains made in the education sector. It compounded the struggles of under-resourced education systems, especially those in crisis contexts. It threatened the education of millions of students, who lost months of learning and have few prospects for regaining what was lost or, for some, of ever returning to school.

Today, the escalating effects of climate change, unprecedented forced displacement, and migration, and a rapid increase in the number, complexity, and length of humanitarian crises have made clear the need for responses that work at the humanitarian-development-peacebuilding nexus to support more resilient education systems. At the same time, the global humanitarian community has made commitments to create more equitable and locally led humanitarian action and demonstrate new ways of working.

This update of the INEE Minimum Standards is therefore especially timely. It addresses emerging challenges by ensuring that the Standards remain relevant, accessible, and adaptable, and continue to support education stakeholders who are striving to meet the collective goal of fulfilling the ambitions set out in Sustainable Development Goal 4 by 2030.

This third edition has been realized through the dedicated engagement of more than 1,600 individuals across 35 countries, representing diverse contexts and experiences. INEE conducted stakeholder-led consultations, both online and in-person, in 17 crisis-affected countries, and received inputs in more than 14 languages.

The three iterations of the INEE Minimum Standards reflect the contributions of more than 5,000 individuals who have worked collectively to achieve the ambition of providing quality education for people of all ages who are living in crisis situations. They are a true example of inter-agency and inter-sectoral collaboration. This 2024 edition continues to build on the goals of improving the quality of education preparedness, response, and recovery; increasing access to safe and relevant learning opportunities; and ensuring accountability to those we serve.

We urge all stakeholders around the globe to take this opportunity to realize these standards, and by doing so, demonstrate the commitment to uphold the right to education at all times.

Audrey Azoulay
UNESCO
Director-General

Catherine Russell
UNICEF
Executive Director

Filippo Grandi
UNHCR
UN High Commissioner for Refugees

ACRONYMS

ADCAP	Age and Disability Capacity Program
CBO	Community-based organization
CHS	Core Humanitarian Standard
CSO	Civil society organization
CVA	Cash and voucher assistance
DRR	Disaster risk reduction
ECD	Early childhood development
ECW	Education Cannot Wait
EiE	Education in emergencies
EMIS	Education management information system
ESP	Education sector plan
GADRRRES	Global Alliance for Disaster Risk Reduction and Resilience in the Education Sector
GCPEA	Global Coalition to Protect Education From Attack
GEC	Global Education Cluster
IASC	Inter-Agency Standing Committee
IDP	Internally displaced person
IFRC	International Federation of Red Cross and Red Crescent Societies
ILO	International Labour Organization
INEE	Inter-agency Network for Education in Emergencies
INEE MS	INEE Minimum Standards
ISP	Information sharing protocol
JENA	Joint education needs assessment
LGBTQIA+	Lesbian, gay, bisexual, transgender, queer, intersex, asexual, and agender
MHPSS	Mental health and psychosocial support

NGO	Non-governmental organization
OCHA	Office for the Coordination of Humanitarian Affairs
OPD	Organization of persons with disabilities
SDG	Sustainable Development Goal
SEEP	Small Enterprise Education and Promotion
SEL	Social and emotional learning
SRGBV	School-related gender-based violence
TEP	Transitional education plan
TVET	Technical and vocational education and training
UN	United Nations
UNESCO	United Nations Educational, Scientific and Cultural Organization
UNHCR	United Nations Refugee Agency
UNICEF	United Nations Children's Fund
WASH	Water, sanitation, and hygiene

INTRODUCTION

Education is a human right for all, and this right continues during emergencies. Education is life-sustaining and life-saving, as acknowledged in the UN General Assembly Resolution on the Right to Education in Emergency Situations.

What is Education in Emergencies?

Education in emergencies (EiE) refers to the provision of equitable, inclusive, and quality learning opportunities for people of all ages in situations of crisis, from preparedness to response, and through to recovery. It includes early childhood development, primary, secondary, non-formal, technical, vocational, higher, and adult education. It can be delivered through different modalities, including in-person teaching and learning and the various approaches to distance education (i.e., high-tech, low-tech, no-tech). It also can occur in a variety of contexts (e.g., offline, online, or hybrid). In an emergency situation and through to recovery, quality education provides physical, psychosocial, and cognitive protection that can save and sustain lives. Common emergencies in which EiE is essential include conflicts, protracted crises, situations of violence, forced displacement, disasters related to natural hazards, and public health crises. EiE is a wider concept than "emergency education response," which is an essential part of EiE.

Education is especially critical for the hundreds of millions of learners affected by crises, but it is often seriously disrupted, leaving them unable to enjoy the transformative effects of inclusive and equitable quality education. EiE promotes dignity and sustains life by offering these children, young people, and adults a safe learning environment. Schools and other learning environments can be an entry point for identifying and supporting learners who need essential services beyond the education sector, such as protection, nutrition, water, sanitation, and hygiene (WASH), and health. For learners with disabilities, education can provide access to early detection, assistive devices and technologies, and intervention services. It can offer education on sexual and reproductive health and rights, as well as referral services for those experiencing gender-based violence, which is particularly important for women and girls who are most at risk of such violence. Education saves lives by physically protecting learners from the dangers and exploitation often common in a crisis environment, and by providing nurturing care. It gives learners life-saving information to help them strengthen their survival skills and coping mechanisms. Collaboration between the education sector and other relevant sectors such as WASH, protection, shelter, and mental health and psychosocial support is important in establishing safe, learner-friendly spaces.

What is quality education?

Understanding of what "quality" means may vary between contexts, and different actors may have their own definitions. Broadly, quality education encompasses seven characteristics.

1. **Rights-based:** Quality education is accessible, equitable, protective, participatory, non-discriminatory, and inclusive of all people.
2. **Contextualized and relevant:** Education systems address the needs of the learners by using culturally and linguistically relevant learning materials.
3. **Holistic development of learners:** Quality education promotes cognitive development, social and emotional skills, mental health and psychosocial wellbeing, values of responsible citizenship, economic sustainability, and peacebuilding.
4. **Teaching and learning:** Teachers receive adequate compensation and relevant training so that they understand pedagogic content and have the knowledge and skills they need to support learners' holistic development.
5. **Enabling resources:** Quality education includes adequate and relevant resources for teaching and learning and fosters links between the resources available in the learning environment, home, and community to improve holistic learning outcomes.
6. **Learning outcomes:** Quality education allows learners to develop the necessary knowledge, skills, and competencies to meet certification requirements, progress through the education system, and access lifelong learning opportunities.
7. **Learning continuity:** Quality education provides sustained learning opportunities across the humanitarian-development-peacebuilding nexus.

Education also can lessen the psychosocial impact of crises by creating structure and routines, and by providing stability and hope for the future. It can help learners adapt and prepare them to thrive in a complex and unpredictable world. Education also helps to strengthen learners' problem-solving and coping skills so they can make informed decisions about how to survive and to care for themselves and others in dangerous environments. It enables learners to develop critical awareness and to assert their agency in discussions of social justice and human rights, and through civic involvement and activism.

Communities also prioritize education during crises, as schools and other learning environments are often at the heart of the community. These spaces symbolize opportunity for future generations and hope for a better life.

Quality education can help learners and their families assert their dignity and build the life and the future they aspire to. It also can contribute directly to the social, economic, and political stability of a society. It reduces the risk of violent conflict by strengthening social cohesion and supporting conflict resolution and peacebuilding. Crisis planning and response can offer opportunities for national authorities, local and national actors, communities, and humanitarian and development actors to work together to create more equitable and inclusive education systems.

Education is always a human right

Human rights and humanitarian and refugee law make up the body of international law and normative standards that guarantee and regulate human rights and other protections, both in peacetime and during crises. The Inter-agency Network for Education in Emergencies Minimum Standards for Education: Preparedness, Response, Recovery (INEE MS) are based on human rights, specifically the right to education, as expressed in key human rights documents, such as the UN Universal Declaration of Human Rights and the Convention on the Rights of the Child (see Annex 3: Relevant Legal Instruments). The INEE MS aim to reflect the legal protections afforded to learners, education personnel, and education institutions by international humanitarian law.

The Education 2030: Incheon Declaration and Framework for Action and the Sustainable Development Goals (SDGs), particularly SDG 4, represent an important global commitment by the international community. These documents have developed and reaffirmed the right to education, giving specific attention to education during crises, including for displaced populations such as refugees, internally displaced persons (IDPs), and asylum seekers. The two documents stress the following:

- Inclusion and equity
- Gender equality
- Providing access to quality early childhood education and to lifelong learning opportunities for all young people and adults
- Improving the quality of existing education programs

The INEE MS are also based on the Sphere Humanitarian Charter, the Protection Principles of the United Nations Refugee Agency (UNHCR), and the Core Humanitarian Standard on Quality and Accountability. The Sphere Humanitarian Charter is based on the principles and provisions of international humanitarian law, international human rights law, refugee law, and the Code of Conduct for the International Red Cross and Red Crescent Movement and Non-Governmental Organizations (NGOs) in Disaster Relief. It expresses the belief that all people affected by crisis have the right to receive assistance and protection in order to ensure that their living conditions enable them to live life with dignity and security. The charter also cites the legal responsibility of states and warring parties to guarantee that right to protection and assistance. When the relevant authorities are unable or unwilling to fulfill these responsibilities, they are obliged to allow humanitarian organizations to provide protection and assistance. It is widely recognized that the provisions of human rights law that are applicable during armed conflict complement the protections afforded by international humanitarian law. In other words, the human rights law standards regarding what constitutes a "quality" education remain relevant in situations of armed conflict.

Human rights are universal and apply fully in emergency contexts. The right to education is both a human right and an enabling right, as education helps people develop the skills they need to achieve their full potential and exercise their rights, such as the right to life and good health. For example, once a person is able to read the safety warnings about landmines, they will know to avoid a field littered with mines. As outlined in General Comment No. 13 of the UN Committee on Economic, Social, and Cultural Rights, education is the primary vehicle by which economically and socially marginalized adults and children can lift themselves out of income poverty and obtain the means to participate fully in their communities. Education also plays a vital role in empowering women, in safeguarding children from exploitative and hazardous labor and sexual exploitation, in promoting human rights and democracy, and in protecting the environment.

Providing quality education to all is the responsibility of national authorities, the main duty bearers. They pass this responsibility on to education authorities, other relevant line ministries, and local education authorities. During emergencies, other actors, such as the UN, national and international NGOs, civil society, the private sector, and community-based organizations (CBOs), also can support education activities and share responsibility for the provision of education. The INEE MS provide a framework of good practice for all stakeholders to help achieve quality education.

In the INEE MS, education planning is based on the language and spirit of human rights law. The INEE MS bring to life the principles of participation, accountability, non-discrimination, and legal protection to provide quality education.

What are the INEE Minimum Standards?

The INEE MS contain 19 standards, each of which includes key actions and guidance notes. The purpose of the INEE MS is to improve the quality of education preparedness, response, and recovery; to increase access to safe and relevant learning opportunities; and to ensure that the actors who provide these services are held accountable.

The INEE MS are designed to be applicable to crisis response in many different situations, including emergencies caused by conflict, by natural hazards such as those induced by climate change, and slow- and rapid-onset crises in both rural and urban environments. No country or education system today is immune from crisis, and the INEE MS provide a common framework that can be applied in any economic, political, or social context.

The primary aims of the INEE MS are to provide a quality, coordinated humanitarian response in the education sector, and to help stakeholders protect the education rights and needs of people affected by crisis in ways that assert their agency and dignity. The INEE MS provide guidance on how to prepare for and respond to emergencies in equitable ways to reduce risk, improve future preparedness, and lay the foundation for providing quality education. This guidance will enable handbook users to build back stronger education systems during recovery and development, and to achieve more cost-effective, sustainable outcomes for crisis-affected communities.

The INEE MS are a key tool for all EiE stakeholders

The INEE MS offer a framework of technical knowledge and good practice for providing equitable and inclusive quality education during emergencies. This includes anticipatory action and prevention, preparedness, response, recovery, disaster risk reduction, and conflict mitigation. The INEE MS are a key tool for convening education stakeholders around common standards and outcomes. They offer a framework for coordinating the work of humanitarian and development organizations, which often work simultaneously to support education. To do so effectively, these actors must work together across the humanitarian-development-peacebuilding nexus.

Using this framework can bring stakeholders together at the country and global levels as they promote the standards, the key actions, and the guidance notes. Stakeholders include but are not limited to:

- Education authorities at the national, sub-national, and local level
- UN agencies
- Bilateral and multilateral donor agencies
- Civil society organizations (CSOs), NGOs, and CBOs, including community education committees
- Teachers and other education personnel and teachers unions
- Young people and youth-led organizations
- Members of inter-agency coordination mechanisms
- Education consultants
- Researchers and academics
- Human rights and humanitarian advocates

Using the INEE Minimum Standards

How are the INEE MS organized?

The INEE MS are organized into five domains related to specific areas of education. Each domain contains standards, and each standard is followed by key actions and guidance notes. Each chapter begins with an overview of the domain being addressed.

Figure 1: The five domains of the INEE MS

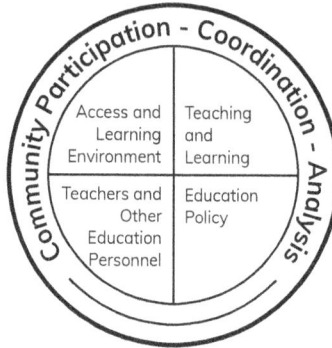

Domain 1: Foundational Standards for a Quality Response. The seven standards (1-7) in this domain form the basis for ways of working across all other domains. To highlight the fact that this domain addresses process standards, it was renamed from "Foundational Standards" to "Foundational Standards for a Quality Response." These process standards are the basis for a quality response that is holistic, locally led, and accountable to the people and communities it supports. They cover the key elements that should be present at all levels and in all types of education programming. The standards in this domain are organized into three sub-categories: community participation (Standards 1-2), coordination (Standard 3), and analysis (Standards 4-7).

Domain 2: Access and Learning Environment. The three standards (8-10) in this domain focus on access to safe and relevant learning opportunities. They highlight the importance of linking with other sectors, such as health, WASH, nutrition, shelter, and protection. These links help to improve security and safety, as well as learners' physical, cognitive, and psychological wellbeing.

Domain 3: Teaching and Learning. The four standards (11-14) in this domain focus on critical elements of teaching and learning, on curricula, and on the assessment of learning outcomes. This domain also addresses teacher training, professional development, and support.

Domain 4: Teachers and Other Education Personnel. The three standards (15-17) in this domain focus on administration and on managing human resources in education, particularly teachers. This includes recruitment and selection, conditions of work, and professional support and training.

Domain 5: Education Policy. The two standards (18-19) in this domain focus on formulating, planning, and implementing national education policies.

What is the difference between a domain, a standard, a key action, a guidance note, and "see also"?

Each section of the INEE MS will follow the same format.

DOMAIN

The INEE MS are organized into five domains related to specific areas of education.

STANDARD

We first set out the **minimum standard**. The standards follow from the idea that populations affected by crisis have the right to a life with dignity and to safe, quality, and relevant education. For this reason, they are qualitative in nature and are meant to be universal and to apply in any context.

KEY ACTION

A number of **key actions** follow under each standard. These actions are suggested ways to achieve the standard and should be adapted to the context. Actors can apply the key actions in order of importance, add new key actions, or leave out those that are not appropriate. The main aim of the actions is to meet the standard in a given context. Actors will have to work out who has the authority and responsibility for implementing the key actions in the most appropriate way; this will depend on the context or on the action itself.

GUIDANCE NOTE

Each key action is accompanied by a **guidance note** that covers specific points to consider when carrying out the action. The guidance notes offer more explanation, provide useful background information, and highlight issues of inclusion and non-discrimination, but they do not say specifically how to act. Each guidance note is connected to a specific key action. Users should read the key actions and guidance notes for each standard together because they build on each other to help achieve the standard.

SEE ALSO

The guidance notes also provide important links to other relevant standards or guidance notes, which are indicated by **"see also."**

Each standard is related to the others, which provides an overview of quality education and shows how interconnected many of the topics and themes are in the INEE MS.

How do I navigate and use the INEE MS?

The INEE MS address many areas of education across the humanitarian-development-peacebuilding nexus. This means that users can approach the various sections of the handbook according to their current needs and goals.

Always use the Foundational Standards for a Quality Response when applying the standards of the other four domains: Access and Learning Environment, Teaching and Learning, Teachers and Other Education Personnel, and Education Policy. Also read the brief introduction to each domain that sets out the major issues in that domain and explains the standards.

In the INEE MS, "education" encompasses different levels and types of formal and non-formal education, including the following:

- Early childhood development (ECD)
- Primary education
- Secondary education
- Tertiary education, which includes technical and vocational education and training (TVET), higher education, and adult education

When a key action or guidance note is particularly relevant to a specific type or level of education, it is stated clearly.

Using the Index

The index presented in Annex 2 is a useful tool when seeking information on a specific theme, issue, or area of work in different parts of the INEE MS. For example, when seeking guidance on curricula, the index will show that it is discussed on pages 139–45.

How do I adapt the INEE MS to my local context?

Contextualization is the process of interpreting or adapting the INEE MS to a context; the process of debating, determining, and agreeing on the meaning of global guidance in a local situation; "translating" the meaning and guidance of the INEE MS for the context of a country (or region) in order to make their content appropriate and meaningful.

Informal contextualization happens when individual users review and adapt the guidance for their particular needs.

Formal contextualization is a collaborative process that engages all education stakeholders in a given context to develop a set of contextualized standards. It differs from informal contextualization in that the outcome is recorded and shared widely to make it available for the use of all education stakeholders in that context.

There will always be tension between universal standards based on human rights and our ability to apply them. The INEE MS are goals we must work toward in our efforts to provide quality education, and the key actions are steps we can take to achieve each standard. Contextualizing the key actions, guidance notes, and indicators is essential if the INEE MS are to be met. Because each context is different, actors need to adapt the content of the standards to each situation to make them concrete and actionable. For example, Standard 15, Key Action

3 states "ensure the number of teachers and other education personnel recruited reflects current needs and finances." To apply this, consult stakeholders about what learning spaces and how many teachers are available, and what the national and local standards are for class size and teacher-student ratio. To understand what is locally acceptable, consider context, including available resources and the stage of the emergency.

Why is contextualization important?

- **Contextualization is an important step toward locally led action**, as it makes the content of the standards relevant to the culture and appropriate to the context.
- **Contextualization ensures that stakeholders have a shared understanding** of a standard and how to meet it within their context.
- **Contextualization promotes accountability** by identifying which stakeholders are responsible for which actions and choosing locally relevant methods to verify those actions (see the INEE Minimum Standard Indicator Framework).
- **Contextualization supports local buy-in**, as it is a collaborative validation process that helps stakeholders from different levels of the education system agree to the importance of a standard and what actions should be taken to meet it. Contextualization can help initiate conversations between stakeholders who have different levels of power and influence, help them determine what aspects of education they value during crises, and begin to move toward a more equitable, inclusive education system.

How do we contextualize the INEE MS?

Formal contextualization can happen at a
- National level
- Sub-national level
- Organizational/institutional level
- School level

It can be organized to support
- The education response to a particular crisis
- Disaster mitigation and preparedness
- The design and implementation of a particular strategy, plan, program, or project
- National education policy and strategies

In general, a formal contextualization follows these seven steps:

Step 1: Map out other education providers in your context
Step 2: Host an INEE MS orientation workshop
Step 3: Set up a working group with representatives from across the education sector
Step 4: Work with a facilitator to guide the contextualization process
Step 5: Define the content of each standard in accordance with the context
Step 6: Synthesize the contextualized standards into one document
Step 7: Host a forum to present the contextualized standards to the stakeholders and practitioners in your context

Stakeholders who are interested in contextualizing the INEE MS should contact the INEE Secretariat (minimum.standards@inee.org) for more guidance and support on planning and reporting.

Ideally, contextualization should happen before an emergency as part of education contingency planning and preparedness. Education authorities working with an education sector coordination mechanism, an education cluster, or a refugee education working group can develop locally relevant actions to meet the standards. The leadership of education authorities as a host partner and/or their endorsement is key to promoting participants' ownership of the process. Previous contextualization exercises have shown that participation, collaboration, and diverse representation of stakeholders from across the education sector are essential to successful contextualization. (To see examples of contextualization of the INEE MS, visit the INEE website.)

Some standards may take longer to achieve than others. During the contextualization process, stakeholders must examine the barriers to providing inclusive and equitable quality education for all and identify realistic, phased strategies to reduce them. Each standard presents a goal for education stakeholders to strive to meet, so contextualization should not lower the standards or alter the rights they are based on. Contextualization instead should aim to reach similar rights-based goals that are aligned with local needs, norms, values, and capacity.

The INEE MS were developed to make education stakeholders more accountable when it comes to education rights and the needs of people affected by crises. The aim is to make a significant difference in the lives of people affected by crisis. No one handbook can do this—it is only possible through the collective action of the global education community.

Tools to help use, apply, and institutionalize the INEE MS

Resources such as the INEE MS Indicator Framework, INEE MS Case Studies, and INEE MS Reference Tool are available on the INEE website.

The INEE MS are also available in digital form on the INEE website, where the INEE MS content, translations, indicator framework, and supporting resources are directly linked.

How are the INEE MS applied in practice?

Since being launched in 2004, the INEE MS have been an effective tool used in many contexts to promote quality education from the onset of an emergency through to recovery. Humanitarian response was previously understood as a continuum involving disaster preparedness before a crisis, response during an emergency, and ongoing assistance in the early stages of recovery. In a global context of increasing conflict, protracted crises, instability, and displacement, this linear development is often not the reality. It is now recognized that humanitarian response should be understood more holistically, and as part of a "triple nexus" that includes development and peacebuilding (see Figure 2). In practice, humanitarian, development, and peacebuilding activities often happen simultaneously, and they intersect in their efforts to achieve the shared goals of alleviating human suffering, strengthening resilience, and preventing conflict. The humanitarian-development-peacebuilding nexus encompasses other terms, such as "humanitarian-development nexus" and "humanitarian-development coherence."

The INEE MS offer a useful framework for analysis and planning. The nexus approach highlights the importance of placing this framework within the dynamic interactions of humanitarian response, development, and peacebuilding activities (for more information, see *Humanitarian-Development Coherence in Education: Working Together in Crisis Contexts*).

Figure 2: Humanitarian-development-peacebuilding nexus

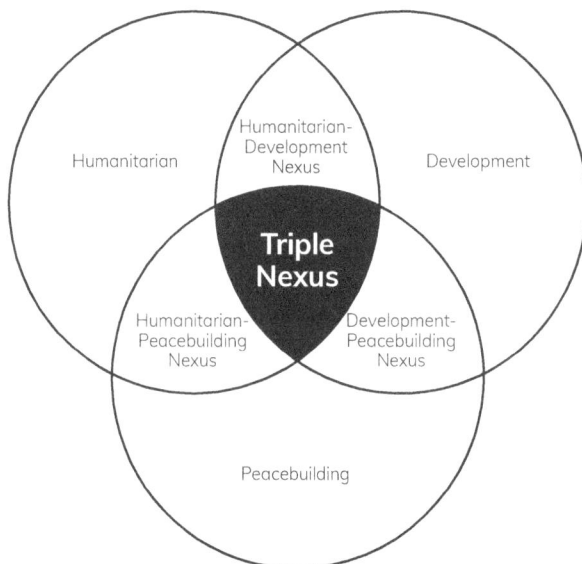

Source: Stockholm International Peace Institute, (2019). Connecting the dots on the triple nexus

The INEE MS were designed to help actors plan, implement, monitor, and evaluate actions during a humanitarian response. The INEE MS are most effective when education stakeholders are already familiar with them and trained to use them. The standards provide a common framework and make it possible for various stakeholders, such as governments, communities, and national and international agencies, to develop shared objectives. Users of the INEE MS report that they help in the following ways:

- Ensuring that communities are meaningfully involved in designing and implementing education programs, both during emergencies and through to recovery
- Coordinating education assessments and response more effectively
- Strengthening national education systems
- Contributing to improved service delivery
- Monitoring and evaluating education work during emergencies, and through to recovery and development
- Building knowledge and skills for implementing high-quality education programs

- Guiding donor investment in the education sector
- Advocating for and negotiating humanitarian spaces and resources, particularly for education as part of humanitarian response

The INEE MS are also a key accountability tool for education providers. Donor agencies are increasingly using them as a quality and accountability framework for the education projects they support.

For case studies of how the standards have been used in specific contexts, visit the INEE website. INEE welcomes new case studies on the implementation of the INEE MS. Readers interested in developing a case study can send an email to minimum.standards@inee.org.

Those interested in participating in a training or in learning more about how to use the INEE MS can send an email to minimum.standards@inee.org.

Frequently asked questions about the INEE MS

How do we make sure that the INEE MS reinforce existing government education standards?

Many countries have national education standards, policies, and frameworks. INEE recognizes and supports national authorities' leading role in creating education laws and policies, and in providing basic education services to all learners living in a country. This includes girls, persons with disabilities, refugees, IDPs, and members of marginalized groups. Where national standards exist, it is important to analyze the differences between those standards and the INEE MS. Experience has shown that the INEE MS are generally compatible with national education standards. They also are a useful tool that can complement, supplement, and help reach national standards. They provide strategies for reaching national standards and guidance specific to emergency situations, which might not be included in national policies or strategies.

The INEE MS set high standards, so why are they called "minimum"?

The INEE MS are based on the right to education as established in many international legal instruments and agreements. This means that the guidance in the INEE MS cannot set aims that are lower than these rights. The standards may seem high because they describe internationally agreed-to human rights and good practice, but they also define the minimum requirements for quality education, equity, and human dignity. When the standards cannot be met, they still apply as universal, agreed-upon benchmarks. They can be used to set ambitious longer-term goals for achieving inclusive and equitable quality education. The INEE MS also enable stakeholders to identify barriers to providing inclusive and equitable quality education for all and to develop realistic, phased strategies to reduce them.

Are there ways to use the INEE MS with limited resources?

The INEE MS are useful in several ways when resources are limited. First, many aspects of the standards define good practices that do not require high spending. For example, standards for community participation can improve the quality of humanitarian and education work. Applying them is a relatively low-cost intervention, helps save time and resources in the long term, and can contribute to more lasting, positive effects. Second, the INEE MS can be used to advocate for increased and more effective funding for education during emergencies and through to recovery. Third, using the INEE MS supports a methodical approach to understanding and responding to evolving needs that can help stakeholders identify critical issues, explore inequalities, and reduce inefficiencies.

Cross-cutting Issues to Consider When Using the INEE Minimum Standards

Below we identify the key issues that were purposely integrated throughout the handbook. They are addressed often throughout the handbook because they must be considered for all levels and types of education programming and through all stages of crises, from preparedness to response, and through to recovery. The term "intersectionality" recognizes that many aspects of identity are complex and interconnected. Identities such as ethnicity, race, gender, sexual orientation, age, disability, language, class or caste, citizenship status, and religion overlap and interact. Individuals and groups may face different forms of exclusion and discrimination as a result. It is important to approach inclusive education responses and systems with this in mind because it highlights how intersecting inequalities affect the barriers and discrimination individuals and groups face.

Protection

Protection and child protection are central to all humanitarian response. The 2013 Centrality of Protection in Humanitarian Action, a commitment made by the Inter-Agency Standing Committee (IASC) Principals, holds the entire humanitarian sector accountable for the protection of those affected by crises and places protection at the center of all aspects of humanitarian response. This means considering the views, capacities, needs, and vulnerabilities of people affected by crises within all sectoral interventions. "Protection" refers to ensuring that the rights of people affected by crisis and the obligations of duty bearers under international law are understood, respected, protected, and fulfilled without discrimination. "Child protection," as part of the larger protection umbrella, refers to the prevention of and response to abuse, neglect, exploitation, and violence against children. Protection and child protection are essential parts of the education response at every level and aspect of programming, including policy, infrastructure, training, and professional development; activities in the learning environment; and accountability to learners, teachers, and their communities.

Crises increase the risk and prevalence of harm, especially to children and communities who are already vulnerable or marginalized. They affect the availability of and access to safe and protective learning environments, the quality of learning environments, and the essential skills and knowledge individuals and communities need to protect themselves. Learners in crisis situations may be unable to access education and thus are denied the protections education can provide. On the other hand, learning environments may present significant risks to child protection, such as corporal punishment, gender-based violence, or violations of children's rights through the inaccurate portrayal of their histories and identities. If these issues are not addressed, schools and other learning environments may become dangerous and stressful, which may lead to dropout and poor attendance, undermine learning, and harm the health and wellbeing of learners and of teachers and other education personnel. Creating a protective, supportive learning environment is essential to preventing and mitigating certain protection risks, and to improving access, retention, and success in learning that contributes to longer-term protection.

Education and child protection services fill important and complementary roles in supporting children's need to survive, develop, and thrive. The education sector provides a unique pathway for the child protection sector to access children and young people and support their wellbeing. Child protection programs often support children who are not accessing education and provide specialized services to children affected by crisis, which enables them to continue or return to their education. Together these two sectors are a key factor in promoting healthy child development, and in protecting the future wellbeing and stability of affected communities. Integrating protection into EiE creates opportunities to better identify, mitigate, prevent, and respond to risk and harm within the school environment, community, and home.

For more guidance on child protection, see the resource collection on Child Protection on the INEE website and the *Minimum Standards for Child Protection in Humanitarian Action*.

Gender

"Gender" refers to the socially constructed roles, responsibilities, and identities of women and girls, men and boys, and gender diverse people, and how they are viewed and valued in society. They vary from culture to culture and often change over time. Gender identities define how women and girls, men and boys, and gender diverse people are expected to think and act. These behaviors are learned from family, at school, through religious teaching, and from the media. Since gender roles, responsibilities, and identities are socially learned, they also can be changed. Gender together with age, sexual orientation, gender identity and expression, and sexual characteristics determine roles, responsibilities, power dynamics, and access to resources and services, including education.

Education needs often change during emergencies, and different barriers for girls, boys, and gender diverse children and young people often emerge. Young women and girls usually experience greater disadvantages and compounding threats to their ability to access safe, quality education. These include targeted attacks on girls' schools, school-related gender-based violence (SRGBV), greater risk of early and forced marriage, early pregnancy, trafficking, carrying a greater burden of unpaid caregiving and domestic labor, and reduced access to sexual and reproductive health services. Men and boys also face threats to their ability to access safe and quality education, including recruitment into armed forces, SRGBV, arbitrary arrest, and family pressure to take up paid employment.

Gender norms also can create significant barriers for people of diverse sexual orientations, gender identities and expressions, and sexual characteristics, such as lesbian, gay, bisexual, transgender, queer, intersex, asexual, and agender (LGBTQIA+) people. People who are LGBTQIA+ regularly face bullying, harassment, and violence in their schools and other learning environments. Violence and persecution on the basis of sexual orientation, gender identity, expression, and sexual characteristics are major factors in causing displacement, and they have a negative impact on the health and wellbeing of people who are LGBTQIA+ around the world.

For more guidance on gender and supporting people who are LGBTQIA+, see the resource collections on Gender and LGBTQIA+ on the INEE website.

Disability

"Disability" is an evolving concept. It results from the interaction between persons with a physical, psychosocial or mental, developmental, or sensory impairment and barriers in the environment that hinder their full and effective participation in society on an equal basis with others. Some disabilities are visible, while others may be invisible or hidden. Persons with disabilities, who often face a greater risk of exclusion, must be able to access education in emergency situations. They often face more challenges to receiving assistance, due to the physical, attitudinal, communication, technological, or organizational barriers that prevent them from accessing food and water distribution points, sanitation facilities, schools, and so on. Crises can increase the vulnerabilities and risks faced by learners and teachers and other education personnel with disabilities, which can limit their ability to access and participate in disability-inclusive programming.

Disability-inclusive education means ensuring that informational, environmental, physical, attitudinal, financial, or any other type of barriers do not inhibit learners with disabilities from participating in education.

For more guidance on disability, see the resource collection on Inclusive Education on the INEE website and the *Humanitarian inclusion standards for older people and people with disabilities.*

Mental health and psychosocial support

Mental health and psychosocial support (MHPSS) refers to any type of local or outside support that aims to protect or promote psychosocial wellbeing and prevent or treat mental conditions in crisis situations. Wellbeing is defined as a condition of holistic health and the process of achieving it. It refers to physical, emotional, social, and cognitive health.

Children and young people in humanitarian contexts are often exposed to adverse and life-threatening events, and thus they face greater psychological challenges and stressors. MHPSS can help to improve their resilience and strengthen their coping mechanisms in times of crisis. Education is an important channel for offering MHPSS, because a safe and supportive learning environment can protect learners against the negative effects of a crisis. Learning environments can create stable routines, foster hope, and reduce stress. Teachers and other education personnel, who often come from the crisis-affected community, may face the same distress as the learners, and it is important that they also receive proper support.

People are affected by a crisis in different ways and require different kinds of support. MHPSS involves creating a system of complementary support to meet the needs of various groups, which includes the following:

- Access to basic needs and safety
- Strong family and community support
- Non-specialized support
- Specialized services

Providing MHPSS requires that education and other sectors, such as protection and health, work together.

For more guidance on MHPSS, see the resource collection on MHPSS and SEL on the INEE website.

Disaster risk reduction and resilience

DRR and resilience are complementary concepts focused on developing individual and community level resilience to risks. Together, DRR and resilience help to ensure that education systems can mitigate the impacts of hazards and shocks of all kinds, provide continuous learning opportunities to the people affected, and contribute to their well-being and long-term development.

DRR is about reducing risks through systematic efforts to analyze and manage the causal factors of disasters. This can include reducing exposure to hazards, reducing the vulnerability of people and property, wisely managing land and the environment, and improving preparedness. Investing in DRR and preparedness can be cost-effective and efficient because it helps education authorities and their partners to plan, coordinate, and respond more effectively.

Resilience refers to the capacity of individuals, communities, and systems to adapt, withstand, and recover from shocks and stresses. It encompasses different dimensions including social, emotional, physical, and cognitive resilience. Resilience aims to mitigate the negative effects of crises on education by strengthening the capacities of individuals, communities, and education systems to cope with the impacts of hazards and shocks, respond effectively to meet local needs, and bounce back stronger. DRR helps make education systems resilient over the long term, which is key to ensuring that education and protection continue, as outlined in the Sendai Framework for Disaster Risk Reduction. It also can limit disruptions to learning in the event of risks and hazards of all kinds.

DRR and resilience play an important role in keeping schools and other learning environments safe during crises. DRR and resilience initiatives can provide schools with strategies to limit disruptions to learning, ensure learning continuity, and protect learners, teachers and other education personnel, and infrastructure from the impacts of hazards and risks.

For more guidance on DRR and resilience, see the resource collection on Risk Reduction and Resilience on the INEE website and the Global Alliance for Disaster Risk Reduction and Resilience (GADRRRES) *Comprehensive School Safety Framework*.

Conflict sensitive education

Education and conflict have a complex and mutually reinforcing relationship. Learning environments can be the targets of violence and attacks, and education is often disrupted during conflicts. Education can contribute to conflict by teaching behaviors and attitudes that worsen tensions or by unevenly distributing education resources and access. However, education also can help to transform a society from one of exclusion to one of inclusion. Conflict sensitive education is a process that includes:

- Understanding the context where education happens
- Analyzing how the context and education programs and policies interact (development, planning, and delivery)
- Reducing the negative effects and increasing the positive effects education policies and programming have on conflict, within an organization's given priorities and mandates

Education policies and programs that integrate attention to conflict together with technical solutions can mitigate the risk of investments in education increasing tensions and will be better aligned with the principle of do no harm. Conflict sensitivity provides a foundation on which humanitarian and development actors can build peace through education. Such interventions can be a bridge that connects activities across the humanitarian-development-peacebuilding nexus.

For more guidance on conflict sensitive education, see the resource collection on Conflict Sensitive Education on the INEE website.

Climate crisis

The climate crisis is an increasing threat to the right to education for learners across the globe. Climate-related hazards and shocks, including drought, heatwaves, wildfires, tropical storms, air pollution, and flooding, may keep children and young people out of school and significantly impact their educational attainment, as well as their overall health and wellbeing. These natural hazards, shocks, and extreme weather events often damage or destroy education infrastructure and are key causes of learner and teacher displacement. The economic impact of the climate crisis causes many families to struggle to get by financially. This may lead learners to drop out of school permanently so they can work to help support the family. This all has a disproportionate effect on the learners already facing inequality and discrimination, including girls, persons with disabilities, members of indigenous communities, and others. Meanwhile, chronic poverty, systemic racism, and legacies of colonialism continue to increase marginalized groups' vulnerability to the climate crisis. This makes the need to address the effects climate change is having on education even more urgent, especially during emergencies.

Providing EiE can help education systems adapt to the negative effects of climate change and contribute to environmental sustainability. Crisis-sensitive planning and DRR can lessen the impact climate shocks have on education infrastructure and access, and make education systems more resilient. TVET and skills building can prepare young people to participate in sustainable and environment-friendly economies. EiE helps at-risk children and young people and those affected by crises to develop skills that increase their resilience. EiE also can enable children and young people to become part of climate change solutions by helping them understand and address the impact of the climate crisis, and by equipping them with the knowledge, skills, values, and attitudes they need to act as agents of change.

For more guidance on the climate crisis, see the resource collection on Climate Crisis on the INEE website.

Centering equity in EiE

Global inequality and injustice are rooted in the legacies of colonialism and racism. Colonialism is widely understood to have shaped the global humanitarian and development systems, both historically and currently; racial and cultural biases are present in and actively shaping the structures and actions in these systems. These forces show up in the ways of working, the practices, and the policies of the humanitarian and development sectors, including the following:

- The language used to talk about people affected by crisis
- Who holds power in decision-making spaces and processes
- Who holds power over money and resources and who has access to them
- Who holds the power to set global agendas and produce knowledge

It is essential to approach EiE and the INEE MS through a lens of equity, decoloniality, and anti-racism. Equity refers to fair and just practices that are achieved by systematically assessing disparities in opportunities, outcomes, and representation, and by addressing these issues through targeted actions. Decoloniality broadly refers to a process that aims to question and transform legacies of colonialism in institutions, structures, and ways of knowing. It involves actively addressing actions, behaviors, and decisions that uphold or reinforce the power dynamics of colonialism. Anti-racism is more than the absence of racism. It is an active process of challenging structures and practices of racism. It is essential for users of the handbook—and the global education community—to engage critically with these concepts, to work for locally led humanitarian action, and take action to dismantle unbalanced power structures and inequality.

For more guidance on the anti-racism and decoloniality, see the resource collection on Anti-racism and Decoloniality on the INEE website.

Developing the INEE Minimum Standards: a consultative process to reflect the evolving EiE landscape

During the development of this handbook in 2004, INEE facilitated a highly consultative process that involved national authorities, practitioners, policy-makers, academics, and other educators from around the world. More than 2,250 individuals from over 50 countries contributed to the development of the first edition of the INEE MS. INEE updated the handbook in 2010 and again in 2024. The 2024 update of the INEE MS builds on the original consultative process and on INEE's diverse membership consisting of representatives from the education, humanitarian, and development sectors. The 2024 update process (October 2021–December 2023) involved more than 1,600 people in 35 countries. The key steps of this process were:

- Analyzing feedback on the handbook
- Engaging in online and offline consultations
- Strengthening cross-cutting issues through expert group consultations
- Conducting stakeholder reviews

The humanitarian and development landscapes have changed significantly since the INEE MS were updated in 2010. At that time, several critical parts of the current humanitarian system did not exist, including the SDGs, the Global Compact on Refugees, and Education Cannot Wait (ECW). Emergency contexts also have changed because of the escalating impact of climate change, the onset of pandemics in an increasingly interconnected world, unprecedented forced displacement, migration, and a rapid increase in the number, complexity, and length of humanitarian crises. Also, the connections between education, child protection, and other sectors have been strengthened since 2010. There are increased calls for new ways of working that emphasize locally led humanitarian action, decoloniality, and the nexus approach to humanitarian, development, and peacebuilding activities. The 2024 update is an effort to make sure that the INEE MS stay relevant and accessible, and that it is easy to adapt and contextualize these standards in a new and changing international humanitarian context.

A critical reflection on the update process

The 2024 update of the INEE MS is based on the principles of universal human rights, cultural diversity, racial equity, community participation, and broad consultation. The primacy of the voices of the people affected by emergencies and the practitioners working most closely with them were at the center of the update process. INEE strove to be inclusive of all EiE stakeholders, including those without access to online services or technology.

And yet, there is tension between producing global standards and capturing the diversity of humankind's lived experiences, perspectives, and ways of knowing that come into play in the work of EiE across the globe. This reality presents challenges, particularly in trying to elevate the voices of those who are historically under-represented in humanitarian and development spaces. This has implications in terms of who holds the power to define and produce knowledge. Operational limitations and complications resulting from the COVID-19 pandemic created additional challenges in reaching out to stakeholders. And, finally, despite conscious efforts, inputs from the disability-inclusive education community were limited.

Language is another essential part of the decoloniality process and a powerful force in determining who produces knowledge. While the update process followed a multicultural and multilingual approach, it is important to reflect on the implications of English being the language used to write and collect feedback on the updated INEE MS drafts, and how this replicates the power imbalances of a global system of knowledge production.

Acknowledging these realities is a necessary step in moving INEE toward a more equitable and inclusive practice and further strengthening the INEE MS as a global public good.

What is new in the INEE MS, 2024 Edition?

If you are familiar with the 2010 edition of the INEE MS, you will note that the structure of the domains and standards in this updated edition is mostly the same. Changes to the structure include aligning key actions and guidance notes so that they are one-to-one, and numbering the standards 1–19 instead of within each domain.

Updates to the content include:

- A section on cross-cutting issues
- A "resources and further reading list" at the end of each standard, with links to relevant guidance
- New guidance on distance education, cash and voucher assistance (CVA), private-sector engagement in EiE, humanitarian and development coherence, EiE coordination, data security and protection, the role of education in addressing environmental emergencies such as climate change, and more
- Strengthening the presence of and guidance related to refugees, child protection, MHPSS, gender, disability, ECD, social and emotional learning (SEL), DRR, conflict mitigation, and inter-sectoral links and collaboration (protection, WASH, health, shelter, and nutrition)
- Emphasis on using inclusive and respectful language when referring to people's identities and circumstances
- Emphasis on using plain language that is easy to read, understand, and translate
- Actively engaging with concepts of anti-racism, decoloniality, and locally led humanitarian action in guidance that emphasizes the agency and knowledge of local actors

A Note on Capacity Sharing

Use of the term "capacity" varies, and different actors in the humanitarian sector use it in different ways. Capacity sharing and related terms, such as "capacity exchange," "capacity strengthening," "capacity building," and "capacity development," may be used interchangeably. Whatever term is used to describe the activity, it is essential that it promotes locally led humanitarian action. Characteristics of a capacity sharing approach include:

- Challenging ways of working that are based on the assumption that local capacity is lacking or needs to be built up
- Putting the diverse strengths and knowledge of local actors and the people affected at the center of humanitarian response (see Annex 1: Glossary for a definition of asset-based approach)
- Acknowledging power imbalances between international, national, and local actors and working to shift power to local actors and communities
- Reflecting the principles of respect, mutual learning, and equitable partnerships

Achieving these things requires first defining how capacity is understood in a context. It is important that the actions taken to address any gaps are a collective process led by communities.

Capacity sharing can happen at different levels; between individuals or communities sharing knowledge and skills, or between organizations strengthening each other's performance, capabilities, and ability to adapt to change. This sharing and learning is multi-directional and can happen between organizations of different types and sizes, with different roles and resources. No individual or organization should be considered the "expert," and partnerships should support participation and new ways of thinking and working (Menashy and Zakharia, 2022). Capacity sharing goes beyond short-term or project-based training and might also involve:

- Two-way capacity assessments or context-wide capacity mapping
- Accompaniment
- Peer-to-peer learning
- Secondments between organizations
- Financial support

Capacity sharing works to fulfill goals set by local actors and communities. It should be tailored to their challenges, opportunities, and values. Informal activities that build trust and communication can supplement the formal, structured activities. This will address and strengthen the resources, systems, and structures needed for sustainable programming that supports the resilience of communities (IASC Localization Taskforce, 2022).

References and further reading

- *Guidance Note on Capacity Strengthening for Localization*, Grand Bargain Localization Taskforce, 2020
- IASC Localization Taskforce (2022). *Capacity Sharing among Local and International Actors to Deliver Humanitarian Action* [Unpublished].
- Menashy, F. & Z. Zakharia. (2022). *Guiding Principles for Promising Partnership Practices in Education in Emergencies*. Policy Brief. Dubai Cares. *https://eiepartnerships.org/publication/policy-brief/*
- *Rethinking Capacity and Complementarity for a More Local Humanitarian Action*, Overseas Development Institute, 2019
- *NEAR Organizational Capacity Assessment Tool*, NEAR Network, 2020

Strategic Links

The INEE MS are part of the Humanitarian Standards Partnership and a companion to the Sphere Standards and the Core Humanitarian Standard

The Sphere Humanitarian Charter, the Protection Principles, and the Core Humanitarian Standard are the foundational chapters of the Sphere Handbook. Together they express what people affected by crises have a right to expect from humanitarian assistance. The Sphere Handbook includes minimum standards in humanitarian response for the following sectors:

- Water supply, sanitation, and hygiene promotion
- Food security and nutrition
- Shelter, settlement, and non-food items
- Health action

The INEE MS echo the core beliefs of Sphere: that we must take all possible steps to alleviate human suffering arising out of calamity and conflict, and that people affected by crisis have a right to live life with dignity. The INEE MS reflect the commitment, as set out in the Core Humanitarian Standard, that organizations will deliver quality, effective, and accountable support and assistance. The 2008 Sphere-INEE Companionship Agreement recognizes that the INEE MS and Sphere Standards are complementary. It reinforces the importance of creating inter-sectoral links between education and the sectors represented by Sphere at the outset of an emergency. The goal is to improve the quality of assistance provided to people affected by crises and to improve the accountability of the humanitarian system in disaster preparedness and response.

Guidance from the Sphere Handbook is cross-referenced throughout the INEE MS. Guidance on education has also been included in the 2018 edition of the Sphere Handbook. Using the INEE MS as a companion to the Sphere Handbook ensures that multi-sectoral needs assessments, followed by joint planning and a holistic response, create inter-sectoral links.

The INEE MS are closely linked with other humanitarian standards as part of the Humanitarian Standards Partnership, which includes the following:

- *Sphere Handbook*
- *Humanitarian inclusion standards for older people and people with disabilities*
- *Minimum Standards for Child Protection in Humanitarian Action (CPMS)*
- *Minimum Standard for Market Analysis (MISMA)*
- *Minimum Standards for Camp Management*
- *The Core Humanitarian Standard (CHS)*
- *Minimum Standards for Education: Preparedness, Response, Recovery (INEE MS)*
- *The Livestock Emergency Guidelines and Standards (LEGS)*
- *Minimum Economic Recovery Standards (MEERS)*
- *Standards for Supporting Crop-Related Livelihoods in Emergencies (SEADS)*

Figure 3: Humanitarian Standards

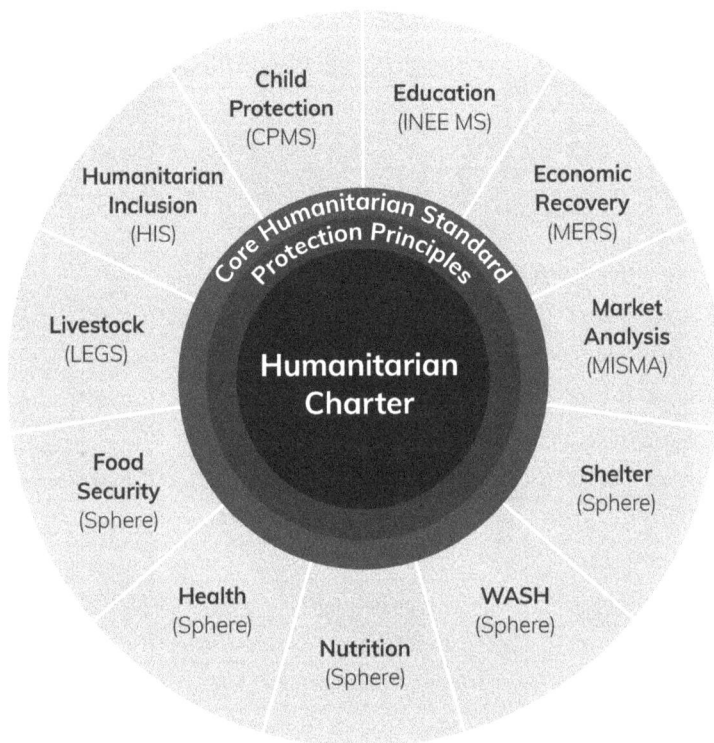

Figure showing concentric circles. Center: **Humanitarian Charter**. Inner ring: Core Humanitarian Standard, Protection Principles. Outer segments: Child Protection (CPMS), Education (INEE MS), Humanitarian Inclusion (HIS), Economic Recovery (MERS), Livestock (LEGS), Market Analysis (MISMA), Food Security (Sphere), Shelter (Sphere), Health (Sphere), Nutrition (Sphere), WASH (Sphere).

For more information on the Sphere Handbook and the Humanitarian Standards Partnership, go to https://hspstandards.org/.

The INEE MS serve as a common framework to promote quality coordination of EiE responses

To meet the complex education needs of crisis-affected children and young people, it is essential to have effective humanitarian coordination systems that involve diverse stakeholders and clearly define leadership, roles, and responsibilities.

These systems and their component mechanisms are essential for effective coordination in complex and dynamic situations, such as emergencies, where multiple actors need to work together to meet the needs of the people affected. Certain systems focus on the needs of target groups, but there is often overlap, which creates the need for actors within these systems to work together.

Depending on the nature of the crisis, different coordination mechanisms may be established, including, but not limited to, the following in the figure below:

Figure 4: Education sector coordination

	Development System	Refugee System	Cluster System
Coordination Mechanism	Local Education Groups	Refugee Education Working Group	Education Cluster
Target group and focus	All children and young people; implementation of Education Sector Plans and achievement of SDG 4	Refugee children and young people in all phases of emergencies, from first phase to durable solutions	IDPs and local crisis-affected children and young people in emergency contexts
Leadership	Global: UNESCO coordinates monitoring of SDG4 Country: MoE as lead, often paired with a rotating donor co-lead	Global: UNHCR Country: National refugee agency or MoE as lead, with UNHCR co-lead	Global: UNICEF and Save the Children Country: Often MoE as chair, with UNICEF and/or Save the Children as co-lead; other NGOs sometimes co-lead

Source: GEC, INEE, UNHCR, (2020). *Education in Emergencies coordination: Harnessing humanitarian and development architecture for Education 2030. Visual adapted from: UNHCR, (2019). UNHCR Refugee Coordination Model*

The INEE MS offer a framework that coordination groups can use to:

- Promote coherent, joined-up education sector coordination that supports continuity of education for children and young people affected by crisis
- Improve the quality of coordination, which promotes inter-agency dialogue and advocacy between coordination group members, donors, and other sectors
- Improve planning and preparedness, DRR, and response, including through joint needs assessments, monitoring, and evaluation
- Train staff members and partners and support capacity-sharing
- Frame how funding appeals are developed

MAP

Minimum Standards for Education:
Preparedness, Response, Recovery

Inter-agency Network for Education in Emergencies

Domain 1: Foundational Standards for a Quality Response

Community Participation
- Standard 1: Participation
- Standard 2: Resources

Coordination
- Standard 3: Coordination

Analysis
- Standard 4: Assessment
- Standard 5: Response Strategies
- Standard 6: Monitoring
- Standard 7: Evaluation

Domain 2: Access and Learning Environment
- Standard 8: Equal and Equitable Access
- Standard 9: Protection and Wellbeing
- Standard 10: Facilities and Services

Domain 3: Teaching and Learning
- Standard 11: Curricula
- Standard 12: Teaching and Learning Processes
- Standard 13: Assessment of Holistic Learning Outcomes
- Standard 14: Training, Professional Development, and Support

Domain 4: Teachers and Other Education Personnel
- Standard 15: Recruitment and Selection
- Standard 16: Conditions of Work
- Standard 17: Support and Supervision

Domain 5: Education Policy
- Standard 18: Law and Policy Formulation
- Standard 19: Planning and Implementation

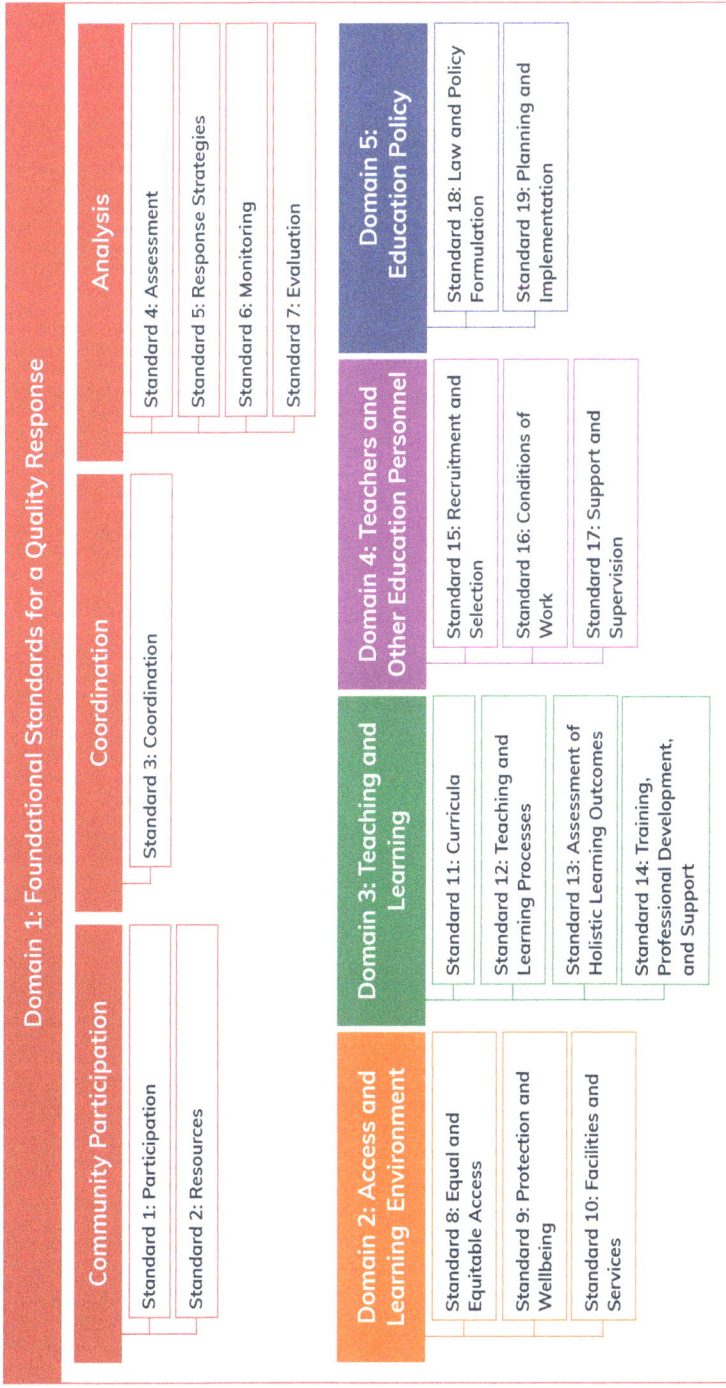

Cross-cutting Issues: Protection - Gender - Disability - Mental health and psychosocial support - Disaster risk reduction and resilience - Conflict sensitive education - Climate crisis - Centering equity in EiE

34

1

Foundational Standards for a Quality Response

Foundational Standards for a Quality Response

Community Participation

Standard 1: Participation

Community members participate meaningfully, transparently, and without discrimination in the analysis, planning, design, implementation, monitoring, and evaluation of the education response.

Standard 2: Resources

Community resources are identified, mobilized, and used to implement age-appropriate learning opportunities.

Coordination

Standard 3: Coordination

Education coordination mechanisms are in place to support the stakeholders who are working to ensure access to and continuity of quality education.

Analysis

Standard 4: Assessment

Timely education assessments of the emergency situation are holistic, transparent, and participatory.

Standard 5: Response Strategies

Inclusive education response strategies include a clear description of the context and of the barriers to the right to education, and strategies to overcome those barriers.

Standard 6: Monitoring

There is regular monitoring of education response activities and of the evolving learning needs of the people affected.

Standard 7: Evaluation

Systematic and impartial evaluations improve education response activities and enhance accountability.

Overview of Domain 1

The foundational standards presented in this domain are essential to providing a quality education response that is both holistic and accountable to the people and communities it supports. These standards are considered foundational because they cover the key elements that should be present at all levels and in all types of education programming, and in all aspects of a response. They apply in all contexts and are the basis for using the standards in the other four domains: Access and Learning Environment, Teaching and Learning, Teachers and Other Education Personnel, and Education Policy.

> **Holistic education responses** take a "whole-child" approach by addressing the diverse and multi-sectoral needs of crisis-affected children and young people to improve their academic outcomes and their mental, emotional, and physical wellbeing.

Each of the standards in this domain relates directly to the commitments set out in the Core Humanitarian Standard on Quality and Accountability (see Figure 5). The two complement each other and, used together, help to ensure a principled, accountable, high-quality education response.

The standards in this domain are organized into three sub-categories: community participation (Standards 1–2), coordination (Standard 3), and analysis (Standards 4–7). These sub-categories reflect actions that stakeholders can take throughout the humanitarian program cycle. The actions build on each other and are the basis of an effective education response. The seven standards in this domain make up a process of related actions that are key to preparing, planning, managing, delivering, and monitoring a collective education response. We discuss the standards below.

Figure 5: The Core Humanitarian Standard

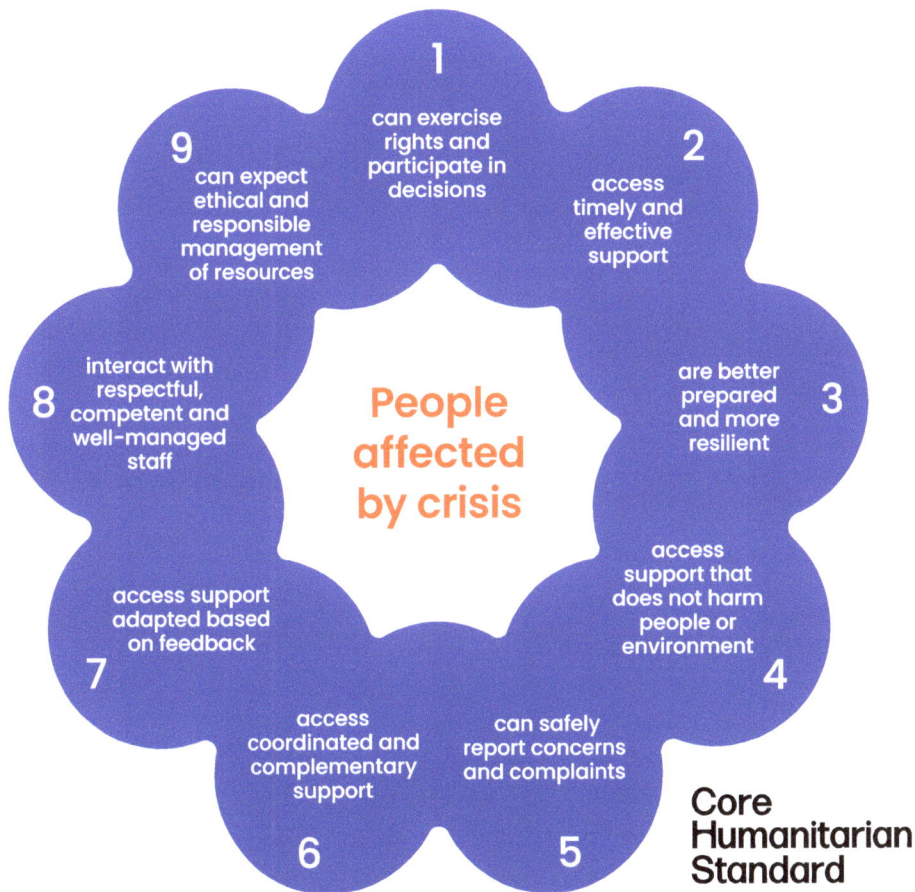

People affected by crisis

1 can exercise rights and participate in decisions

2 access timely and effective support

3 are better prepared and more resilient

4 access support that does not harm people or environment

5 can safely report concerns and complaints

6 access coordinated and complementary support

7 access support adapted based on feedback

8 interact with respectful, competent and well-managed staff

9 can expect ethical and responsible management of resources

Core Humanitarian Standard

Community participation (Standards 1–2) is essential to an effective emergency response

The key actions in these standards involve actors such as:

- Communities affected by crisis, including children and young people, teachers and other education personnel, parents and caregivers, community leaders, and CBOs
- National, sub-national, and local education authorities
- Inter-agency coordination mechanisms
- Stakeholders involved in the education response, including local and national CSOs and NGOs, faith-based organizations, humanitarian and development partners, donors, and private sector actors

Community participation involves parents and caregivers, children and young people, CSOs, local NGOs and community groups, teachers unions, traditional leaders, and indigenous communities. It is important to recognize that a community is a complex network of relationships and individuals. It can be understood in different ways, depending on the context. In settings of displacement, climate emergency, migration, or protracted crises, community structures and networks may be disrupted or change over time. When established community life is disrupted by a crisis and/or displacement, new communities are formed.

Community participation involves enabling communities affected by crisis to use their power to make decisions and influence education issues. The community must be involved in the decision-making, planning, and implementation of education activities, which takes time.

Community ownership and involvement in an EiE response will help with the following:

- Improving accountability through meaningful engagement
- Strengthening the mobilization of local resources
- Maintaining education services over the long term
- Making it possible to identify local education issues and ways to address them

Community participation is important at all stages of an education response: analysis, planning, design, implementation, monitoring, and evaluation. Children and young people have the right to participate in response activities in ways that are appropriate to their age and capacities. This is important to ensure that their specific needs and experiences guide the education response. It can be difficult to achieve equitable and inclusive participation during a crisis, but it is key to making a response effective.

Community participation should include opportunities for capacity sharing led by community members. Communities already have the necessary capabilities, resources, and resilience, and external stakeholders should use these as the starting point for development. Many affected communities will, on their own, start education programming, mobilize resources, build temporary learning environments, teach, manage supplies, support learners, maintain the facilities, and keep them safe. To be locally led, a response must support local initiatives and strengthen the resources, systems, and structures needed for sustainable programming that supports the resilience of communities.

Coordination (Standard 3) brings stakeholders together to provide a coherent, principled education response

The key actions in this standard involve actors such as:
- National education authorities and/or agencies that lead the coordination of the education response
- Members of inter-agency coordination mechanisms
- Stakeholders involved in the education response, including local and national CSOs and NGOs, faith-based organizations, humanitarian and development partners, donors, and private sector actors

Coordination is a critical element of any humanitarian response and the key to making sure a response is predictable. It also ensures that there is an effective partnership in place that makes accountability possible. Stakeholders involved in an education response should work together in a transparent, results-oriented way so that they are accountable to the people affected and deliver humanitarian assistance that is relevant and equitable.

National and sub-national education authorities are responsible for fulfilling the right to education for all and should lead or co-lead the coordination of the education response. However, their preparedness to lead coordinated education planning and response in a crisis can vary, so leadership may be assigned, by agreement, to an inter-agency coordination mechanism. This coordination mechanism should represent all actors and ensure that there is a coordinated approach to needs assessment and analysis, strategic planning, advocacy and resource mobilization, monitoring and evaluation, and capacity sharing.

Coordination mechanisms could include an education cluster, refugee education working group, local education group, and others. The main education coordination mechanisms used in crises have different mandates and structures, and multiple coordination mechanisms can exist within the same context. Education clusters, under the IASC cluster system, coordinate education for IDPs and local emergency responses. In refugee situations, UNHCR works with governments to coordinate the education response through sectoral coordination groups, also known as refugee education working groups, in line with the Refugee Coordination Model. In mixed settings, where the population of humanitarian concern includes IDPs, refugees, and other people affected in the same geographic location, joint coordination arrangements will be put in place to meet the specific needs of the context. (For more information on education coordination systems, see Figure 4 in Introduction to the INEE MS.)

A key step is to create linkages between coordination mechanisms within the education sector and across sectors to make sure that education responses are predictable, holistic, equitable, and well-coordinated. Inter-sectoral collaboration supports joint and integrated programming, which is key to addressing the interconnected needs of crisis-affected children and young people and to ensuring the Centrality of Protection in humanitarian action. Promoting engagement between cluster and refugee coordination mechanisms and linking education coordination mechanisms in a humanitarian-development-peacebuilding nexus approach can lead to the following:

- Better coverage so that fewer refugee and crisis-affected children and young people are out of school

- Greater access to uninterrupted quality education
- More efficient use of resources through information sharing and planning

Analysis (Standards 4–7) puts the people affected at the center of humanitarian response

The key actions in these standards involve actors such as:

- National, sub-national, and local education authorities
- Education coordination mechanisms and coordination mechanisms from other relevant sectors
- Stakeholders involved in the education response, including local and national CSOs and NGOs, faith-based organizations, humanitarian and development partners, donors, and private sector actors

In order to respond effectively and make sure that an education response does no harm, stakeholders must properly understand the local context, how the crisis is developing, and how it is affecting education. Education authorities, communities, and learners should play a central role in identifying the impacts of the crisis and developing response strategies. Stakeholders should analyze the education sector along with other humanitarian sectors, including a review of the following:

- Economic conditions
- Religious and cultural beliefs
- Ethnic demographics
- Social practices, including gender relations and attitudes toward disability
- Political and security factors
- Coping mechanisms and expected future developments

Assessments should be coordinated and phased, beginning with a multi-sectoral rapid needs assessment and continuing with a comprehensive inter-agency assessment focused on education. An assessment should identify the needs, rights, vulnerabilities, and capacities of the people and institutions affected, and include available local resources. It also should collect information on the economic barriers to education access, gaps in education services, protection risks for all levels and types of education, and for all learners and for teachers and other education personnel. It is important to consider the barriers to education access from both the demand side and the supply

Demand-side barriers are those at the household or child level. They include times when a family cannot afford to pay tuition or other education costs, or if they lose income by sending a child who was working to school.

Supply-side barriers are those related to the education services being provided. They include a damaged or low-quality learning environment and a shortage of qualified teachers.

(for more information see Figure 6: Barriers to Accessing Education in Domain 2: Access and Learning Environment)

side. Conducting integrated assessments—which involves looking at both sides—will help determine the most appropriate modality of assistance, such as CVA, in-kind, direct service delivery, or a combination of these.

Assessments should produce transparent, publicly available, disaggregated education data that will be relevant during all stages of an emergency and through to recovery. The data should be managed ethically and in keeping with data protection policies and the principle of do no harm.

Evidence from the initial assessments must drive the response strategies. The changing situation and needs of the community and the systems should be assessed regularly to make sure they are reflected in the response. Response strategies should be harmonized with national education programs, and they should include activities that make the education system more resilient to prevent, prepare for, and respond to future emergencies. Response strategies also should incorporate community members' knowledge of local hazards and the skills they have to prevent or manage crises, and include ways to support them.

Education stakeholders should collect information on the needs and outcomes of crisis-affected learners and include this information in the national education management information system (EMIS). To do this, education authorities and partners may need to jointly identify needs and share capacities at the national, sub-national, and local levels to ensure that data can be designed, collected, disaggregated, analyzed, presented, and shared among all education stakeholders.

The data collected for and produced during the monitoring and evaluation stages is key to achieving the goals and objectives of EiE programs. Regular monitoring and evaluation of the education response and of the affected community's evolving education needs should be inclusive and transparent. Evaluation and monitoring reports should be shared, including lessons learned, to improve future education responses. They should be shared in a form that is understandable and accessible to all, including community members.

STANDARD 1: PARTICIPATION

Community members participate meaningfully, transparently, and without discrimination in the analysis, planning, design, implementation, monitoring, and evaluation of the education response.

Key actions
(please read with guidance notes)

1. **Inclusive community participation:** Ensure that a range of community members meaningfully participate in prioritizing, planning, designing, implementing, monitoring, and evaluating EiE activities.

2. **Do no harm:** Promote community participation in a way that is transparent, equitable, and does no harm.

3. **Participation in analysis:** Ensure that a wide range of community members participate in the analysis of EiE activities, including assessments, context analyses, social audits, joint budget reviews, and DRR and conflict mitigation activities.

4. **Capacity sharing:** Engage in capacity sharing activities with community members, education authorities, and other education stakeholders.

5. **Community education committees:** Include representatives of all vulnerable and marginalized groups in community education committees, to the extent possible.

6. **Community-based education action plan:** Engage in a participatory process to create a community-based education action plan.

7. **Participation of children and young people:** Invite children and young people to meaningfully participate in the development, implementation, monitoring, and evaluation of EiE activities.

Guidance notes

1. **Inclusive community participation:** Education authorities and other education stakeholders should make sure that a range of community members participate in EiE activities so that education is delivered safely, effectively, and equitably. Any member of the affected community should be able to participate meaningfully, regardless of age, gender, ethnicity, race, social class, religion, sexual orientation, disability, displacement status, civil documentation, political affiliation, HIV status, health status, or other factors. In the early stages of an acute response, participation might only be possible with a limited number of the people affected.

There should be more opportunities over time for more people and groups to become involved in decision-making.

No group of people should be excluded from participating because they are difficult to reach or need assistance. Different forms of participation should be available, based on age, ability, language, and culture. Education actors should pay special attention to accessibility issues, security conditions, or other local circumstances that can affect the participation of marginalized or vulnerable groups. Local community groups, such as women's and men's organizations, elders and community leaders, faith leaders and organizations, refugee-led organizations, youth-led organizations, and OPDs can help to identify and remove barriers that may prevent vulnerable community members from participating in decision-making (for more guidance, see *Sphere Handbook*, Commitment 4; *Humanitarian inclusion standards for older people and people with disabilities*, education inclusion standard 3; and *INEE Guidance Note on Gender*).

Community members' knowledge is key to identifying appropriate and protective education services. It should guide education authorities and other education stakeholders when identifying the following:

- The education needs and economic barriers to education access for all children and young people, and the preferred modality of assistance to address these (CVA, in-kind, and direct service delivery)
- The financial, material, and human resources that are available locally
- Existing and changing gender relations
- Power dynamics in the community, including between dominant groups and marginalized groups
- Security issues, risks, threats, and ways of protecting education institutions, staff members, and learners
- Protection concerns in the learning environment, including SRGBV
- Local hazards, safe and accessible locations for schools and other learning spaces, and approaches to DRR
- Ways of including life-saving and conflict sensitive messages into the education response, including messages about major health issues in the community
- Strategies to promote social cohesion, build peace, and address the root causes of conflict and disasters

Education authorities and other education stakeholders should work with local stakeholders to strengthen or develop links between families, the community, schools, universities, or other learning environments in a participatory, inclusive, and consultative way.

See also Standard 4, Guidance Note 7; Standard 5, Guidance Notes 2 and 4; Standard 8, Guidance Note 9; Standard 9, Guidance Note 6; Standard 10, Guidance Notes 1 and 6; Standard 19, Guidance Notes 2 and 5

2. **Do no harm:** External stakeholders should promote community participation in EiE activities in a transparent and equitable way to avoid contributing to existing inequalities or conflicts. This requires a thorough understanding of community dynamics. Education actors should conduct a community-level context analysis to help determine the most relevant and appropriate ways to promote community ownership of education activities.

Understanding the dynamics within a community is key to taking a "do no harm" approach. Where multiple communities are present in the same geographic location, it is important to understand and work with the network of communities. For example, in situations of displacement, the community members may include refugees or migrants who are living in a host community.

Make sure that participating in EiE activities does not harm any person or group, especially vulnerable groups or those most at risk of discrimination, such as women and girls, people who are LGBTQIA+, or ethnic and linguistic minorities. Identify who is at risk of discrimination or exclusion and why, and determine how to include them safely.

Community members must be clear about what is involved in participating and why particular groups are asked to be represented in planning and decision-making. Education actors must make it clear to communities and individuals how the information they gather will be used and if there will be any follow-up actions. People should understand that they can share information freely and confidentially, but also that they do not have to participate. If participating will expose people to risks or inconveniences, that must be made clear to all (for more guidance, see *INEE Guidance Note on Conflict Sensitive Education; Minimum Standards for Child Protection*, Standard 17; *Sphere Handbook*, Commitment 3).

> See also Standard 2, Guidance Note 4; Standard 4, Guidance Note 7; Standard 5, Guidance Note 3

3. **Participation in analysis:** Local communities and groups are important partners in understanding barriers to participation in education. Analyzing educational activities is an essential way for the community to participate in education planning and problem-solving.

Social audits are community-based evaluations of an education program. They can help to do the following:

- Work out which people, funding, and materials are available
- Identify gaps in services
- Monitor how effective a program is

It may not always be possible to carry out social audits at the beginning or in the middle of an emergency. However, in protracted or chronic crises or in the early recovery stages, social audits can help communities improve their ability to monitor education programs and keep a record of rights violations. Participating in social audits is particularly important for young people, especially girls, learners with disabilities, and learners who are not participating in formal or non-formal education. Education actors should share the results of social audits with all community members and the relevant authorities (for more guidance, see A *Practical Guide to Social Audit as a Participatory Tool to Strengthen Democratic Governance, Transparency, and Accountability*).

See also Standard 2, Guidance Note 1; Standard 4, Guidance Notes 4, 7, and 9; Standard 6, Guidance Note 3; Standard 7, Guidance Note 2

4. **Capacity sharing:** Capacity sharing is a key part of community participation that involves respecting and building on the knowledge and expertise already present in a community. Community members can help to identify education experts, including teachers and other education personnel, who can share their cultural and contextual knowledge with external stakeholders. Their diverse knowledge and strengths should guide the planning and implementation of programs. If contextual expertise cannot be found, or if people are not able or willing to support the (re)establishment of the education system, community members and external stakeholders should then work together to develop capacity sharing activities.

Assessments should look at the different capacities, needs, and responses of children, young people, and adults in the community. This includes vulnerable groups such as girls, gender diverse children and young people, and persons with disabilities. External stakeholders also should assess their own capacities and gaps to identify where the expertise of local actors and communities can guide them. Capacity sharing activities among education personnel and community members should focus on roles and responsibilities for the long term. These activities should promote the community's ownership of the education program, help to maintain it, and promote coordination with other sectors. Capacity sharing activities may cover areas such as resource mobilization and management, facility maintenance, disability awareness, and special measures taken to ensure the participation of children and young people. External stakeholders should prioritize using contextually relevant training resources, and working with institutions within the community that can provide recognized credentials for those who are participating in training.

See also Standard 5, Guidance Note 6; Standard 7, Guidance Note 2

5. **Community education committees:** Communities organize themselves in a variety of ways. One forum for community participation is a community education committee, which refers to a group of community members who identify and try to meet the education needs and rights of all learners in a community. This includes learners in non-formal education. These committees may also be called parent-teacher associations and school management committees. In some contexts, they may be formally recognized in national laws as part of school governance structures. A community education committee or similar group is key to making sure that education approaches come from and are led by the community. External stakeholders should support existing community education committees. If one does not exist, external stakeholders should encourage the community to form one, in collaboration with education authorities and the inter-agency coordination mechanism.

The community education committee should represent all groups in the community, which may include:

- Teachers, head teachers, and other education personnel
- Parents and caregivers
- Children and young people
- Representatives from tertiary education, including learners, faculty, and staff members from higher education and TVET programs
- Representatives from local NGOs, CSOs, and CBOs
- Representatives from local and indigenous communities
- Cultural, religious, and community leaders
- Staff members from other sectors, including health, protection, etc.

It is essential to include representatives of all marginalized and vulnerable groups. Formally recognized groups may need to add members to be truly representative. Community education committee members should be chosen through a participatory process that is locally accepted and allows all community members to participate equitably.

During complex crises, where distinctions like ethnicity, tribe, religion, and race can be divisive, the community education committee should work with all parties in a way that does not risk harming any person or group. The committee members' aim should be for everyone in the community to receive an education that is safe, impartial, and appropriate. They should have firsthand knowledge of changes in the socioeconomic, political, and safety and security context and share this with decision-makers at all levels.

The roles and responsibilities of community education committee members should be clearly defined and aligned with national and sub-national education systems, where they exist. The roles and responsibilities may include:

- Communicating with local and national education authorities and the duty bearers who are responsible for providing access to quality education

- Defining the roles, responsibilities, and expectations of humanitarian actors in community-led education activities
- Negotiating education approaches that consider age, gender, language, ability, and culture so that education programs respect learners' needs and rights; examples include flexible school calendars and age-appropriate curricula
- Organizing financial and in-kind contributions from communities
- Identifying what is needed for capacity sharing and helping to design these activities
- Monitoring who is and is not participating in learning opportunities, and the quality of teaching and learning
- Strengthening the safety and security of staff members and learners going to and from school
- Including DRR, conflict sensitivity, and climate risk management in the provision of education, including disaster preparedness plans that are disability-inclusive

See also Standard 2, Guidance Note 1; Standard 4, Guidance Note 7; Standard 8, Guidance Notes 2 and 5; Standard 12, Guidance Note 4; Standard 19, Guidance Note 5

6. **Community-based education action plan:** A community-based education action plan should build on the education sector plan (ESP), if there is one. It should have a framework for improving formal and non-formal education programs that are in line with the country's education policies, strategies, and plans. It should reflect the needs, rights, concerns, and values of the affected community, particularly those who belong to vulnerable groups, so it should be developed in a participatory manner. Community-based education plans can be developed through the community education committee with support from local education authorities and humanitarian partners.

An education action plan focuses on ensuring continuity of education. It may have several objectives, including the following:

- Developing a shared vision of what the teaching and learning environment might become
- Adapting curricula to the context, which may include conflict sensitivity, gender-responsiveness, DRR, and climate risk management
- Agreeing on how to recruit, supervise, train, compensate, and support teachers and other education personnel, if there is not already a national system
- Taking a human rights-based approach to reduce discrimination and promote a shared understanding that education must be inclusive and equitable

- Reaching agreement on how to develop a safe and supportive learning environment and committing to do it, including protecting education from attack and SRGBV
- Outlining tasks and responsibilities for the education authorities who are legally responsible for protecting the right to education, and other education stakeholders; this can include organizing resource mobilization, maintaining and developing infrastructure, and coordinating with outside agencies and other sectors, including protection, food security, health, nutrition, and WASH

Action plans should include regular community monitoring and assessment of EiE activities to maintain broad community participation in the response.

> Q See also Standard 4, Guidance Note 7; Standard 9, Guidance Notes 5 and 10; Standard 11, Guidance Note 1; Standard 15, Guidance Note 2; Standard 16, Guidance Note 1; Standard 17, Guidance Note 3; Standard 18, Guidance Note 5; Standard 19, Guidance Note 2

7. **Participation of children and young people:** Article 12 of the UN Convention on the Rights of the Child states that all children and young people have a right to express their views on issues that affect them. This gives children and young people the right to participate in all stages of the education response and to take part in decision-making around the development and management of the education system. Stakeholders should support children's and young people's participation in activities and discussions in a safe, secure, and welcoming environment that encourages constructive dialogue. Child-friendly engagement strategies should be used to help children and young people express themselves in ways that acknowledge and respect their age and culture, such as through art, music, and drama. Children and young people are experts in their own lives, and understanding their specific needs and experiences is essential to providing a quality education response. Education authorities and humanitarian actors should consult them when designing and conducting assessments. Young people in particular should meaningfully participate at all stages of data collection and analysis, monitoring, and evaluation. This will also give them an opportunity to learn skills such as data collection, communication, and evidence-based advocacy for themselves and their communities. Participation should be inclusive of gender, ability, and language to ensure that a diverse range of needs and voices are heard. It should be flexible enough to accommodate the needs of individual children and young people (for more guidance, see *INEE Guidance Note on Gender; Humanitarian inclusion standards for older people and people with disabilities*, education inclusion standard 3).

Involving children and young people in any type of process should serve the best interests of the child, adhere to the principle of do no harm, and follow the basic requirements for children's effective and ethical participation, as outlined in General Comment No. 12 (2009) The right of the child to be heard. Actors who work with children and young people must have safeguarding and referral mechanisms in place to address child protection concerns and any MHPSS needs that may arise. This is a standard requirement for anyone working with children, and important when working with vulnerable or marginalized groups, such as young women, gender diverse learners, learners with disabilities, and ethnic minorities (for more guidance, see *Minimum Standards for Child Protection*, Principles 3 and 4; *Supporting Integrated Child Protection and Education Programming in Humanitarian Action*).

Education actors should encourage children and young people to participate in co-curricular activities and programs that teach them ways to protect and support their own and their community's physical, emotional, social, and cognitive wellbeing. Participation in these activities gives young people positive alternatives to becoming involved in armed groups or criminal gangs or other negative coping mechanisms. It also promotes personal development and enables the participating young people to develop useful skills, self-efficacy, and good interpersonal relationships. Such programs also encourage the community to appreciate the contributions their children and young people make.

Involving children and young people in the planning, monitoring, and evaluation of their education programs, especially skills and livelihoods training, makes it more likely that the programs will meet their current and future needs. Youth-led organizations can help identify ways to engage young people in creating positive change, including peacebuilding, social cohesion, addressing the root causes of conflicts and disasters, and becoming part of climate change solutions. Opportunities for young people to participate can include the following:

- Participating in structured volunteer activities and civic engagement
- Engaging in peer mentoring, peer mediation, or conflict resolution
- Helping to develop comprehensive school safety plans or age-appropriate learning activities on relevant topics such as climate change

(For more guidance, see *Minimum Economic Recovery Standards*, Enterprise and Market Systems Development Standards and Employment Standards.)

See also Standard 2, Guidance Note 3; Standard 4, Guidance Notes 4 and 9; Standard 6, Guidance Note 3; Standard 7, Guidance Note 2; Standard 8, Guidance Note 9; Standard 9, Guidance Note 3; Standard 17, Guidance Note 6; Standard 18, Guidance Note 1

References and further reading

Links to these and additional resources are available on the INEE website.

- *A Practical Guide to Social Audit as a Participatory Tool to Strengthen Democratic Governance, Transparency, and Accountability,* United Nations Development Programme, 2016

- *Guidance Note on Capacity Strengthening for Localization,* Grand Bargain Localization Workstream, 2020

- *Humanitarian inclusion standards for older people and people with disabilities,* Age and Disability Capacity Program (ADCAP), 2018

- *IASC Guidelines on Working with and for Young People in Humanitarian and Protracted Crises,* IASC, 2020

- *INEE Guidance Note on Conflict Sensitive Education,* INEE, 2013

- *INEE Guidance Note on Gender,* INEE, 2019

- *Minimum Economic Recovery Standards,* SEEP Network, 2017

- *Minimum Standards for Child Protection in Humanitarian Action,* Alliance for Child Protection in Humanitarian Action, 2019

- *Participation Handbook for Humanitarian Field Workers,* ALNAP, 2009

- *Supporting Integrated Child Protection and Education Programming in Humanitarian Action,* Alliance for Child Protection in Humanitarian Action and INEE, 2022

- *The Adolescent Kit for Expression and Innovation,* United Nations Children's Fund (UNICEF), 2015

- *The Core Humanitarian Standard on Quality and Accountability,* CHS Alliance, Group URD, and the Sphere Project, 2014

- *The Nine Basic Requirements for Meaningful and Ethical Children's Participation,* Save the Children, 2021

- *The Sphere Handbook: Humanitarian Charter and Minimum Standards in Humanitarian Response,* Sphere, 2018

STANDARD 2: RESOURCES

Community resources are identified, mobilized, and used to implement age-appropriate learning opportunities.

Key actions
(please read with guidance notes)

1. **Community resources:** Identify, analyze, and mobilize local resources to support EiE activities.

2. **Safety, access, and quality:** Work with communities, education authorities, and humanitarian actors to strengthen the safety of, access to, and quality of education.

3. **Community contributions:** Recognize existing skills and knowledge within the community and design EiE programs that build on them.

4. **Disaster risk reduction and conflict mitigation:** Use community resources to develop, adapt, and deliver education that includes DRR and conflict mitigation.

Guidance notes

1. **Community resources:** Community resources include the cultural, intellectual, linguistic, monetary, and material resources in a community. Examples of this are technological infrastructure related to distance education, such as radio or mobile phone coverage, and internet access and connectivity. When designing and planning an education response, education authorities and humanitarian actors should identify and analyze the locally available resources to work out how they can contribute to the response. It is important to recognize a community's local and indigenous knowledge systems. A social audit or capacity assessment can help identify what local resources are available. It is important not to overwhelm communities, and to provide support as requested to manage incoming financial and material resources so they can provide the maximum benefit to the community. However, community resources are not a replacement for the national authorities' legal responsibility to protect and fulfill the right to education.

Community resources can contribute to education in several ways, such as providing physical spaces for ECD centers, schools, and other learning environments, and the material and labor needed to build, maintain, and repair them. Communities also play an important role in promoting protection and supporting the emotional, physical, social, and cognitive wellbeing of learners, teachers and other education personnel, and parents and caregivers. This includes providing sufficient compensation to help teachers maintain their practice, motivation, and wellbeing. Although the national authorities have the ultimate responsibility for managing appropriate teacher compensation, in some cases communities can mobilize what resources are available to support teachers, such as in-kind or cash compensation gathered by the community education committee (for more guidance, see INEE Guidance Note on Psychosocial Support; INEE Guidance Note on Teacher Wellbeing in Emergency Settings).

To provide and monitor transparency and accountability, it is essential to keep records of the resources communities mobilize. Monitoring must include mechanisms that safeguard children, such as those that identify and track practices that may harm or exploit children, such as child labor. Other important indicators are those that identify and track instances where women or socially or economically marginalized groups are unfairly relied on to perform tasks or provide resources (for more guidance, see Minimum Standards for Child Protection).

> See also Standard 1, Guidance Notes 3 and 5; Standard 4, Guidance Note 2; Standard 8, Guidance Notes 9 and 11; Standard 10, Guidance Note 5; Standard 11, Guidance Note 6; Standard 16, Guidance Note 1; Standard 17, Guidance Note 1; Standard 19, Guidance Note 3

2. **Strengthening safety, access, and quality:** Community resources can improve the safety of, access to, and quality of education. Education authorities, the local community, and humanitarian actors should encourage community members to identify and help vulnerable children and young people gain access to learning opportunities and continue to higher education levels.

Communities and education authorities should work together to make schools, ECD centers, and other learning environments safe and protective places for children and young people. This can include organizing safe access and transportation, and reaching out to those living in isolated and remote areas. Community members can help teachers by serving as classroom assistants or school focal persons, or by taking on non-teaching tasks like preparing resources. Learners will benefit from having community members of all genders serve as ECD caregivers and classroom assistants, or from having them provide security support to ensure that all learners will be safe on the way to and from school. Providing childcare in learning spaces can help caregivers, particularly girls and young women who are mothers or are caring for younger siblings, to continue their education. Young children also benefit from having both female and male early childhood caregivers. Communities and other stakeholders should ensure that strong role models of all genders are involved across the learning continuum (for more guidance, see INEE Guidance Note on Gender).

Where distance education programs are being used, neighbors, extended family, and siblings can help support both teachers and learners. For example, the community can provide homes or community spaces as learning centers. Bringing this about may first require raising community awareness about the benefits of and support needed to provide distance education (for more guidance, see INEE Background Paper on Distance Education in Emergencies).

In areas where formal education opportunities that meet the needs and demands of young people are not available, the community can advocate for non-formal education programs. This might include accelerated education, catch-up classes, lessons in basic literacy and numeracy, TVET, and small business development training. To ensure that non-formal education programs are recognized, the education authorities should lead their design, with support from the community. Where relevant, development and humanitarian partners should also be involved in developing these programs (for more guidance see *Minimum Economic Recovery Standards*, Enterprise and Market Systems Development Standards).

> See also Standard 8, Guidance Notes 5 and 6; Standard 9; Standard 19, Guidance Notes 1 and 5

3. **Community contributions:** When education authorities or other stakeholders plan, implement, and report on activities, they should include information on community contributions. Strong community contribution shows a sense of ownership and helps create long-term support. However, contributions from the community should not be a condition for receiving support, as the national authorities have a legal responsibility to fulfill the right to education.

It is important that children and young people, especially those from marginalized groups, participate in the design and needs assessment stages of education planning. Stakeholders should encourage and recognize their participation in and contributions to peer education, community mobilization, and community development initiatives.

> See also Standard 1, Guidance Note 7

4. **Disaster risk reduction and conflict mitigation:** National authorities, the local community, and humanitarian actors should use local resources to develop, adapt, and share information on DRR education and community response preparedness. When community resources are used to develop, adapt, and deliver education, it is important to draw from and strengthen positive local coping strategies, technical and scientific knowledge, and capacities for disaster risk management. For example, engaging community members and using local materials to design, rebuild, or retrofit learning environments makes it easier for the community to take responsibility for maintaining these spaces over the long term. Local and indigenous knowledge of the land and how to adapt to environmental changes can support DRR, building resilience, and sustainable development.

When actors mobilize resources in an environment where resources are scarce, they must adhere to conflict sensitive and "do no harm" principles (for more guidance, see *INEE Guidance Note on Conflict Sensitive Education*). To assess whether resources are being mobilized in conflict sensitive ways, it is important to consider the following:

- Who is providing the resource
- How the resource affects the relationship between the education activity and dynamics of the conflict or crisis
- How the resource will affect the provision of equal and equitable access to education for all learners

See also Standard 1, Guidance Note 2; Standard 5, Guidance Notes 3 and 6; Standard 9, Guidance Notes 2 and 10; Standard 10, Guidance Notes 2 and 3

References and further reading

Links to these and additional resources are available on the INEE website.

- *EiE-GenKit: a core resource package on gender and education in emergencies*, ECW, INEE, and UNGEI, 2021
- *INEE Background Paper on Distance Education in Emergencies*, INEE, 2022
- *INEE Guidance Note on Conflict Sensitive Education*, INEE, 2013
- *INEE Guidance Note on Gender*, INEE, 2019
- *INEE Guidance Note on Psychosocial Support*, INEE, 2018
- *INEE Guidance Note on Teacher Wellbeing in Emergency Settings*, INEE, 2022
- *Minimum Economic Recovery Standards*, SEEP Network, 2017
- *Minimum Standards for Child Protection in Humanitarian Action*, Alliance for Child Protection in Humanitarian Action, 2019
- *The Sphere Handbook: Humanitarian Charter and Minimum Standards in Humanitarian Response*, Sphere, 2018

STANDARD 3: COORDINATION

Education coordination mechanisms are in place to support the stakeholders who are working to ensure access to and continuity of quality education.

Key actions
(please read with guidance notes)

1. **Education authorities' leadership:** Education authorities, where appropriate, assume a leadership role in the education response, which includes convening and participating in inter-agency coordination mechanisms with other education stakeholders.

2. **Inter-agency coordination mechanism:** Coordinate needs assessment and analysis, strategic planning, advocacy and resource mobilization, monitoring and evaluation, and capacity sharing through the inter-agency coordination mechanism and consider all levels and types of education in its activities.

3. **Wide representation and meaningful participation:** Ensure that local and national actors are widely represented, participate meaningfully, and guide decision-making in the inter-agency coordination mechanism.

4. **Collaboration across coordination mechanisms:** Collaborate with the various inter-agency coordination mechanisms in the education sector and other sectors, from preparedness to response, and through to recovery.

5. **Resource mobilization and financing:** Use coordinated, timely, transparent, and equitable financing structures to support EiE activities.

6. **Transparent information and knowledge management:** Establish transparent mechanisms for sharing information about planning and coordinating the EiE response in the education coordination mechanism and across coordination mechanisms in other sectors.

7. **Principled coordination to achieve results:** Adhere to principles of equity, transparency, responsibility, and accountability to ensure that the EiE response achieves results.

📋 Guidance notes

1. **Education authorities' leadership:** National or sub-national education authorities, and in some cases non-state actors, are responsible for fulfilling the right to education for all, and they should assume a leadership role in coordinating the education response. Government-led coordination mechanisms, which may exist prior to a crisis, have a mandate to coordinate support to the education sector. However, their preparedness to lead coordinated education planning and response in a crisis can vary. Sometimes a government will lead the coordination and at other times it will co-lead or participate in a coordination mechanism, with support from the international community. Humanitarian actors should engage in capacity sharing with education authorities and other local and national actors, but they should be careful not to infringe on others' legitimate roles. Sometimes it may not be appropriate for education authorities to coordinate humanitarian assistance, such as in contested areas or if they are party to the conflict (see Guidance Note 2 below).

2. **Inter-agency coordination mechanism:** If education authority preparedness is limited or constrained, coordination of the education response may be temporarily assigned, by agreement, to an inter-agency coordination mechanism. In this case, an existing education coordination mechanism should be given the responsibility, or, if the IASC cluster system is activated, the Humanitarian Coordinator and the Humanitarian Country Team will decide whether to activate an education cluster, in consultation with national partners. Decisions around cluster activation are based on an analysis of humanitarian needs, the nature of the crisis, and the size and complexity of the response. In situations concerning refugees, a refugee education working group coordinates the education response in line with UNHCR's Refugee Coordination Model. In any case, when appropriate, an education authority representative should actively participate in decision-making. Where the government cannot be a member of the coordination mechanism, the leads or co-leads are responsible for communicating and engaging with the government.

   Depending on the nature of the crisis, coordination groups at the national and sub-national levels may be needed. Education coordination mechanisms should always respect national and local approaches and structures and make proactive efforts to identify, link with, and work with local coordination and leadership structures, including local and national actors. The terms of reference should establish the committee members' roles and responsibilities.

   All levels and types of formal and non-formal education should be considered in coordination activities, including ECD, primary, secondary, technical and vocational, and higher and adult education.

🔍 See also Standard 8, Guidance Note 4

---

3. **Wide representation and meaningful participation:** If an inter-agency coordination mechanism is established, it is essential to have wide representation and the meaningful participation of local and national actors. This is an important step toward locally led humanitarian action and decoloniality. Their participation and leadership in decision-making and in all aspects of the program cycle is essential to ensure accountability to the people affected and to make sure that the assistance provided is relevant. Local and national actors are the first responders in humanitarian crises. They have firsthand knowledge of local challenges and solutions, and a deeper connection to both the affected people and local networks. Local and national actors are a diverse group that includes the following:

    - Local governments
    - National NGOs
    - CSOs
    - CBOs, including OPDs, refugee-led organizations, youth-led organizations, women-led and women's rights organizations, and faith-based organizations
    - Private sector actors
    - Teachers unions

    Local, national, and international stakeholders should participate equitably in coordination mechanisms and have proportionate and gender-responsive representation. The stakeholders' relationships should be based on partnership, mutual learning, trust, and respect. It is essential that organizations representing marginalized groups are encouraged to participate and supported when they do so. These groups may face multiple barriers, such as language, discrimination, power imbalances, the political environment, logistical and technological obstacles, security challenges, physical obstacles, and resource and capacity constraints. It is important to take all steps necessary to ensure that coordination mechanisms offer a safe and enabling environment. This includes removing any barriers to the meaningful participation of local and national actors and supporting their lead in decision-making. These steps can include the following:

    - Reflecting on how power imbalances shape the relationships between local, national, and international actors, and how power imbalances may be linked to gender imbalances and gender inequality among local and national actors
    - Identifying steps to shift power to those who are typically excluded
    - Sharing information on education coordination mechanisms and how to work with them, including induction for new members
    - Clarifying expectations about participation, including the technical capacity required and how much time it takes
    - Running meetings in the local or national languages
    - Reducing and explaining jargon or technical language

- Holding meetings in accessible, appropriate spaces and having the option to attend remotely. This includes accommodations for persons with physical disabilities, including those with hearing, sensory, or visual impairments
- Sharing information in locally acceptable ways

> Q See also Standard 5, Guidance Note 6

4. **Collaboration across coordination mechanisms:** It is important to create connections and promote collaboration between the coordination mechanisms in the education sector and other sectors. Identifying opportunities for collaboration between coordination mechanisms will help create a more holistic and equitable education response.

Coordination mechanisms can promote and facilitate collaboration across sectors by setting the priorities and approaches for each sector. For example, inter-cluster coordination provides a platform where clusters can work together on shared strategic objectives. The child protection and education sectors provide services to many of the same learners, have partners in common, and often implement actions in the same spaces. Additionally, the Centrality of Protection outlines the obligations of all humanitarian actors, including coordination mechanisms, to ensure protection from sexual exploitation and abuse and other child safeguarding violations, and to mitigate risks of gender-based violence. This makes it critical for education and protection coordination mechanisms to work together and coordinate their activities to address learners' interconnected needs, barriers, and risks. This may include these sectors sharing responsibilities for training and capacity sharing to have a wider reach. Education coordination mechanisms should also work with any cash working group present to figure out if and how CVA might be used to support education activities. Coordinated needs assessments are an opportunity to promote inter-sectoral links (for more guidance, see *Minimum Standards for Child Protection*, Standard 1 and Standard 23; *Education in Emergencies - Child Protection Collaboration Framework*).

In the education sector, a key priority is to promote dialogue and engagement between humanitarian coordination mechanisms and national coordination mechanisms, such as a local education group. It is important that national and humanitarian plans align so that the national ESP can meet the needs of crisis-affected learners. This will ensure that the humanitarian plans are in line with and supportive of the national priorities and processes. Joint planning is also important for areas such as teacher management, compensation, and professional development. Aligning key processes, such as education data management and budgeting, will also help ensure that crisis-affected learners are visible and accounted for in the national systems (for more guidance, see *Humanitarian-Development Coherence in Education: working together in crisis contexts*).

In situations where humanitarian concerns include IDPs, refugees, and affected people in the same geographic location, the humanitarian coordination mechanisms—education clusters and refugee education working groups—should work together. In these settings, joint coordination arrangements may follow the guidelines provided in the Joint UNHCR-OCHA Note on Mixed Settings, or be adapted to the specific context in keeping with global mandates. This can improve the efficiency, timeliness, and quality of an education response. The appropriate level of collaboration depends on the situation, the composition of the population affected, and how close different populations are to each other. It is important to make sure there is collaboration between education cluster and refugee coordination mechanisms (for more guidance, see *Education in Emergencies coordination: Harnessing humanitarian and development architecture for Education 2030*).

> See also Standard 4, Guidance Note 10; Standard 5, Guidance Notes 4 and 7; Standard 8, Guidance Note 1; Standard 10, Guidance Note 9; Standard 14, Guidance Note 1; Standard 16, Guidance Note 1; Standard 17, Guidance Note 3; Standard 18, Guidance Note 5; Standard 19, Guidance Note 4

5. **Resource mobilization and financing:** Significant funds are required to implement quality education programs during emergencies and through to recovery in a successful and timely manner. Education coordination mechanisms play a key role in mobilizing resources and advocating for funding for cross-cutting issues in EiE pooled funds vetting criteria. Education systems affected by crisis are funded in several ways, most importantly by national governments. When there is a funding gap, humanitarian and development assistance can complement national and local resources. Financing should be managed in an inclusive, transparent, and coordinated way, such as through the UN flash appeal and consolidated appeals processes. ECW and the Global Partnership for Education are two global funds dedicated to education response. In acute emergencies, the UN Central Emergency Response Fund, UN Country-Based Pooled Funds, ECW First Emergency Response, and other emergency response funds, such as NGO-led funds, can provide education funding. The Refugee Response Plan is the key document used for raising funds in refugee situations. The Humanitarian Response Plan is the main appeal and response document used in situations affecting IDPs and crisis-affected children and young people. Humanitarian actors should prioritize and facilitate local partners' direct access to resources to reduce transaction costs and ensure successful outcomes for the people affected. This includes advocating with donors to achieve more direct and sustainable funding that will support access to education at all levels.

Emergency financing arrangements should reflect national and regional labor market conditions and traditions. They should not set precedents that cannot be maintained. To avoid fueling division in conflict situations, the allocation of resources should be based on a context analysis. A coordinated policy is needed to ensure that teachers' and other education personnel's compensation is not interrupted. To support sustainable interventions across the humanitarian-development-peacebuilding nexus, it is important to harmonize emergency financing arrangements with longer-term arrangements. This may include international financing institutions, multi-donor trust funds, or development financing options, such as pooled funding or national financing.

Private sector funding may supplement local and national resources and international assistance. The Abidjan Principles outline governments' human rights obligations to regulate private involvement in education. Private financing should not undermine national and local ownership of education programs or replace locally recognized credentialing requirements. The national or sub-national education authorities and inter-agency coordination mechanism should discuss how to coordinate their operations with private sector funding, including longer-term funding and exit strategies, for example cluster deactivation.

International humanitarian actors should make sure their assistance complements assistance from community-based and civil society funding, faith-based giving, and South-South cooperation. The funding parties should work closely with the local community to do a needs assessments, followed by ongoing consultation (for more guidance, see INEE Guidance Notes on Teacher Compensation; INEE Reference Guide to External Education Financing; Minimum Economic Recovery Standards, Financial Services Standards).

> See also Standard 5, Guidance Notes 5 and 7; Standard 8, Guidance Note 11; Standard 15, Guidance Note 3; Standard 18, Guidance Notes 5 and 9; Standard 19, Guidance Note 3

6. **Transparent information and knowledge management:** Information and knowledge management includes:

- Assessing needs, capacities, and coverage in a participatory and inclusive way
- Collecting, storing, analyzing, and sharing sex-, age-, and disability-disaggregated data
- Monitoring and evaluation
- Reflecting on lessons learned to inform future work

Information and knowledge management includes different levels and types of education data. This may include response-based reporting, general education information management through an EMIS, or learner data. How these various types of education data are collected, analyzed, shared, and used will vary.

Effective information and knowledge management systems should aim to build on and strengthen national systems and avoid duplicating them. It is essential to involve national and local partners who work in relevant sectors such as child protection, gender/gender-based violence, MHPSS, shelter, nutrition, WASH, health, food security, livelihoods, and early recovery and to share information across sectors. National and local authorities should design information and knowledge management systems and oversee them over the long term.

Sharing information and data in a coordinated way can strengthen an education response. Not doing so may cause data to be collected multiple times or misused. On the other hand, sharing data between organizations can also increase the risk of mismanagement and affect communities negatively. To prevent this, humanitarian actors should establish an information sharing protocol (ISP) to ensure a responsible exchange of information and data. ISPs are usually established system-wide, but also at the cluster/sector and organization level (for more guidance, see *Minimum Economic Recovery Standards*, Core Standard 2).

> See also Standard 4, Guidance Notes 6 and 11; Standard 6, Guidance Note 6; Standard 7, Guidance Note 3; Standard 18, Guidance Note 8

7. **Principled coordination to achieve results:** A results-oriented approach means that all actors coordinate their education responses to produce the desired results. Different actors have different mandates and missions, but all should agree to accountability in coordination and information sharing. This means being transparent about collecting and using information to plan the work. If there are critical gaps in the education response, the education cluster, refugee education working group, and other mechanisms will take responsibility for encouraging stakeholders to fill the gaps and cover the highest-priority needs.

Inter-agency coordination mechanisms should regularly monitor and evaluate the coordination of the education response to identify and address any gaps in coordination. Information about the outcomes of coordinated monitoring and evaluation work should be shared openly, including with the people affected. Doing this will highlight where more work is needed, such as respecting cultural diversity, promoting anti-racist initiatives, and protecting the rights of indigenous people. It also will help support people using the INEE MS and related humanitarian principles. Any national human rights institutions involved in a response should monitor their national authorities' obligation to guarantee the right to education for all. National international humanitarian law committees, supported by the International Committee of the Red Cross, may also help national authorities meet their responsibility to fulfill the right to education.

> See also Standard 6, Guidance Note 1; Standard 7, Guidance Note 1; Standard 19, Guidance Note 3

References and further reading

Links to these and additional resources are available on the INEE website.

- *Education in Emergencies: Child Protection Collaboration Framework*, Child Protection Area of Responsibility and Global Education Cluster (GEC), 2020
- *Education in Emergencies coordination: Harnessing humanitarian and development architecture for Education 2030*, GEC, INEE, and UNHCR, 2020
- *Guidance for Education Cluster Teams: Practical Coordination Steps toward Humanitarian–Development Nexus*, GEC, 2022
- *Guidance Note on the Participation of Local Actors in Humanitarian Coordination Groups*, Grand Bargain Localization Workstream, 2020
- *Guide to Coordinated Education in Emergencies Needs Assessments and Analysis*, GEC, 2020
- *Humanitarian Coordination and the Cluster Approach: A Quick Guide for Local and National Organizations*, GEC, Save the Children, and Translators without Borders, 2020
- *Humanitarian-Development Coherence in Education: working together in crisis contexts*, INEE, 2021
- *IASC Guidance on Strengthening Participation, Representation and Leadership of Local and National Actors in IASC Humanitarian Coordination Mechanisms*, IASC, 2021
- *INEE Guidance Notes on Teacher Compensation*, INEE, 2009
- *INEE Reference Guide on External Education Financing*, INEE, 2012
- *Inter-Agency Toolkit on Localization in Humanitarian Coordination*, Child Protection Area of Responsibility, Save the Children, and Street Child, 2022
- *Refugee Coordination Model*, UNHCR, 2019

STANDARD 4: ASSESSMENT

> Timely education assessments of the emergency situation are holistic, transparent, and participatory.

Key actions
(please read with guidance notes)

1. **Rapid needs assessment:** Conduct a rapid needs assessment as soon as possible, with consideration for the security and safety of the assessment team and the people affected.

2. **Comprehensive assessment:** Conduct a comprehensive assessment of education needs and resources for the different levels and types of education.

3. **Cash and voucher assistance:** Conduct a needs assessment to collect information on the economic barriers to accessing education.

4. **Assessment teams:** Form an assessment team with balanced representation and ensure that team members receive proper training before they collect data.

5. **Disaggregated data:** Collect disaggregated data that identify the perceived purpose and relevance of education for the local community, barriers to education access, and priority education needs and activities.

6. **Data responsibility:** Collect, store, share, analyze, and use data safely, ethically, and effectively.

7. **Context analysis:** Conduct a context analysis to ensure that the EiE response is appropriate, relevant, and sensitive to the potential for risks and conflict.

8. **Community resilience:** Identify local capacities, resources, and strategies for education, crisis mitigation, preparedness, and recovery before and during the emergency.

9. **Participation in assessments:** Ensure that representatives of the people affected and the education authorities participate in the design and implementation of data collection.

10. **Collaboration within the education sector and with other sectors:** An inter-agency coordination mechanism coordinates education assessments with those by other sectors and actors.

11. **Assessment findings:** Share assessment findings promptly with a wide range of stakeholders, especially the people affected by the crisis.

Guidance notes

1. **Rapid needs assessment:** Data collection and needs assessments should be kept to a minimum in the early stages of a response. When a crisis arises, data should be collected through a multi-sectoral rapid needs assessment. This should be done as soon as it is safe for the assessment team and the people affected. Multi-sectoral assessments minimize cost, increase efficiency, and reduce the burden on the people affected. The goal of a multi-sectoral assessment should be to create a first snapshot of what the people affected need and understand their priorities. Stakeholders such as the national government, the UN Office for the Coordination of Humanitarian Affairs (OCHA), UNHCR, or United Nations Development Programme have specific mandates to do this work and thus should lead or coordinate multi-sectoral assessments.

   It is essential that education is represented in multi-sectoral assessments. In countries with an active, formal rapid response mechanism, education questions should be integrated into that mechanism's assessment question bank. Humanitarian actors can use the rapid response question bank in the GEC's *Strengthening Rapid Education Response Toolkit* to contextualize education questions in a rapid response mechanism assessment. Assessment and analysis should continue in the later stages of a response, and should include girls, children with disabilities, and other potentially vulnerable children and young people. Humanitarian actors can use an environment assessment tool, such as the NEAT+, to ensure that a response is sustainable. This kind of tool will help actors identify environmental concerns before they design longer-term emergency or recovery interventions.

   > See also Standard 3, Guidance Note 7; Standard 5, Guidance Notes 1 and 4; Standard 8, Guidance Note 11

2. **Comprehensive assessments:** After completing the rapid needs assessment, EiE stakeholders should conduct a comprehensive inter-agency assessment of the education sector, such as a joint education needs assessment (JENA). National education authorities and the education coordination mechanism should coordinate and manage joint assessments. A rapid JENA may take place up to a month after the onset of a crisis, followed by a more detailed JENA later on. A JENA aims to determine the impact of the emergency on learners, communities, and the education system. It should collect information on education capacities, resources, vulnerabilities, and gaps and challenges to the right to education for all, across all levels and types of education. A joint inter-agency needs assessment is the highest standard for an education assessment, but the type, depth, and scope of an assessment will depend on contextual factors, such as the resources available, capacity, and decision-making time frame. Emergencies are complex, and the needs of the people affected change over time. After the initial assessment, EiE

stakeholders should regularly update the data through monitoring and evaluation to determine achievements, limits, and unmet needs. The findings for each phase of a crisis should guide the design and focus of later assessments.

Assessments should make the most of existing information sources. This is known as secondary data, which can include published research, government reports, online material, and data that has already been analyzed for other purposes. Assessment teams should analyze the secondary data before collecting primary data. The primary data collection should be limited to what is needed to fill urgent knowledge gaps and guide critical decisions. If access to some secondary data is restricted, other sectors or pre-crisis databases can provide useful secondary data. Pre-crisis data provides a measure against which to compare the emergency situation. Local leaders and community networks can help assessment teams reach members of the community to collect primary data. Stakeholders conducting the assessment should respect local and indigenous communities and knowledge systems and include them in the assessments.

Preparedness for assessments is usually led by the inter-agency coordination mechanism in cooperation with education authorities. Education authorities and the inter-agency coordination mechanism should standardize data collection tools in country so it is possible to coordinate projects and minimize the demand on the people sharing information. Relevant stakeholders should aim to develop and agree on the assessment tools they will use during preparedness planning. Training people to use these tools is also an important part of preparedness and contingency planning. The tools should include space to add information the local respondents consider important, which will enable them to express their needs fully. Collection tools should be developed using the method and software best suited to the situation. This may be a paper-based collection tool or a mobile/electronic tool. The time frame, budget, and capacity of the assessment team are also important to consider. (For more guidance and resources on planning, coordinating, and conducting needs assessments, see *EiE Needs Assessment Package*.)

> See also Standard 2, Guidance Note 1; Standard 3, Guidance Note 2; Standard 5, Guidance Notes 1 and 4; Standard 6, Guidance Notes 1 and 4; Standard 7, Guidance Note 1; Standard 8, Guidance Note 2; Standard 11, Guidance Note 6; Standard 19, Guidance Note 2

3. **Cash and voucher assistance:** Inter-agency coordination mechanisms should assess education needs in an integrated way, from both the demand-side and supply-side perspectives. To determine whether CVA is an appropriate response modality, the assessments should collect specific information on the economic barriers to education.

Multi-sectoral assessments and comprehensive education assessments should include cash-related questions, where the situation allows. This will help to determine how education costs and negative coping mechanisms might be addressed with CVA. Information on CVA can help stakeholders identify the following:

- The education services available
- The benefits of using CVA instead of or in addition to in-kind and direct service delivery
- The delivery modalities that the people affected prefer, such as CVA, in-kind, or direct service delivery
- The physical access those affected have to markets

Additional assessments are needed to determine if CVA is feasible in a particular area. If a non-education CVA feasibility assessment is planned, education stakeholders should advocate including education-related questions. If this is not possible, they should work with the cash working group or other sectors (e.g., child protection, food security, livelihoods) and organizations with strong CVA expertise to adapt cash feasibility assessment tools to collect information on CVA in the education sector. Feasibility assessments of both types can help stakeholders identify the following:

- The capacity and functioning of markets for education-related goods and services, such as uniforms, school materials, and transportation
- The protection and operational risks associated with CVA
- The options available to transfer money to the people affected

> See also Standard 5, Guidance Note 1; Standard 8, Guidance Note 3; Standard 16, Guidance Note 1

4. **Assessment teams:** When forming an assessment team, it is important to consider the team members' profiles. The teams should include people from the affected community, as they will bring their knowledge of the local context and understand how to operate effectively in that context. This also will help with the data collection because members of the community have connections to local networks. The teams should have a balance of genders to reflect the experiences, needs, concerns, and capacities of learners, teachers and other education personnel, and parents and caregivers of all genders. An inter-agency assessment team should have a balanced representation of languages and organizational affiliations, and national and international staff members. Systems should be in place to counter any explicit or implicit bias that might affect the way assessments are planned and conducted, and the way information is analyzed.

Assessment team members should receive proper training before they collect data. The training should cover the goal of the assessment, the methodology and tools, and the code of conduct. It should also teach the team how to get informed consent and to address concerns about protection. This includes their responsibilities in terms of child safeguarding and protection from sexual exploitation and abuse and gender-based violence. If some respondents will be children, the training should cover child safeguarding and child-friendly skills to ensure that the children's participation is safe and meaningful (see Annex 1: Glossary for a definition of child-friendly) (for more guidance, see *EiE Needs Assessment Package; Minimum Standards for Child Protection*).

> 🔍 See also Standard 1, Guidance Notes 3 and 7; Standard 6, Guidance Note 3

5. **Disaggregated data:** Teams should collect disaggregated data to guide the education response and assess any ongoing risk. Education stakeholders should design assessment tools to collect and analyze relevant information on different social groups, including their vulnerabilities, risks, and the effect the crisis has on education. Disaggregated data is important in understanding how different marginalized groups are affected by the crisis. The data should be disaggregated by sex, age, and disability status at a minimum, but can also include language, location, displacement or international protection status, ethnicity, and more. Teams also should collect disaggregated data related to other sectors that are linked to education, such as child protection, MHPSS, ECD, WASH, health, and nutrition. They should use secondary data sources as much as possible to collect this information (for more guidance, see *INEE Guidance Note on Gender; INEE Guidance Note on Psychosocial Support; INEE Guidance Note on Teacher Wellbeing in Emergency Settings*).

The varying nature of crises can make the data on vulnerable populations or on certain characteristics quite sensitive. This information can include religious or ethnic origins, language, political opinions, religious beliefs, physical or mental health conditions, and sexual orientation. Teams should take extra care when collecting potentially sensitive information.

> 🔍 See also Standard 5, Guidance Note 8; Standard 6, Guidance Note 4; Standard 7, Guidance Note 1

6. **Data responsibility:** The basic principles of respect and non-discrimination should be the foundation of any assessment. It is important to handle the data lifecycle— which includes collecting, storing, analyzing, sharing, and using data—safely, ethically, and effectively. All stakeholders who work with and manage humanitarian data should adhere to the following principles:

   ○ **Do no harm:** Collecting information can put people at risk. Their information may be sensitive, and even just participating can put them at risk. Team members must ensure that personal information is protected in line with accepted frameworks. This may fall under national and regional data protection laws or organizational data protection policies. "Do no harm" also includes addressing any ongoing or observed protection issues and following child safeguarding protocols. If there is concern that children's participation might cause them harm, team members should consult child protection actors.

- **Informed consent or assent:** Those collecting information must protect participants and inform them of the following:
  - Why they are collecting the data
  - That they have the right not to participate
  - That they can stop at any time without consequences
  - That they have the right to confidentiality and anonymity

Parents and caregivers should give consent for their children to participate. The children should also be asked if they want to participate.

- **Purpose driven:** Data should be collected to strengthen the education response and collected only if there is a clear reason. Doing otherwise could create unnecessary risk and waste resources.
- **Confidentiality:** It is essential to keep participants' data confidential throughout the data cycle. Stakeholders should take all necessary steps and safeguards to avoid violating confidentiality. Whenever feasible, personal data should go through an anonymization process.
- **Transparency and accountability:** Stakeholders should make the following clear to participants:
  - What data they are collecting
  - How they will keep it confidential
  - How they will use it
  - Whom they may share it with and how they will share it
  - How they will keep it safe
  - How individuals can ask for their personal data to be removed

(For more guidance, see IASC Operational Guidance on Data Responsibility in Humanitarian Action; Minimum Standards for Child Protection, Standard 18.)

Data analyses should clearly identify the following:
- Indicators
- Data sources
- Collection methods
- Data collectors
- Data analysis procedures

Where data collectors face security risks, the analysis should refer to the types of organizations involved in the data collection and not the names of the data collectors. The collectors should note any limitations of the data collection or analysis that could affect the reliability of the findings or how useful they may be in other situations. If the data shows that certain groups or issues are not included in programs and monitoring systems, the collectors should make a note of that.

To reduce bias and strengthen validity, stakeholders should collect data using several sources and then compare them. Sources can include classroom observations, focus group discussions, community group discussions, key informant interviews, and household surveys. Before drawing conclusions, the team members should consult with the most affected groups, including children and young people of all genders and persons with disabilities. To prevent the education response from reflecting the perceptions and priorities of people external to the context, local perceptions and knowledge should be central to the analysis.

See also Standard 3, Guidance Note 6; Standard 6, Guidance Note 4; Standard 7, Guidance Note 3

7. **Context analysis:** Context analysis is a key step in the assessment process and usually part of a multi-sectoral assessment. It complements other assessment activities. Analysis of the context, including disaster risk and conflict analysis, can ensure that an education response is appropriate, relevant, and sensitive to the potential for conflict and disaster. Education stakeholders should consider the medium- and long-term implications of an intervention, including learners' ability to integrate into formal programs, to complete certified non-formal programs, or to re-enter the education system in their country of origin. In refugee situations, the context analysis should include information on the education systems in the country of origin and the host country. It should document the differences and similarities in the curriculum, language, requirements, and structure of the two systems, at what levels certification exams are given, and trends in enrollment and completion in each country, disaggregated by age, sex, disability, and education level. The analysis should look at how these factors could affect refugees' access to education, and at the legal framework that governs access to the national education systems or refugees' access to education.

Risk analysis should consider all aspects of the context that may affect the health, security, and safety of learners, especially children and young people. This will help to make education a protective measure rather than a risk factor. A risk analysis assesses all hazards and risks to education, which may include the following:

- Insecurity, poor governance, and corruption
- Biological and health hazards, such as pandemics, communicable diseases, and air pollution
- Natural and climate change-induced hazards, such as earthquakes, floods, and wildfires
- Technological hazards, such as a toxic gas release or chemical spill
- Conflict and violence
- Risks related to gender, age, race, disability, ethnic background, and other relevant factors

A risk analysis report proposes strategies for managing the risks created by natural and human-made hazards, including conflict. These strategies can include prevention, mitigation, preparedness, response, reconstruction, and rehabilitation. For example, the risk analysis report may note that schools and other learning environments should have contingency and security plans to prevent, reduce, and respond to emergencies. It also could suggest that schools and other learning environments prepare a risk map that shows potential threats and highlights what may affect learners' vulnerability and resilience. A useful starting point is the safe schools context analysis, as described in the *Comprehensive School Safety Framework*. This can help education stakeholders identify strengths and weaknesses, opportunities and threats, and guide national or sub-national strategic planning for school safety.

Conflict analysis assesses the presence or risk of violent conflict to prevent education interventions from increasing inequalities or worsening a conflict. This is necessary in both conflict and disaster situations. Conflict analysis should ask the following questions:

- Who is directly or indirectly involved in a conflict?
- Who is being affected by a conflict or is at risk of being affected?
- What has caused the actual or potential conflict?
- How do actors interact and what are the dynamics, including education stakeholders?

Research organizations often conduct conflict analyses for a region or country, which education actors should review from an education perspective. If no such analysis is available or applicable, education stakeholders can carry one out by holding a workshop in the affected area, or through a desk study. Education stakeholders should advocate for the right agencies to do a comprehensive conflict analysis that includes education-specific information, and to share their findings with all interested parties.

> See also Standard 1, Guidance Note 1; Standard 9, Guidance Note 2; Standard 10, Guidance Note 1; Standard 14, Guidance Note 3; Standard 18, Guidance Note 7; Standard 19, Guidance Note 2

8. **Community resilience:** Education actors should complement the context analysis with an assessment of context-specific education capacities, resources, and strategies, including community resilience and coping efforts. The assessment should include digital literacy and technological infrastructure related to distance education, such as internet access and connectivity. If possible, education stakeholders should use preparedness and mitigation activities both before and after an emergency to assess and strengthen community knowledge, skills, and capacities for disaster mitigation, preparedness, and recovery. Local and indigenous knowledge systems should be included in the context analysis and assessment efforts. These unique ways of knowing can create a foundation for locally appropriate, sustainable development and help to guide community-based DRR and resilience strategies.

See also Standard 2; Standard 5, Guidance Note 6; Standard 9, Guidance Note 10; Standard 10, Guidance Notes 1–3 and 5; Standard 18, Guidance Note 4

9. **Participation in assessments:** Education authorities and representatives of people who are affected by a crisis should participate in the design and implementation of assessments. When possible, EiE actors should encourage and support children's and young people's participation by conducting peer assessments, school risk mapping, etc. Their involvement should be contingent on the situation being safe and secure.

When conducting assessments, it is important to communicate in all languages used in the community, including sign language and braille, where applicable. Qualified translators and interpreters should facilitate communication.

See also Standard 1, Guidance Notes 3 and 7

10. **Collaboration within the education sector and with other sectors:** To make assessments as comprehensive and useful as possible, it is important that education stakeholders collaborate within the education sector and with other sectors. To avoid duplication, they should conduct harmonized or joint assessments and coordinate field visits with other emergency response providers through the inter-agency coordination mechanism. This will prevent the inefficient use of resources and over-assessment of certain people or issues. Coordinated assessments encourage humanitarian stakeholders to share information and ensure that all affected groups are accounted for. This improves accountability and results in stronger evidence of the impact of an emergency and a more coherent response.

The education sector should work with other sectors to guide the education response to threats and risks and to determine what services are available. This may include coordination with the following:

- **The child protection sector** to conduct joint assessments and learn about the risks facing children who are accessing education and those who are not. Risks include gender-based violence, children who are unaccompanied or separated from their caregivers, harmful traditional practices, barriers to education, and a lack of social and MHPSS services (for more guidance, see *Minimum Standards for Child Protection*, Standard 23; *Supporting Integrated Child Protection and Education Programming*)
- **The health sector** to get epidemiology and other health data and information about the threat of health emergencies and to learn what basic health services are available, including services for sexual and reproductive health, for rehabilitation or early intervention for children with disabilities, and for HIV prevention, treatment, care, and support

- **The nutrition sector** to learn about school-based, community-based, and other nutrition services
- **The WASH sector** to make sure there is a reliable water supply and appropriate sanitation in the learning environment (for more guidance, see *Sphere Handbook*)
- **The cash working group or food security sector** to advocate for including education-related costs in the minimum expenditure baskets, to align CVA modalities, or to share information on payment mechanism options
- **The shelter and camp management sectors** to coordinate finding safe and appropriate locations for learning; building, rebuilding, and accessing learning and recreation spaces; and providing non-food items for the learning environment (for more guidance, see *Minimum Standards for Camp Management*)
- **The logistics sector** to organize the procurement and delivery of books and other supplies
- **The ECD sector**, which is often cross-cutting and embedded within existing sectoral interventions and may or may not have a coordination mechanism at the national or subnational levels. It is important to collect information on ECD efforts in education and other sectors during assessments to understand young learners' and caregivers' needs and determine who will lead overall ECD coordination across and/or within sectors.

> See also Standard 3, Guidance Notes 2 and 4; Standard 10, Guidance Notes 1 and 7–9; Standard 19, Guidance Note 4

11. Assessment findings: The actors managing the assessment should make the assessment findings available as soon as possible to a wide range of stakeholders, including local and national governments, national NGOs, UN agencies, CSOs, CBOs, and the people affected. Pre-crisis data and post-crisis assessments that identify resources and education needs should also be made available. This information will enable stakeholders to plan education activities and determine whether education authorities, NGOs, humanitarian agencies, and communities are fulfilling the right to education. When possible, local and national education authorities should share and coordinate the assessment findings. If they cannot, an inter-agency coordination mechanism, such as the education cluster or refugee education working group, can manage this process. Data sharing agreements such as an ISP should be established and be in line with national or regional data protection laws.

The actors managing the assessment should share assessment findings using a form of communication appropriate to the context to ensure that they reach local stakeholders and the people affected. Possible formats include presentations, printed summary sheets, simplified/child-friendly reports, workshops, or links to a public online posting. Sharing assessment findings can be connected to education-related activities in the community, such as community education committees, parent-teacher association meetings, and other forums. Sharing information with the people affected, especially those who participated in the assessment, is a critical step toward accountability. Sharing information with people affected by the crisis may require more time and resources, but it is important so that they can engage meaningfully with the findings. Assessment reports and products should be standardized and made available in languages, formats, and channels that are easily accessible.

See also Standard 3, Guidance Note 6

References and further reading

Links to these and additional resources are available on the INEE website.

- *Comprehensive School Safety Framework*, GADRRRES, 2022
- *Considerations for Cash and Voucher Assistance in Education in Emergencies Needs Assessments Checklist*, GEC, 2019
- *Considerations for Cash and Voucher Assistance in Rapid Needs Assessment and Analysis*, GEC, 2021
- *EiE-GenKit: a core resource package on gender and education in emergencies*, ECW, INEE, and UNGEI, 2021
- *IASC Gender with Age Marker* [Website]
- *IASC Operational Guidance on Data Responsibility in Humanitarian Action*, IASC, 2021
- *INEE Guidance Note on Conflict Sensitive Education*, INEE, 2013
- *INEE Guidance Note on Gender*, INEE, 2019
- *INEE Guidance Note on Psychosocial Support*, INEE, 2018
- *INEE Guidance Note on Teacher Wellbeing in Emergency Settings*, INEE, 2022
- *Listen and Learn: Participatory Assessment with Children and Adolescents*, UNHCR, 2012
- *EiE Needs Assessment Package*, GEC, 2020
- *Nexus Environmental Assessment Tool (NEAT+)*, UNEP/OCHA Joint Environment Unit
- *Questionnaire Design for Needs Assessments in Humanitarian Emergencies*, ACAPS, 2016
- *Strengthening Rapid Education Response Toolkit*, DG-ECHO, GEC, UNICEF, Save the Children, UNESCO-IIEP, REACH, NORCAP, and Translators without Borders, 2022
- *The Washington Group Short Set on Functioning*, Washington Group on Disability Statistics, 2022
- *UNICEF Guide to Conflict Analysis*, UNICEF, 2016

STANDARD 5: RESPONSE STRATEGIES

> Inclusive education response strategies include a clear description of the context and of the barriers to the right to education, and strategies to overcome those barriers.

Key actions
(please read with guidance notes)

1. **Evidence-based response strategies:** Reflect the assessment findings accurately in response strategies.

2. **Response planning:** Ensure that the education response progressively enables the people affected to access inclusive and equitable quality education.

3. **Do no harm:** Design and implement response strategies in ways that do not harm the community or service providers.

4. **Updates to response strategies:** Regularly update information collected from the initial assessment and context analysis to guide the education response.

5. **Donor response:** Provide enough funds for the response to ensure that the minimum level of education access and quality can be met.

6. **Education system resilience:** Include activities in response strategies that support the education authorities, local and national actors, and community members to prepare for, prevent, and respond to future crises.

7. **Harmonization with national programs:** Ensure that EiE response strategies complement and align with national education programs.

8. **Baseline data:** Collect baseline data systematically at the start of a program.

Guidance notes

1. **Evidence-based response strategies:** Response strategies must be based on evidence and driven by a needs analysis of both the demand side and the supply side. It is important to consider the assistance modality, such as CVA, in-kind, and direct service delivery. Education stakeholders should carefully analyze and interpret the assessment data, and their response strategies should reflect the key findings and major priorities. They should also be aware of biases and assumptions about

what people need, and of the most appropriate way to meet those needs. To ensure that the learners', educators', and education systems' specific needs are met, stakeholders may need to adapt and contextualize their response approach to be in line with the information gathered during the assessments.

> See also Standard 4, Guidance Notes 1–3

2. **Response planning:** Education stakeholders should develop a rapid response plan as soon as possible after the onset of a new crisis, or if an existing crisis suddenly worsens. A rapid response plan is typically a condensed version of a broader response strategy. It is implemented during the first phase of a response, usually up to three months. Education should be included in all multi-sectoral rapid response mechanisms. In some situations this may not happen due to contextual constraints, so a separate but complementary education rapid response should be planned, coordinated, and implemented through the education coordination mechanism. Rapid response activities should focus on essential services that address the immediate wellbeing and learning needs of learners and of teachers and other education personnel. These may include providing temporary infrastructure and recreational, creative, and academic materials; conducting initial assessments to determine learning levels to tailor the response; and interventions such as MHPSS, SEL, school meals, and child-friendly spaces. The rapid response services should connect with longer-term programming as soon as possible. It is important to base response strategies on preparedness or contingency plans or, if there are none, to develop these plans with the meaningful and inclusive participation of sub-national or local education authorities and communities (for more guidance, see *Strengthening Rapid Education Response Toolkit*).

After the first phase of a response, rapid response plans should blend into the broader education response programming. The voices and perspectives of all learners, teachers, and community members should guide the design and implementation of the response strategies. It is also important to acknowledge that programs are implemented within a national policy context which will also influence what response options are available. Increasing learning and protection should be a priority of response strategies. Response strategies can outline the different levels, languages, and types of education, identify the risks and hazards, and indicate whether other agencies or sectors are supporting education activities. The budget for implementing a response strategy should include essential education activities, including baseline data collection, monitoring, and evaluation.

Response strategies should be as flexible as possible to allow education stakeholders to carry out key activities, including the following:

- Analyzing and working to remove barriers to access for all levels and types of education
- Assessing learning levels

- Adapting learning opportunities to meet the needs of all learners
- Providing multiple learning pathways
- Connecting to essential services beyond the education sector, such as protection, MHPSS, nutrition, WASH, health, and food security

> See also Standard 1, Guidance Note 1; Standard 8; Standard 18, Guidance Note 5; Standard 19, Guidance Notes 2 and 3

3. **Do no harm:** During an EiE response, resources like training, jobs, supplies, and food are introduced or distributed in what are often resource-scarce environments. To some, these resources can represent power and wealth. They can become a part of the conflict, worsen the effects of the emergency, or contribute to existing inequalities within the community, such as marginalization or discrimination. In a conflict situation, some people may try to control and use these resources to support their side and weaken the other side, or to gain personally. Stakeholders can use risk and conflict analysis to help ensure that resources are distributed equitably and that the EiE response maximizes positive impact and minimizes negative impact (for more guidance, see *INEE Guidance Note on Conflict Sensitive Education*).

Transferring resources and conducting an EiE response can also strengthen local actors' capacity to build peace or promote social cohesion. Awareness raising activities can lessen division and tension by building on or creating ties that bring a community together. For example, teacher professional development programs can unite teachers in their professional identities as educators that bridge ethnic divides. Ensuring the inclusion of marginalized groups in community activities can promote more equitable community relations. Awareness raising efforts also can improve attitudes about the education of persons with disabilities and the contributions they make to the community.

> See also Standard 1, Guidance Note 2; Standard 2, Guidance Note 4; Standard 3, Guidance Note 5; Standard 4, Guidance Note 7; Standard 8, Guidance Note 7; Standard 10, Guidance Note 7

4. **Updates to response strategies:** Education stakeholders should regularly review and update their response strategies during emergencies, and through to recovery. Updates should reflect the state of learner's learning and protection, changes in strategy and what has been achieved, as well as changes in the emergency and security situation. Feedback from learners and teachers on how the response has or has not met their needs and rights should guide the strategy updates. Changing needs should also be reflected in the updated strategy. Education programming should promote progressive improvements in learning, inclusion, equity, coverage, sustainability, and shared ownership. To ensure that education activities are gradually handed over to the relevant parties, updated response strategies should have transition plans and exit strategies in place at all levels of education.

Reviewing and updating response strategies can provide opportunities for cross-sectoral collaboration. This may include coordinating and identifying common activities between child protection and the education response, between the ECD response and nutrition programming, or between TVET programs and economic recovery activities.

> See also Standard 1, Guidance Note 1; Standard 3, Guidance Note 4; Standard 4, Guidance Notes 1 and 2; Standard 6, Guidance Note 1

5. **Donor response:** Humanitarian partners and donors need to regularly review the quality and coverage of the EiE response to ensure that it meets the minimum levels of access and quality. They should pay particular attention to how many learners from vulnerable groups enroll and continue to go to school to ensure that they have equal access to education. "Equal access" means that all children, young people, and adult learners have equal education opportunities, particularly those marginalized because of ethnicity, language, gender, disability, race, or class. Funding for the education response should be available as early as possible when a crisis occurs and should be given the same priority as the water, food, shelter, and health responses. Donors and humanitarian partners must adhere to do no harm principles to ensure that their assistance does not negatively impact communities hosting refugees and/or IDPs, for example by contributing to social tension through unequal support. Adequate funding is critical to fulfilling the right to education for all. Short-term funding cycles should not limit the run of EiE programs, which should continue well into the recovery period.

> See also Standard 8, Guidance Notes 1 and 11; Standard 15, Guidance Note 3

6. **Education system resilience:** The EiE response should include activities led by education authorities to build a more resilient system for the future. They should strive to create an inclusive education system for all learners, including those from marginalized groups.

Education authorities, local and national actors, humanitarian and development partners, and donors should work together through coordination mechanisms to promote and support activities for disaster risk management and emergency preparedness. Local and national actors are in the best position to lead an emergency response from preparedness through to recovery, and to guide the transition from a rapid response to a longer-term response. Investment in disaster risk management and preparedness will enable education authorities and their partners to plan, coordinate, and respond more effectively. Measures taken before a crisis and during recovery can include:

- Providing support for education authorities to update or create emergency preparedness plans and contingency plans

- Working with school communities to choose safe sites and buildings, or to repair, rebuild, and retrofit schools, early childhood centers, and other learning environments
- Helping set up early warning systems at the community level

Response strategies should include capacity sharing between education authorities, local and national actors, communities, and external stakeholders. In order to prepare for, prevent, and respond to future crises, capacity sharing should build on challenges and goals identified by communities. This can include:

- Supporting local stakeholders, community members, and young people to implement response activities, such as assessments of the education sector that include data collection and analysis
- Creating professional development opportunities with teachers and other education personnel that focus on comprehensive school safety, teaching social and emotional skills, training learners in DRR, and educating them on climate change at every level of education
- Capacity sharing between local and national actors and international actors and donors to adapt funding policies and procedures to increase partners' access to direct funding and support continuity and sustainability between crises or programs

> See also Standard 1, Guidance Note 4; Standard 2, Guidance Note 4; Standard 3, Guidance Note 3; Standard 4, Guidance Note 8; Standard 14, Guidance Note 3; Standard 18, Guidance Notes 4–5; Standard 19, Guidance Note 2

7. **Harmonization with national programs:** It is important to harmonize the EiE response with the national education policies, strategies, and programs reflected in the existing ESP, transitional education plan (TEP), or other national education plans. This is key to ensuring the continuity of learning processes and practices, to creating sustainable exit strategies and/or transition plans, and to supporting the leading role of education authorities. Harmonization can involve national and local education planning, analysis, assessment, coordination, administration and management, and physical infrastructure. For example, the amount spent to compensate teachers and buy equipment should be harmonized across organizations so that spending levels are sustainable over the long term.

Humanitarian organizations with specific mandates and missions, such as supporting children, primary education, or refugees, should make sure that their education response complements those of the education authorities and other education stakeholders. The overall education response strategy should be equitable and inclusive and cover the following:

- ECD and caregiver support
- Primary education

- Education opportunities for young people, including skills building, secondary, higher, technical and vocational, and livelihood education
- Accelerated education and non-formal programs
- Adult education
- Disability-inclusive and gender-responsive education
- Pre-service and in-service teacher training

Response strategies for adult learners should include education literacy and numeracy programs. Survival skills and awareness training are also important in terms of safety and security, such as landmine awareness. Response strategies in situations of displacement or areas with returnee refugees should include longer-term support, such as accelerated education, catch-up classes, bridging programs, vocational training, and higher education opportunities.

See also Standard 3, Guidance Notes 4 and 5; Standard 8, Guidance Note 2; Standard 14, Guidance Note 1; Standard 16, Guidance Note 1; Standard 17, Guidance Note 2; Standard 18, Guidance Note 5; Standard 19, Guidance Note 2

8. **Baseline data:** Baseline data offers evidence-based insight into the education situation before EiE programs and activities began. The baseline data makes it possible to monitor and evaluate the effects of programs and should be collected systematically. The key data for a strong baseline includes disaggregated population data, school attendance rates, and teacher-student ratios. Data specific to an intervention can also be helpful. For example, if the aim of a program is to improve girls' school attendance, the baseline is their attendance rates before the program began.

References and further reading

Links to these and additional resources are available on the INEE website.

- *Cash and Voucher Assistance for Education in Emergencies: Synthesis Report and Guidelines*, Cash Learning Partnership Network, 2019
- *Comprehensive School Safety Framework*, GADRRRES, 2022
- *Disability-Inclusive Humanitarian Action Toolkit*, UNICEF, 2022
- *EiE-GenKit: a core resource package on gender and education in emergencies*, ECW, INEE, and UNGEI, 2021
- *Guidance Note on Capacity Strengthening for Localization*, Grand Bargain Localization Workstream, 2020
- *Guidelines on Mental Health and Psychosocial Support in Emergency Settings*, IASC, 2007
- *INEE Guidance Note on Conflict Sensitive Education*, INEE, 2013
- *INEE Guidance Note on Gender*, INEE, 2019
- *INEE Minimum Standards Indicator Framework*, INEE, 2021
- *INEE Reference Guide on External Education Financing*, INEE, 2012
- *MHPSS and EiE Toolkit*, MHPSS.net, REPSSI, and the International Federation of Red Cross and Red Crescent Societies (IFRC) Reference Centre for Psychosocial Support, 2021
- *Risk-Informed Education Programming for Resilience: Guidance Note*, UNICEF, 2019
- *Strengthening Rapid Education Response Toolkit*, DG-ECHO, GEC, UNICEF, Save the Children, UNESCO-IIEP, REACH, NORCAP, and Translators Without Borders, 2022
- *Supporting Integrated Child Protection and Education Programming in Humanitarian Action*, Alliance for Child Protection in Humanitarian Action and INEE, 2022
- *The Washington Group Short Set on Functioning*, Washington Group on Disability Statistics, 2022

STANDARD 6: MONITORING

There is regular monitoring of education response activities and of the evolving learning needs of the people affected.

Key actions
(please read with guidance notes)

1. **Regular monitoring:** Establish effective systems to regularly monitor education response activities from the onset of an emergency through to recovery.

2. **Safety and security:** Monitor education response activities to ensure the safety and security of all learners and teachers and other education personnel.

3. **Participation in monitoring:** Regularly consult and involve representatives of the community affected in monitoring activities and provide opportunities for training in data collection methodologies, as requested.

4. **Education management information system:** Maintain education management information systems so it is possible to compile disaggregated education data and use it to guide the education response.

5. **Learning outcomes:** Monitor learning outcomes regularly and use them to guide program design.

6. **Monitoring findings:** Analyze and share education data regularly with all stakeholders, especially the communities affected, and marginalized and vulnerable groups.

Guidance notes

1. **Regular monitoring:** Monitoring is an ongoing process that regularly measures progress toward the goals and objectives of education programs. It also helps to determine whether programs are meeting the changing education needs of the people affected and responding to the changing context. Monitoring can happen at the response or program level. Stakeholders at each level can monitor inputs, outputs, activities, outcomes, and, where possible, impacts. Monitoring can be used to do the following:

   - Track the coverage and quality of programs
   - Identify possible areas for improvement
   - Determine information flow and related roles and responsibilities
   - Contribute to knowledge sharing and learning between organizations and programs

- Promote accountability at different levels, such as when gathering feedback from the people affected or reporting the responsible use of donor funds

For monitoring at the response level, the inter-agency coordination mechanism should coordinate, collect, and share information on the collective education response. Monitoring the quality and coverage of education responses should be a multi-sectoral, inter-agency effort. Education authorities and humanitarian and development actors should collaborate when developing monitoring plans, tools, and indicators. The 4Ws/5Ws (who is doing what, where, when, and for whom) are typically used to monitor a response at the cluster or sector level, but agencies should also have their own internal monitoring plans and tools. During the acute or early stages of a response, regular monitoring can be challenging. In the early stages, it may be necessary to adopt a light and flexible approach to monitoring that focuses on priority information. This may include the changing emergency context and needs, the number of goods and services that are delivered, or how they are being used. Alternative strategies might include collecting data remotely instead of in person or using paper-based collections tools instead of electronic. As the situation becomes more stable, monitoring teams can shift to a more structured approach including real time monitoring that focuses on program outcomes or objectives.

Monitoring at the program level can show what planned and unplanned effects education programs have. This is important information, as it can prevent a program from unintentionally increasing marginalization, discrimination, conflict, or the impact of natural and climate change-induced hazards. It can be useful to collect various types of information from schools and other education programs on a sample basis, for example disaggregated data on school enrollment and dropout. Both announced and unannounced monitoring can improve the validity of the data and give a quick overview of any needs and challenges.

In cases where CVA is being used, the following information can be collected:
- Whether the modality and payment mechanisms are still appropriate
- Any protection concerns linked to the program
- The prices of key education-related items in local marketplaces, which help to ensure that the value of assistance is still appropriate

Education stakeholders can monitor out-of-school children and young people through visits to a random sample of households. Household data can indicate why they do not enroll in or go to school. It also can be gathered in collaboration with child protection programs to monitor child protection risks, especially those associated with financial constraints, such as child labor. Data on ethnicity or other characteristics may be too sensitive or difficult to collect on a comprehensive basis. In such cases, sample surveys and qualitative feedback gathered, for example, through informal conversations can highlight challenges specific groups face.

See also Standard 3, Guidance Note 8; Standard 4, Guidance Note 2; Standard 5, Guidance Notes 4 and 8; Standard 7, Guidance Note 1; Standard 19, Guidance Note 3

2. **Safety and security:** Monitoring and reporting systems can also be valuable accountability mechanisms. They can make it possible to report violations of the safety and wellbeing of learners and of teachers and other education personnel. They also make it possible to evaluate the condition of the education infrastructure. This is particularly important if there is a risk of schools being used for military purposes, or of being targeted for armed attack, abduction, child recruitment into armed forces and armed groups, or of being threatened by disasters associated with natural hazards, or if infrastructure increases the risk of gender-based violence. For this aspect of monitoring, education stakeholders may need to work with local and national authorities, or with UN agencies or NGOs responsible for security, justice, protection, and human rights. It is important to consider the sensitivity of the information reported and to share it in accordance with data protection policies and ISPs (for more guidance, see *Minimum Standards for Child Protection*, Standard 6).

> See also Standard 9, Guidance Note 9; Standard 18, Guidance Note 3

3. **Participation in monitoring:** Those involved in monitoring should be able to collect information from all people affected in a culturally sensitive way. The team should be fluent in local languages, culturally aware, and include enumerators and data collectors of all genders. They should be able to accommodate the needs of different groups so they are able to participate meaningfully, including women, persons with disabilities, and members of a marginalized community. This may include family escorts, translation support, transportation, etc. The team will also need training on ethical and responsible data collection, including safeguarding and specific skills and principles related to working with children or persons with disabilities.

Representatives of the affected community, including young people and youth-led organizations, should be involved as early as possible in monitoring the effectiveness of the education programs that affect them directly. This is particularly important with non-formal education programs for specific groups, such as adolescent girls, gender diverse people, or learners with disabilities. Communities also can identify monitoring mechanisms that are already in place before new ones are created. It is important to involve members of the affected community in monitoring, but it is also important not to overburden them with reporting responsibilities or duplicate efforts. Multiple partners may ask community members to participate in assessment and monitoring activities, so stakeholders should keep requests to a minimum. Stakeholders should coordinate their monitoring work with communities through the inter-agency coordination mechanism.

> See also Standard 1, Guidance Notes 3 and 7; Standard 4, Guidance Note 4

4. **Education management information system:** An EMIS is usually managed by national authorities. An EMIS makes it possible to store, aggregate, and analyze education data at all levels of an education system. It may track data at the learner or school level. It can be a useful entry point for strengthening the humanitarian-development-peacebuilding nexus and for promoting alignment, collaboration, and long-term planning. An EMIS that is operational and adapted to crisis and risks should have the capability to track trends and collect comparable system-wide data that is useful for emergency preparedness, response, and recovery. A capable and relevant EMIS should be supported by and, where possible, interoperable with other data management systems. This includes those used by national statistics offices and line ministries.

An EMIS may be disrupted by an emergency or unable to be adapted to the data demands related to the emergency response and recovery. To develop, upgrade, or adapt a national EMIS or the equivalent, it is important for education authorities and humanitarian actors to collaborate across the data lifecycle. They should jointly identify and address needs at a national, regional, and local level, which includes the capacity to do the following:

- Define outcomes related to crises and risks that the EMIS is tied to in order to adapt indicators so they can be measured systematically to track trends and progress over time
- Strengthen and institutionalize data management roles and processes to drive longer-term commitment, limit the fragmentation and duplication of data among stakeholders, and optimize existing capacities
- Adapt data collection tools and infrastructure according to the in-country data needs and priorities while prioritizing sustainable systems that are adapted to the context (i.e., low tech)
- Support actively using, sharing, and re-using data, including feedback mechanisms, to drive evidence-based decision-making

Start as early as possible so that a functioning EMIS is in place by the recovery phase, ideally one within a government body. When certain areas cannot be reached or EMIS coverage is incomplete, a national or regional bureau for statistics or partner agency may be able to fill the gaps and provide support. Partners should collaborate with education authorities at all levels to produce, manage, and share data, including during education needs assessments. This will provide an opportunity to align with any existing EMIS. It will also help education authorities define the priorities and opportunities for adapting the EMIS to meet data needs during crises and for managing future risk.

In some contexts, an EMIS does not capture education data on the displacement or protection status of learners, those with disabilities, or certain geographic areas. This can make it challenging to collect accurate data on whether crisis-affected learners are participating in education. Inter-agency coordination mechanisms should have monitoring systems in place to ensure that data on crisis-affected learners is being collected. This can supplement the EMIS by collecting data more frequently or by collecting data on populations that the EMIS often does not cover, such as out-of-school children and young people. It is important to consider compatibility with the EMIS so that data the coordination mechanism's partners collect can eventually be included or used to update a national EMIS, if appropriate. In contexts where crisis-affected learners are not recognized in a national EMIS, humanitarian and development actors can advocate for and work with education authorities to strengthen inclusion.

An EMIS requires standard policies and procedures for collecting, managing, and using data in line with national or regional data protection laws. Compatible software and hardware are essential. National and local education offices and other education sub-sectors, such as national training institutes, should have compatible equipment, protocols, and standards so they can exchange information. Mobile phones with special software can improve data collection, but a lack of technology should not prevent data collection in under-resourced areas. It is important that EMIS-related data processes are purpose-driven with a clear rationale of how the data is intended to benefit learners' education. This will help avoid unnecessary data production, which increases the risks of overburdening teachers, wasting school leaders' time, and exposing data subjects to risks without a clear benefit.

> See also Standard 4, Guidance Notes 2 and 5–6; Standard 8, Guidance Note 8; Standard 13, Guidance Note 5; Standard 18, Guidance Note 8

5. **Learning outcomes:** It is important to monitor learners while they are learning and after they complete or leave a program. The information collected should be comparable for learners at different stages of a program, which requires systematic planning. Quantitative and qualitative assessments can measure the following:

- Gross and fine motor skills, cognitive development, and social and emotional development in young children
- The literacy and numeracy skills of primary age learners
- Children's and young people's awareness and use of key social and emotional skills
- Increases in levels of attainment through formative and summative assessments
- Learners' access to post-literacy reading materials
- The rates at which learners continue their education (e.g., secondary or higher education)
- Employment rates for learners after completing TVET or higher education

Monitoring learners post-program provides valuable program design feedback for all types and levels of education (for more guidance see *Minimum Economic Recovery Standards, Employment Standards*).

> See also Standard 13, Guidance Note 1

6. **Monitoring findings:** Findings from monitoring a program or response should be shared regularly among all stakeholders involved, especially the communities affected and vulnerable groups. This should be done in an accessible and meaningful way. Education stakeholders can use feedback from the populations affected to guide changes in the response activities. Partners often have their own organizational feedback mechanisms, but education authorities and coordination mechanisms should encourage their partners to harmonize how feedback is collected and analyzed. This will in turn guide changes made to the collective education response. It is critical to determine how to communicate these changes and decisions most effectively to the communities. This is an essential aspect of accountability.

> See also Standard 3, Guidance Note 6

References and further reading

Links to these and additional resources are available on the INEE website.

- *Accelerated Education Program Monitoring & Evaluation Toolkit*, AEWG, 2020
- *A Roadmap for Measuring Distance Learning*, USAID, 2021
- *Designing and Monitoring Distance Teaching and Learning Interventions: A Guide for Projects and Implementers*, EdTech Hub and UK Girls' Education Challenge, 2021
- *Core Humanitarian Standard Guidance Notes and Indicators*, CHS Alliance, Group URD, and Sphere Project, 2018
- *INEE Minimum Standards Indicator Framework*, INEE, 2021
- *INEE Technical Note on Measurement for Education during the COVID-19 Pandemic*, INEE, 2020
- *Minimum Economic Recovery Standards*, SEEP Network, 2017
- *Toolkit for Collecting and Analyzing Data on Attacks on Education*, Global Coalition to Protect Education from Attack (GCPEA), 2023

STANDARD 7: EVALUATION

> Systematic and impartial evaluations improve education response activities and enhance accountability.

Key actions
(please read with guidance notes)

1. **Evaluation of education response activities:** Conduct regular evaluations of education response activities to produce credible and transparent data to guide future education activities.

2. **Participation in evaluation:** Involve all stakeholders, including representatives of the community affected and education authorities, in evaluation activities.

3. **Evaluation findings and lessons learned:** Share lessons learned and good practices widely among all relevant stakeholders and partners so that they can shape future advocacy, programs, and policies.

Guidance notes

1. **Evaluations of education response activities:** Evaluation measures program outcomes and determines whether the expected results have been achieved. External or independent evaluators usually conduct evaluations in the middle or at the end of a program or project cycle. Evaluations can also help determine whether activities were relevant to the project's stated priorities, policies, and legal instruments, and if the programs were implemented efficiently. Evaluation is separate from monitoring, but the two processes are related and both are key to achieving the goals and objectives of education programs. Monitoring results should guide evaluation.

Those who evaluate education response activities and EiE programs should use approaches and methods that promptly produce credible evidence of program outcomes and identify impacts that can guide future action. "Impact" refers to the measurable change a program has made in people's lives. In a crisis, a rigorous evaluation may not be possible or practical. A quicker and simpler approach, such as remote data collection, may be needed to determine how a program is impacting the lives of affected people. Both qualitative and quantitative data are important, and they should be disaggregated at a minimum by sex, age, and disability status. Where feasible, it also is important to look at trends across different groups of learners. Quantitative data is about things that can be counted, such as enrollment, attendance, and dropout rates, and achievement measures. Qualitative data is about things that cannot be measured numerically. It can provide insights into the lived experiences of learners and teachers, information on what happens in schools or other learning environments, and why learners enroll, attend school, or drop out. Stakeholders can collect qualitative data from several sources, including focus group discussions, interviews, and classroom observations.

> See also Standard 3, Guidance Note 8; Standard 4, Guidance Notes 2 and 5; Standard 5, Guidance Note 8; Standard 6, Guidance Note 1

2. **Participation in evaluation:** Any evaluation budget should include capacity sharing workshops with stakeholders, such as education authorities, community representatives, and learners. The workshops should include all learners, including girls and young women and those with disabilities. The workshops should introduce and explain the concept of evaluation. They also are a place to develop evaluation plans in a participatory and transparent way, and where participants can review and interpret findings together. Learners and teachers and other education personnel should participate in the evaluation process to make data collection more accurate. This will also help make the evaluation recommendations more realistic. For example, teachers and other education personnel can share their views on the practical issues that should be considered when implementing recommended actions.

> See also Standard 1, Guidance Notes 3–4 and 7

3. **Evaluation findings and lessons learned:** It is important to share key findings in evaluation reports, particularly recommendations and lessons learned, in a way that is understandable and accessible to all stakeholders, including community members and persons with disabilities. These findings should shape future work. The stakeholders in charge of managing data must handle sensitive data ethically and responsibly to avoid contributing to the emergency or conflict, or putting at risk any participants who contributed sensitive information. When sharing information, they should adhere to national or regional data protection policies and ISPs.

> See also Standard 3, Guidance Note 6; Standard 4, Guidance Note 6; Standard 19, Guidance Note 3

References and further reading

Links to these and additional resources are available on the INEE website.

- *Accelerated Education Program Monitoring & Evaluation Toolkit*, AEWG, 2020
- *A Roadmap for Measuring Distance Learning*, USAID, 2021
- *Core Humanitarian Standard Guidance Notes and Indicators*, CHS Alliance, Groupe URD, and the Sphere Project, 2018
- *Designing and Monitoring Distance Teaching and Learning Interventions: A Guide for Projects and Implementers*, EdTech Hub and UK Girls' Education Challenge, 2021.
- *INEE Minimum Standards Indicator Framework*, INEE, 2021
- *INEE Technical Note on Measurement for Education during the COVID-19 Pandemic*, INEE, 2020
- *Toolkit for Collecting and Analyzing Data on Attacks on Education*, GCPEA, 2023

For resources to help you with the implementation of the standards in Domain 1, visit inee.org/minimum-standards.

Access and Learning Environment

Foundational Standards for a Quality Response: Community Participation, Coordination, Analysis

Access and Learning Environment Domain

Standard 8: Equal and Equitable Access

All individuals have access to quality and relevant education opportunities.

Standard 9: Protection and Wellbeing

Learning environments are secure and safe, and they promote the protection and psychosocial wellbeing of learners and teachers and other education personnel.

Standard 10: Facilities and Services

Education facilities promote the safety and wellbeing of learners and teachers and other education personnel, and are linked to health, nutrition, psychosocial, and protection services.

Overview of Domain 2

The standards presented in this domain address the importance of creating an inclusive, equitable, and protective learning environment for all during a crisis. They highlight the importance of making sure that, during an emergency, everyone has access to education and can learn in an environment that provides protection and promotes wellbeing. This means that education facilities are safe for learners and teachers and other education personnel, and that they have access to other social services that are important to their holistic development.

To achieve this standard for EiE, it is essential to collaborate with other sectors. To achieve education for all in a protective environment, collaboration with child protection is especially important. It enables actors to identify protection risks and gaps more effectively, and to prevent abuse, neglect, exploitation, and violence against children and young people. It also makes it possible to design and deliver education programs that result in improved outcomes for crisis-affected learners. The *Minimum Standards for Child Protection* are a relevant reference for all standards in this domain.

The key actions in this domain involve actors such as:

- National, sub-national, and local education authorities
- Education planners and policy-makers
- Communities affected by crisis
- School leaders and teachers and other education personnel
- Stakeholders involved in the education response, including local and national CSOs and NGOs, faith-based organizations, humanitarian and development partners, donors, and private sector actors
- Actors from child protection, WASH, shelter, MHPSS, food security, health, nutrition, disaster management, and other relevant sectors

Access to education without discrimination is a human right for all

Education is a human right for everyone at all times, regardless of their legal status, gender, disability, race, religion, or any other personal characteristics. SDG 4, which addresses quality education, aims to eliminate all discrimination in education by 2030. Article 5 of the UNESCO Universal Declaration on Cultural Diversity states that every individual is entitled to quality education and training that fully respects their cultural identity. The right to education without discrimination is anchored in the International Covenant on Economic, Social and Cultural Rights (1966), the Convention on the Elimination of All Forms for Violence Against Women (1979), and the Convention on the Rights of Persons with Disabilities (2006), among others. These rights apply equally in situations of crisis.

Children, young people, and adults may encounter many barriers to education, which can vary, depending on their individual or collective identities. The discrimination or exclusion individuals or groups face based on their identity overlap and interact. On the demand side, income poverty presents a major barrier to education at all levels. Even when education is free, many families will be unable to meet education-related costs, such as uniforms, books, exam fees, and school materials. Some families may not be able to afford the opportunity cost of sending their children to school, as they need them to work and contribute to the household income. On the supply side, common barriers include a lack of schools or qualified teachers, limited online connectivity, and the language of instruction. Social norms may also lead to exclusion, particularly when society does not prioritize the education of certain groups such as women and girls, gender diverse children and young people, or children and young people with disabilities. As the illustration below indicates, barriers to education can be grouped into four categories, under the supply and demand sides.

Figure 6: Barriers to accessing education

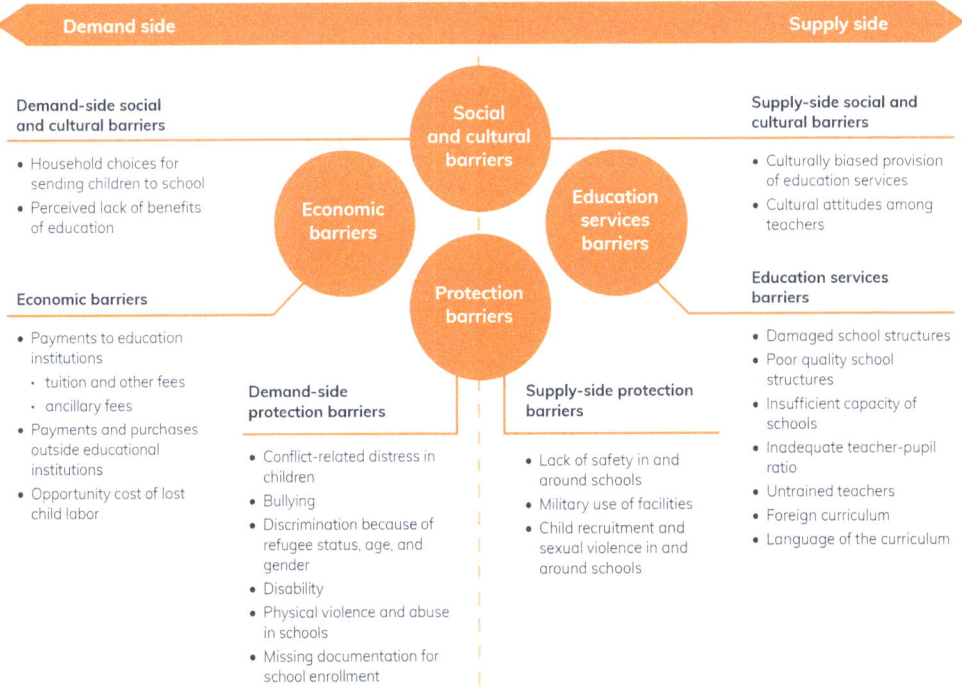

Demand side

Supply side

Demand-side social and cultural barriers

- Household choices for sending children to school
- Perceived lack of benefits of education

Social and cultural barriers

Economic barriers

Education services barriers

Protection barriers

Supply-side social and cultural barriers

- Culturally biased provision of education services
- Cultural attitudes among teachers

Economic barriers

- Payments to education institutions
  - tuition and other fees
  - ancillary fees
- Payments and purchases outside educational institutions
- Opportunity cost of lost child labor

Demand-side protection barriers

- Conflict-related distress in children
- Bullying
- Discrimination because of refugee status, age, and gender
- Disability
- Physical violence and abuse in schools
- Missing documentation for school enrollment

Supply-side protection barriers

- Lack of safety in and around schools
- Military use of facilities
- Child recruitment and sexual violence in and around schools

Education services barriers

- Damaged school structures
- Poor quality school structures
- Insufficient capacity of schools
- Inadequate teacher-pupil ratio
- Untrained teachers
- Foreign curriculum
- Language of the curriculum

Source: CALP Network, (2019). Cash and Voucher Assistance for Education in Emergencies: Synthesis Report and Guidelines

Barriers to education may increase during crises

Fulfilling the right to education can be difficult in emergency situations, since the barriers to education faced by children, young people, and adults may increase as a result of a crisis. A crisis may exacerbate barriers on both the demand side and the supply side. It may result in damaged schools, displaced learners and teachers, and increased insecurity. Crisis and displacement may also mean a loss of income, livelihoods, and safety nets, which can negatively affect access to education. Displacement can result in a prolonged absence or exclusion from education entirely. A crisis that results in widespread school closures, such as the Ebola outbreak and the COVID-19 pandemic, can lead to learning loss and have a detrimental impact on the wellbeing of learners, teachers and other education personnel, and communities.

Protection risks often increase during emergencies, especially when children and young people are not in school. Those who are out of school may face greater risks of gender-based violence, early marriage, early pregnancy, and recruitment into or association with armed forces or armed groups.

Integrated programming, including the provision of CVA, may help address barriers to education and enable people affected by crisis to enroll, continue, and complete their education. When schools close down because of an insecure situation, a health emergency, or a disaster associated with natural hazards, it is important to find alternatives that allow education to continue, such as distance education. Communities' local and indigenous knowledge systems are important in identifying locally appropriate solutions for education continuity, DRR, and resilience.

Safe and inclusive learning environments are essential

National authorities, communities, and humanitarian actors have a responsibility to make sure that everyone can access relevant, quality education, from ECD through tertiary. This includes providing a safe learning environment and taking the needs of all learners into consideration. In a crisis situation, policy and practice might have to be adjusted to enable all learners to enroll and learn.

To create equal access to education for all, it is essential to identify individuals or groups that are or may be excluded and to create programs that actively promote their inclusion. To meet the differing education needs and aspirations of all individuals, education authorities and partners should provide different types of flexible formal and non-formal education opportunities. Out-of-school and over-age children and young people may need alternative education opportunities. Education authorities, humanitarian actors, donors, and communities should plan how to include displaced learners, including refugees, in the national school system. This may require the expansion of school facilities and the provision of specific learning supports, such as language assistance and MHPSS.

The physical safety and psychosocial wellbeing of learners and of teachers and other education personnel may be at risk during emergencies. It is essential to create a safe and protective learning environment that promotes a sense of belonging and meets everyone's wellbeing, mental health, and learning needs. Children and young people have specific rights and vulnerabilities that the learning environment must address. There should be no violence, bullying, or discrimination in the learning environment, and education facilities must be safe and able to mitigate any possible hazards. The learning environment should provide holistic support to learners and teachers and other education personnel. This will require having links to WASH, health, nutrition, protection, MHPSS, shelter, and other relevant services. Collaboration with child protection actors may help education actors identify protection risks, gaps, and responses that ensure the safety of learners and teachers and other education personnel.

STANDARD 8: EQUAL AND EQUITABLE ACCESS

All individuals have access to quality and relevant education opportunities.

Key actions
(please read with guidance notes)

1. **Accessible learning opportunities:** Put plans in place to ensure that education opportunities are accessible and available to all.

2. **Discrimination and exclusion:** Ensure that no individual is denied access to education because of exclusion or discrimination.

3. **Enrollment barriers:** Remove barriers to enrollment in order to accommodate learners affected by crisis and systemic inequalities.

4. **Multiple education opportunities:** To fulfill the education needs of people affected by crisis and put them on a pathway to continued learning, gradually provide them with a range of formal and non-formal education opportunities.

5. **Adaptations to allow access, participation, and completion:** Plan and deliver EiE programs in a way that enables learners to access, remain in, and complete their education and to make the transition to the next level, when relevant.

6. **Pathways to continued learning:** Create opportunities for learners to enter or re-enter formal education systems as soon as possible after a crisis has disrupted learning.

7. **Systems strengthening:** Strengthen the capacity of education systems and local learning environments to deliver education to host and displaced communities in times of crisis.

8. **Integration of refugee, displaced, and migrant populations:** Enable displaced and migrant populations, including refugees, to access recognized and equitable formal and non-formal education through the national education system.

9. **Community participation:** Involve communities in designing and leading approaches that ensure access to quality education for all, respect social and cultural norms, and address injustice.

10. **Avoiding use of education facilities as temporary shelters:** Develop and/or maintain emergency preparedness plans to avoid the use of schools as shelters during emergencies.

11. **Well-resourced education programs:** Provide enough resources to the education response to support continued access to inclusive and equitable quality education for all people affected.

Guidance notes

1. **Accessible learning opportunities:** SDG 4 aims to ensure access to inclusive and equitable quality education and lifelong learning opportunities for all, including free primary and secondary education. ESPs and government policies should guarantee equitable quality education for all. Countries that host refugees are encouraged to promote the inclusion of refugees into all levels of their national education system, in line with the vision of the Global Compact on Refugees. This will require that the additional costs per learner are supported through the national budget or donor financing. ESPs should be gender-responsive, disability-inclusive, and ensure equitable access. Inter-sectoral approaches, such as social protection schemes, may be necessary, especially to reach individuals or groups who are excluded from education. Education authorities and humanitarian partners should work closely to coordinate and align humanitarian response plans and refugee response plans with national ESPs. This will help to ensure the continuity of quality education across the humanitarian-development-peacebuilding nexus. It is essential that all objectives are planned and budgeted for. Civil society can play an important role in advocating to include marginalized children and young people in national and humanitarian planning.

   During acute onset emergencies and displacement, learners may be provided with temporary options to engage in center-based programming, including child-friendly spaces. It is imperative that education actors collaborate with other sectors and providers, specifically child protection, to ensure that there are clear pathways for learners to participate in appropriate non-formal and formal education as soon as possible. Stakeholders should take every opportunity to promote structured learning activities, including play-based, arts-based, sports-related, and learner-centered approaches in the temporary programming (for more guidance, see *Minimum Standards for Child Protection*).

   > See also Standard 3, Guidance Note 4; Standard 5, Guidance Note 5; Standard 18, Guidance Note 1; Standard 19, Guidance Notes 4–5

2. **Discrimination and exclusion:** No individual or social group should be denied access to education or have limited ability to participate and succeed in educational opportunities. Discrimination may be intentional, such as policies and practices that ban pregnant learners from attending school. They also may be unintentional, such as when the design of a learning environment fails to include access for learners with disabilities. Barriers to education often increase during a crisis, and children and young people also may experience new vulnerabilities and protection risks.

   Some children and young people may experience discrimination and exclusion more often than others because of their individual or collective identities, including the following:

- Persons with disabilities
- People with severe mental health conditions and psychosocial disabilities
- Refugees, IDPs, and stateless and migrant communities
- Girls and women
- People who are LGBTQIA+
- Children and young people who are entering education as older learners or who have aged out of existing formal education opportunities
- Children associated with armed forces and armed groups
- Pregnant girls, teenage parents, or child and adolescent heads of household
- Children from families experiencing income poverty or those involved in child labor
- People with long-term health issues that prevent their regular and full participation, or who are perceived as a threat to others' health, including those who have HIV/AIDS
- People with particular social identities, including race, ethnicity, caste, language, tribal affiliation, religious affiliation, political affiliation, and indigenous heritage

Children and young people who are experiencing intersecting inequalities may be at even greater risk of discrimination and exclusion. For example, a teenage parent engaged in child labor or an indigenous young person with a disability may face different challenges. The immediate and long-term impact of discrimination and exclusion can be significant. Children and young people who experience discrimination may be at greater risk of abuse, neglect, exploitation, and violence. If a particular gender, ethnic, linguistic, geographic, or age group has no access to learning, it can create or continue tensions that may worsen a conflict. It also can negatively impact longer-term economic and social development at both the individual and national levels.

On the other hand, a crisis can create opportunities for positive change. Stakeholders must carefully plan and implement their activities to ensure that they do no harm and are conflict sensitive. Opportunities to mitigate and prevent discrimination and exclusion can include the following:

- **Understand patterns of exclusion and discrimination:** Education stakeholders should identify the children and young people who are not accessing education, work to understand the barriers they face, and learn what their education aspirations are. An education assessment will provide information on the vulnerability, protection concerns, needs, and priorities of the people affected, which will allow education actors to work towards removing the barriers and providing equal and relevant education opportunities for all.

- **Identify and correct discriminatory policies and practices:** National authorities are responsible for having and implementing inclusive policies across all aspects of the education system. Orientation and training to counter implicit bias and explicit discrimination should be included in the policies and referral mechanisms at all levels of policy-making and service provision. Communities, including community education committees, can help identify exclusionary and discriminatory practices, including structural discrimination, racism, and sexism. External stakeholders should consult people who are affected by such policies or who experience discrimination. Communities and civil society can advocate for explicit policies to prevent discrimination, give voice to people who face discrimination, and promote EiE activities that are designed and delivered with all individuals in mind.

- **Provide holistic programming:** National authorities and humanitarian actors should take a holistic approach to education and healthy development. Learners' needs will vary according to their age and stage of development. Holistic programming looks at the whole child or young person and creates joint or collaborative connections with other service providers and sectors to support the multiple aspects of healthy development and wellbeing. Education intersects closely with child protection, livelihoods, health and nutrition, and other sectors. Holistic programming can significantly improve the ability of marginalized children and young people to participate and engage in learning. This can include providing CVA or take-home food rations in the schools.

- **Inclusive curriculum:** Education authorities are responsible for ensuring that the curriculum, including teaching and learning materials, promotes respect for diversity, is non-discriminatory, and does not promote stereotypes linked to gender, race, or abilities. Choosing the language of instruction is critical, as it can exclude some individuals and groups.

- **Train teachers and other education personnel:** Teachers and other education personnel should receive training on creating safe, inclusive learning spaces and addressing discrimination and exclusion in and around the learning environment. All teacher training should include orientation in protective reporting policies and practices.

- **Address social norms:** Communities, community education committees, religious leaders, women's rights organizations, and other actors can help identify and challenge the social norms, attitudes, and power dynamics that drive exclusion and discrimination. The education system can, in turn, have a positive effect on social norms by establishing more inclusive practices and education content. Social norms related to gender, such as prioritizing education for boys over girls or acceptance of forced marriage, should be addressed.

(For more guidance, see *Supporting Integrated Child Protection and Education Programming in Humanitarian Action*.)

See also Standard 1, Guidance Note 5; Standard 4, Guidance Note 2; Standard 5, Guidance Note 7; Standard 9, Guidance Note 4; Standard 10, Guidance Note 6; Standard 11, Guidance Note 4; Standard 18, Guidance Note 2; Standard 19, Guidance Notes 4–5

3. **Enrollment barriers:** Policies and regulations regarding who can register for education and what resources and documentation are needed to enroll might need to be removed to protect some people's right to education. Waiving enrollment criteria is often a policy decision. Thus, it requires negotiation and advocacy at the policy level, and putting in place administrative processes that support this. Waiving enrollment criteria can be especially important for refugees, migrants, IDPs, those who have experienced gaps in their education, those who were unable to start their education at the right age, and those who do not have access to the required documentation. It is important that any actions taken are designed and implemented in ways that do not harm the community, and that they mitigate or address how the crisis has affected education access. Removing enrollment barriers might include:

- **Removal of financial requirements:** Ensure that the principles of free and compulsory primary education, available and accessible secondary education (made progressively free), and equal access to higher education on the basis of capacity (made progressively free) are upheld. This can be done by eliminating additional costs such as uniforms, exam fees, books, and supplies, and providing these items for free when possible. An analysis of education costs will help education actors understand and address the financial burdens families may be facing. Policy and program approaches may vary and require collaboration with other sectors. A CVA feasibility assessment should be conducted to determine whether CVA is relevant in a context, as it can be an important support for children experiencing poverty or vulnerability. In alignment with the IASC cash coordination model, education stakeholders should collaborate with the cash working group or other sectors and organizations with strong CVA expertise, such as child protection, food security, and livelihoods, to determine the relevance of CVA.

- **Flexible entrance age:** It may be necessary to temporarily or permanently change restrictive age-specific enrollment policies. It is important to support the development and implementation of policies and practices that ensure appropriate safeguarding and protection, consider cultural norms, and accommodate the specific developmental and learning needs of children and young people in multi-age settings. Alternative education pathways, such as accelerated education or catch-up programs, may be an alternative for over-age learners.

- **Flexibility around what documentation is required:** There should be flexibility around what documents children and young people need to enroll in an education program. During emergencies, people may not have their citizenship or birth certificates, other identity papers, or school records. Education actors and school officials should work together to make sure that documentation requirements are not an unnecessary barrier to education access. In some contexts, UN agencies or other specialized organizations may be able to help displaced populations access or replace their documents, in collaboration with relevant national authorities. When handling sensitive and confidential information, stakeholders must follow safeguarding policies to protect children, young people, and their families and communities.

- **Allowing gaps:** Learners should be given academic support to help them return to an age-appropriate level in formal education. For a short gap in education, support can include remedial or catch-up classes. Children and young people with longer gaps in their learning should be given alternatives that allow them to return to formal education or enroll in non-formal education opportunities, such as accelerated education.
- **Advocacy:** Communities, civil society, an education cluster, or refugee education working group can advocate for lifting enrollment barriers in education programs and policies. This includes advocating for policy changes to ensure the sustainability and acceptance of flexible education models.

> See also Standard 4, Guidance Note 3; Standard 18, Guidance Note 1; Standard 19, Guidance Note 5

4. **Multiple education opportunities:** A range of relevant formal and non-formal quality education opportunities are needed for crisis-affected children, young people, and adults. The aim is to meet the education needs of all learners at all education levels, and to leave no one behind. These opportunities should be relevant to the learners and to the context, and may include access to:

- Child-friendly or other safe learning spaces during an acute crisis
- ECD
- Primary education
- Secondary education
- Tertiary education which includes TVET, higher education, and adult education
- Literacy and numeracy classes
- Skills building
- Accredited alternative education, including accelerated education

Creating child-friendly spaces or other safe learning spaces is often the first response during an acute crisis when it is not yet possible to return to formal schooling. Child-friendly spaces protect and promote the wellbeing (including SEL) of children and young people and prepare them for structured learning in formal or non-formal settings. Education stakeholders should plan child-friendly spaces in collaboration with child protection actors (for more guidance, see *Child Protection Minimum Standards*, Standard 15).

Education authorities are responsible for ensuring that education policies address the needs of excluded populations. This includes providing relevant programs for children and young people who have had long gaps in their education or who did not enroll at the right age. Catch-up or bridging programs may be an option for learners who have experienced gaps in their education but may be able to re-enter and continue in formal education at the appropriate grade and age level. Remedial classes can be provided to learners who are already enrolled but need additional support in specific subjects. Civil society and communities can advocate for the provision of such programs and support their implementation.

Formal education may not be a realistic or relevant option for all learners, especially those who are over age and have missed out on significant periods of education. Non-formal education is often a relevant alternative, such as accelerated education, or literacy, numeracy, and SEL programs. When possible and appropriate, non-formal education should be recognized and certified by education authorities. It is the responsibility of education actors to coordinate with education authorities throughout the design and implementation of their non-formal programs to work towards certification and recognition. Non-formal education should offer a pathway to formal education, livelihood, or employment opportunities (for more guidance, see *Supporting Integrated Child Protection and Education Programming in Humanitarian Action*).

> See also Standard 3, Guidance Note 2; Standard 18, Guidance Notes 1–2

5. **Adaptations to allow education access, participation, and completion:** Education stakeholders should make learning opportunities flexible and adapt them to the situation so they meet all learners' needs and aspirations. The goal is for all learners to be able to fully access and complete their education. Adaptations may mitigate disruptions to learning and enable learners to attend school regularly. Examples of adaptations include:

- Flexible class schedules, hours, shifts, and annual timetables to suit groups of learners who have other responsibilities
- Alternative modes of delivery, such as self-study, distance or blended learning, accelerated education, or catch-up learning programs
- Learner-centered pedagogy that accommodates differentiated learning
- Child-care services for learners who are parents or caregivers for younger siblings
- CVA to reduce negative coping mechanisms that may affect learners' chances of accessing and completing their education, such as child labor or forced marriage

Education actors and community members, including learners, parents, and caregivers, should discuss and agree on what adaptations are needed and appropriate when learning is disrupted. It is important to involve people at risk of being excluded from education, such as children and young persons with disabilities, refugees, and IDPs. Education authorities must be actively involved so that the suggested adaptations will be accepted and recognized.

Targeted adaptations for those who are challenged by contextual circumstances or discriminatory policies should include policies and programs that are responsive to learners' and teachers' rapidly changing needs. Contingency plans should include strategies for dealing with a large-scale disruption of learning, which may create a need for adjustments across the education system, such as distance education and bridging programs. If an emergency prevents learners from going to school, having plans in place to adjust the mode of delivery will ensure that learning can continue. Examples include a change from in-person learning to blended or distance learning.

To provide distance education that enables all learners to have access to learning, it is important to consider multiple modalities and choose carefully how to deliver them, including high-tech, low-tech, and no-tech approaches. Education stakeholders must also protect learners' digital safety and protect them from harmful content. Learners who are living in poverty or facing social exclusion often do not have electricity, access to technology, or the skills to use digital devices. They also may lack other resources, such as books. Education stakeholders should provide these resources to ensure that they can continue learning, including additional support to women and girls, as they often have less access to technology, devices, and internet connectivity than their male peers. Encouraging parents and caregivers to get involved in their children's education is key to ensuring that learners' engaging in distance education are well supported. Where learners are not able engage in-person with their peers or teachers, it is important to give extra attention to supporting their mental health and wellbeing.

> See also Standard 1, Guidance Note 5; Standard 2, Guidance Note 2; Standard 11, Guidance Note 1; Standard 12, Guidance Note 1; Standard 13, Guidance Note 5; Standard 19, Guidance Note 2

6. **Pathways to continued learning:** Governments, education stakeholders, and communities should take all possible actions to continue learning during a crisis. Where learning is interrupted, it should be brought back as quickly as possible, whether through blended learning approaches or creating new safe spaces. If needed during an emergency, child-friendly spaces and non-formal education programs can prepare learners to later join or rejoin the formal education system as soon as possible (see guidance note 9). When possible, non-formal education programs should be certified and accredited. For refugees who are returning to their country of origin or re-settling in a new country, governments, UN agencies, and other relevant actors may advocate for the recognition of refugees' education across countries, including recognition and equivalency of education documents and credentials from prior learning.

> See also Standard 2, Guidance Note 2; Standard 11, Guidance Note 2; Standard 13, Guidance Note 5; Standard 19, Guidance Note 5

7. **Systems strengthening:** Education authorities and humanitarian and development partners should work together to strengthen national education systems at all levels—community, sub-national, national—to offer education to children and young people in crisis-affected communities, including host communities. Crisis-affected learners must be included in national education plans and budgets. Education preparedness and response plans should reflect the aspirations, relevant policies, and protocols of the national system. They also must be designed and implemented in ways that do not harm the community or providers, and do not worsen the impact of the emergency. All authorities from the relevant sectors, including those with financial decision-making and oversight, should work together to ensure that responses are holistic and address the diverse and multi-sectoral needs of crisis-affected learners. Additional services may be needed to expand equitable access rapidly. These can be delivered by humanitarian actors and may include the following:

- **Facilities and services:** Additional education infrastructure may be needed, such as temporary structures that can be set up rapidly. Ideally, they can later be used as semi-permanent and permanent learning structures, community centers, or buildings used for other purposes. When the number of learners increases, it is important to provide additional WASH facilities in order to meet national or international standards. Stakeholders should carefully consider the context, relevance, and best use of any learning environment. All structures should accommodate the age and ability of all learners. When needed, a double shift system can be put in place to make the best use of a learning environment. This can include morning and afternoon classes or other shifts in the schedule, as needed. It is also important to consider the principle of do no harm, as a shift in schedule may lead to reduced classroom learning time and a higher workload for teachers and other education personnel. It also may mean that children and young people must walk to and from school outside daylight hours, which will require considering and addressing additional protection concerns, in collaboration with the protection sector.

- **Teaching and learning:** Relevant education options and integration policies should aim to mitigate exclusion and discrimination. They may include providing language support or remedial education.

- **Teachers and other education personnel:** Stakeholders may need to recruit additional teachers and teaching assistants to maintain a reasonable teacher-student ratio. Training for teachers and teaching assistants should include pedagogy, child protection, MHPSS, subject content, human rights, and other relevant topics. In a situation of rapid influx, teachers should be prepared for teaching multiple grades or managing large classes.

- **School improvement plans:** Education stakeholders should empower communities and schools to increase their enrollment capacity by providing school grants or other types of financial support linked to school improvement plans.

- **Conflict sensitivity:** It is important for education stakeholders to actively address potential tensions between host communities and displaced or migrant populations. This includes addressing the potential negative consequences of integrating additional learners into host education programs, which may result in overcrowded classrooms, shorter instruction time, longer teaching hours, additional learning needs, and a strain on infrastructure. Teachers should be given training on how to promote social cohesion and a sense of belonging for their learners. Partners should monitor and share information about how providing access to additional learners interacts with conflict dynamics (for more guidance, see *INEE Guidance Note on Conflict Sensitive Education*).

Education for refugees and displaced populations should be part of national policy frameworks and plans and be included in budgets. Civil society, communities, and coordination mechanisms, such as education clusters and refugee education working groups, can advocate for the inclusion of these populations into national education systems and hold governments accountable.

> See also Standard 5, Guidance Note 3; Standard 10, Guidance Note 1; Standard 11, Guidance Note 1; Standard 14, Guidance Note 2; Standard 18, Guidance Notes 1–2; Standard 19, Guidance Note 5

8. **Integration of refugee, displaced, and migrant populations:** Governments, education stakeholders, and communities should work together to include displaced populations equitably and sustainably in the national education system. These populations include migrants, refugees, asylum seekers, returnees, stateless persons, and IDPs. UN agencies and humanitarian organizations can work with the authorities to ensure that education access is provided through a recognized system that provides certification and opportunities to transition to the next education level. Humanitarian actors, civil society, and communities can advocate for the provision of multiple education pathways where this does not already exist. When possible, displaced populations should be reflected in an EMIS and be included in national learning assessment surveys.

National legal systems should reflect the rights and accommodations made for internally displaced and migrant learners and teachers and other education personnel. While IDPs have the right to access national schools by virtue of their citizenship, the host country may not have policies in place to support the inclusion of refugees in the national system. In keeping with the protections and rights of refugees, as articulated in global treaties and agreements, efforts should be made to ensure that refugees can be integrated into national education systems in the host country as much as possible. This requires removing policy barriers to accessing education, supporting the use of the host country curriculum, providing opportunities for the official certification of learning, and having refugee learners attend schools alongside those in the host community. Humanitarian and development actors, civil society, and other relevant stakeholders can advocate for the inclusion of refugees in national plans, systems, and budgets. Education stakeholders should make sure that schools and teachers have the support they need to integrate refugee learners and create a supportive learning environment, such as classes to learn the language of instruction. Over-age and out-of-school refugees should have the opportunity to participate in recognized, flexible, non-formal education programs that will enable them to integrate into formal education.

> See also Standard 6, Guidance Note 4; Standard 13, Guidance Note 5; Standard 14, Guidance Notes 1 and 5; Standard 18, Guidance Notes 1–2; Standard 19, Guidance Note 5

9. **Community participation:** Communities should be involved in designing and leading initiatives that ensure that everyone can access quality education in a way that respects their social and cultural norms and deals with injustice. When designing and implementing education policies and programs, policy-makers and education actors should consult with communities. Communities can help ensure equal access to education for all by:

- Identifying individuals and groups made vulnerable by exclusion
- Promoting the participation of all relevant groups, especially those facing social exclusion
- Identifying where alternative learning opportunities may be needed
- Mobilizing extra resources
- Dealing with security, protection, and psychosocial concerns
- Dealing with communication gaps

Community leaders can be powerful advocates for education. This can involve challenging social norms that may lead to exclusion, such as those that devalue education for girls and children and young persons with disabilities. To collect a wide range of perspectives, community members with different backgrounds and vulnerabilities should be engaged in this advocacy. Networks led by children and young people can provide important information about their realities and aspirations. Communities and external stakeholders can work together to support local goals and strategies for advancing access to education and promoting children's and young people's development and wellbeing. When relevant, communities and external stakeholders can organize training on relevant international legal frameworks and standards.

> See also Standard 1, Guidance Notes 1 and 7; Standard 2, Guidance Note 1

10. **Avoiding use of education facilities as temporary shelters:** Schools and education facilities should not be used as shelters or evacuation centers. Using schools as temporary shelters denies displaced learners and learners from the host community access to safe learning environments and their right to education.

National authorities should only allow the use of education spaces as shelters or evacuation centers for displaced people if there are no other options. They should seek out alternative locations during preparedness planning. Civil society and communities can advocate for emergency preparedness plans that minimize the use of learning environments as shelters and call for the following:

- Using schools as shelters only as a last resort
- Using education facilities for the shortest time possible and agreeing on a date for returning the facility to its original function
- Planning and budgeting to ensure that education facilities are returned in a usable or improved state, such as renovated sanitation facilities
- Having continuity plans for learners even when learning facilities are occupied, such as by providing temporary learning spaces where teachers can continue to reach learners

When education facilities must be used to provide temporary shelter, education actors should work with the shelter and protection sectors to minimize negative effects and potential protection risks. When a school is being used for shelter, education or school officials should inform the inter-agency coordination mechanism. While the learning space is being used as a shelter, humanitarian actors can work with the community to plan and provide alternative learning locations or distance education. When an education facility is used as a temporary shelter, it is important to protect school property, including textbooks, libraries, furniture, school records, technological infrastructure, and recreational equipment (for more guidance, see *Supporting Integrated Child Protection and Education Programming in Humanitarian Action*).

See also Standard 18, Guidance Note 4

11. **Well-resourced education programs:** National authorities are responsible for providing education during emergencies. This involves coordinating and providing sufficient financial, material, and human resources. If there is a funding gap, humanitarian and development assistance can complement national and local resources. Other funding sources include global mechanisms such as ECW, the UN Central Emergency Response Fund, UN Country-Based Pooled Funds, donors, international and local NGOs, communities, faith-based organizations, civil society groups, and other development partners.

EiE has long been under-funded. The lack of funding means that, while stakeholders work to address urgent needs and fulfill the right to education for all crisis-affected learners, they should have clear priorities that reflect the reality of the funding situation. Plans to mobilize and allocate funds strategically to meet critical needs may include the following:

- **Contingency and emergency preparedness plans:** Education authorities and partners, including authorities from other sectors that support infrastructure and services linked to education, should include preparedness and contingency plans in the national ESP. This should include funding for EiE within government frameworks and civil society networks. Education authorities and humanitarian and development partners should also identify opportunities to work across the humanitarian-development-peacebuilding nexus to prepare for future crises.

- **Early assessments:** Initial rapid assessments should include education to ensure that education needs are identified, planned, and budgeted for at the onset of an emergency. Education needs and funding should be included in any refugee response plan or humanitarian response plan.

- **Advocate for education in national budgets:** When relevant, communities, civil society, and other stakeholders can advocate for education to be a high priority in the national budget. This is in keeping with international benchmarks, as outlined in the Incheon Declaration, and it may include dedicated funding for EiE responses.

- **Advocate with donors:** Education stakeholders should advocate for flexible, predictable, and sustained funding to support education interventions and systems throughout a response. They may call for collaboration between development and humanitarian donors, with the aim of reducing gaps, ensuring the continuity of systems and interventions, and strengthening the humanitarian-development-peacebuilding nexus.

- **Prioritize funds for identified needs:** Allocation of resources should be informed by a needs assessment. This will ensure that resources are allocated where there is the greatest need, in keeping with humanitarian principles. International actors and donors should prioritize local partners' access to resources and facilitate this as directly as possible to improve outcomes for the people affected and reduce transaction costs.

- **Cross-sectoral collaboration:** Humanitarian actors across sectors and systems should collaborate on efforts to obtain adequate funding to address the holistic needs of all learners and teachers and other education personnel.

See also Standard 2, Guidance Note 1; Standard 3, Guidance Note 5; Standard 4, Guidance Note 1; Standard 5, Guidance Note 5; Standard 11, Guidance Note 6; Standard 15, Guidance Note 3; Standard 17, Guidance Note 1; Standard 18, Guidance Note 5; Standard 19, Guidance Notes 3–5

References and further reading

Links to these and additional resources are available on the INEE website.

- *Checklist for ICT Interventions to Support Education in Crisis and Conflict Settings*, INEE and USAID, 2018
- *Double-Shift Schooling: Design and Operation for Cost-Effectiveness*, UNESCO-IIEP, 2007
- *Education 2030: A Strategy for Refugee Education*, UNHCR, 2019
- *EiE-GenKit: a core resource package on gender and education in emergencies*, ECW, INEE, and UNGEI, 2021
- *Humanitarian inclusion standards for older people and people with disabilities*, ADCAP, 2018
- *Inclusive Distance Education Toolkit*, INEE, 2023
- *INEE Accelerated Education Resource Collection* [Website]
- *INEE Background Paper on Distance Education in Emergencies*, INEE, 2022
- *INEE Guidance Note on Conflict Sensitive Education*, INEE, 2013
- *INEE Guidance Note on Gender*, INEE, 2019
- *Minimum Standards for Child Protection in Humanitarian Action*, Alliance for Child Protection in Humanitarian Action, 2019
- *Operational Guidance for Child Friendly Spaces in Humanitarian Settings*, IFRC, 2018
- *Principles for Digital Development*, Principles for Digital Development Working Group, 2019
- *Supporting Integrated Child Protection and Education Programming in Humanitarian Action*, Alliance for Child Protection in Humanitarian Action and INEE, 2022
- *The Washington Group Short Set on Functioning*, Washington Group on Disability Statistics, 2022
- *UNESCO Qualifications Passport for Refugees and Vulnerable Migrants* [Website]

STANDARD 9: PROTECTION AND WELLBEING

Learning environments are secure and safe, and they promote the protection and psychosocial wellbeing of learners and teachers and other education personnel.

Key actions
(please read with guidance notes)

1. **Psychosocial and physical wellbeing:** Promote learning environments that nurture the wellbeing of learners and of teachers and other education personnel.

2. **Protective learning environments:** Protect learners and teachers and other education personnel from dangers in and around the learning environment and promote their awareness of these risks.

3. **Knowledge of referral mechanisms:** Train teachers and other education personnel how to report and follow-up on protection violations, and how to safely refer learners who have protection needs.

4. **Positive classroom management:** Support and train teachers to create a safe, inclusive, equitable, and violence-free learning environment for all.

5. **Prevention of school-related gender-based violence:** Establish mechanisms to prevent and respond to SRGBV.

6. **Community participation in protection:** Develop systems and policies to make school surroundings safe, in collaboration with families and community members.

7. **Risk reduction in insecure areas or situations:** Develop plans to protect learners, teachers and other education personnel, and education infrastructure in insecure areas or situations, and ensure that the routes learners travel to and from school are safe and accessible.

8. **Proximity of learning sites:** Locate schools and other learning environments, temporary learning spaces, and child-friendly spaces close to the people they serve.

9. **Prevention of military use and attacks:** Ensure that learning environments are free from military use and attacks.

10. **Disaster and climate risk management:** Implement disaster and climate risk management activities to keep learning environments safe from hazards and risks of all kinds.

Guidance notes

1. **Psychosocial and physical wellbeing:** Wellbeing is a significant precursor to learners' improved developmental outcomes. Therefore, supporting wellbeing is an essential part of an EiE response. To promote a safe, secure, and nurturing learning environment, stakeholders should support the wellbeing of learners and of teachers and other education personnel.

A person's wellbeing is affected by many factors and systems. Any MHPSS activities should be informed by the socio-ecological model (see Figure 7). When designing MHPSS interventions, education stakeholders should keep in mind how risk and support factors at one level interact with factors at another level to influence a child's wellbeing. Actors across the education system and other sectors should do their best to ensure that MHPSS interventions are complemented and synchronized at other levels of the social ecology. For example, a new policy intended to promote holistic and sustainable changes in corporal punishment may be accompanied by or aligned with school-level initiatives to promote nonviolent classroom-management techniques and establish protection referral systems and complaint mechanisms.

Figure 7: Program areas across socio-ecological levels

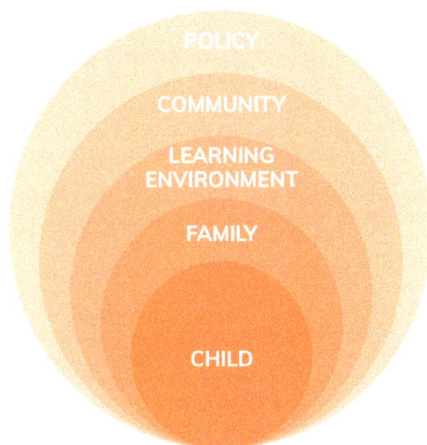

POLICY

COMMUNITY

LEARNING ENVIRONMENT

FAMILY

CHILD

The provision of MHPSS is multi-layered and multi-sectoral and should be delivered in close coordination with other sectors. Humanitarian actors can ensure good coordination by connecting to a cross-sectoral MHPSS technical working group, if already established. If none exists, stakeholders can advocate with the education and health clusters, World Health Organization, or government organizations.

The IASC pyramid is widely used to demonstrate the multi-layered nature of the MHPSS response (see Figure 8). MHPSS, which includes SEL, can take place in a learning environment across layers 1–3 of the pyramid. By teaching children a range of social and emotional competencies, SEL programs can reduce risky behaviors and support positive development, greater attachment to school, and academic success.

Figure 8: IASC MHPSS Pyramid

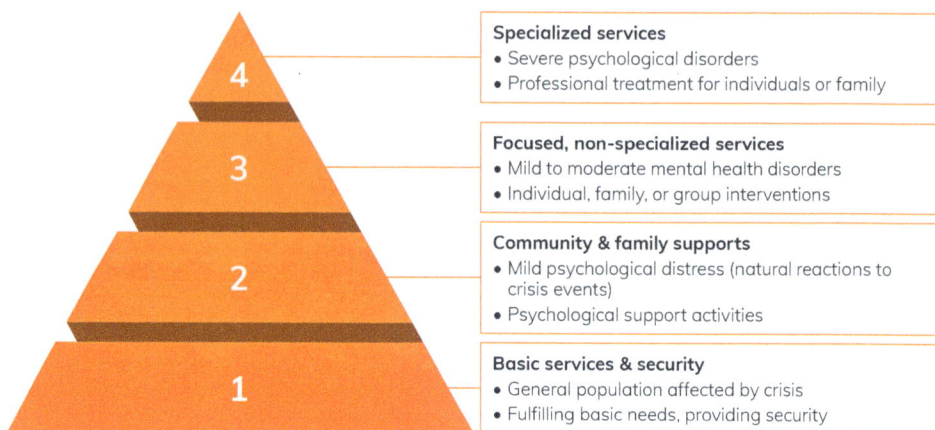

4 — Specialized services
- Severe psychological disorders
- Professional treatment for individuals or family

3 — Focused, non-specialized services
- Mild to moderate mental health disorders
- Individual, family, or group interventions

2 — Community & family supports
- Mild psychological distress (natural reactions to crisis events)
- Psychological support activities

1 — Basic services & security
- General population affected by crisis
- Fulfilling basic needs, providing security

Source: IASC, (2007). IASC Guidelines on Mental Health and Psychosocial Support in Emergency Settings

Support at each layer of the MHPSS pyramid should target all learners and teachers. Activities at layer 1 can include:

- Ensuring that learning environments are physically safe, secure, and gender-responsive
- Setting up referral mechanisms with other sectors, including child protection and health
- Creating and maintaining inclusive and caring learning environments through the integration of SEL
- Advocating for the minimum conditions and standards of health, safety, and learners' and teachers' dignity

Activities for learners at layer 2 should be provided by skilled teachers or facilitators and can include:

- Providing recreational, play-based, or extracurricular activities (arts, sports, music, drama) that promote relationship building, emotional regulation, and communication
- Providing structured SEL activities that help learners develop social skills, problem-solving, and coping mechanisms
- Encouraging and supporting parents and caregivers to get involved in their children's educational activities by helping them with homework, reading to them, or joining school governance bodies

Activities at layer 3 include interventions for high-risk individuals who do not meet the criteria for a mental health diagnosis but have detectable symptoms of a mental, emotional, or behavioral condition. These interventions should be undertaken only by highly trained and qualified staff members, such as clinical social workers, psychologists, psychosocial workers, nurses, or school-based MHPSS providers. Activities they may offer include:

- Family-based interventions
- Structured group sessions
- School-based clinical interventions

Activities at layer 4 include interventions that can only be provided by mental health clinicians and social service professionals. Teachers and other education personnel should be trained to understand the referral mechanisms and to recognize when a learner needs support from other sectors.

There can be stigma around mental health and psychosocial wellbeing in some cultures and contexts. MHPSS professionals should ensure that any services provided are contextually and culturally relevant and build on existing structures and supports (for more guidance, see *INEE Guidance Note on Psychosocial Support; INEE Guidance Note for Teacher Wellbeing in Emergency Settings*).

> See also Standard 11, Guidance Note 3; Standard 13, Guidance Note 1; Standard 14, Guidance Notes 2 and 7; Standard 17, Guidance Note 5

2. **Protective learning environments:** Protective learning environments promote the wellbeing of learners and of teachers and other education personnel and enable learners to engage fully in the learning process. A safe learning environment protects against threats, danger, injury, or loss, and is free from physical or psychosocial harm. It is important that learners and teachers and other education personnel are aware of potential dangers, and that they have the knowledge needed to protect themselves and their surroundings. Potential dangers for learners and teachers and other education personnel in and around the learning environment may include the following:

- Violence and bullying
- Gender-based violence, including sexual exploitation and abuse
- Arms, ammunition, landmines, and unexploded ordnance
- Armed personnel, crossfire, and other military threats, including abduction and recruitment into armed forces or armed groups
- Attacks on schools and other learning environments, learners, and teachers and other education personnel at or on the way to school
- Natural and environmental hazards
- Political insecurity
- Xenophobia, racism

During an emergency, children face additional risks because of their age. They may be more vulnerable to abuse, neglect, exploitation, and violence. Learners who are facing social exclusion and discrimination can be at even greater risk of abuse and violence. The child protection and education sectors should work together to strengthen the protection of children and young people and put in place policies and practices that reduce harm and risks.

Risk assessments help education actors understand the potential hazards and protection risks that should inform programming. Community members, learners, young people, parents and caregivers, and teachers and other education personnel can play a leading role in such assessments. The risk assessment findings should inform the development of protective policies and practices. Specialized organizations can help identify people who are at particular risk and give advice about how to mitigate those risks. Education stakeholders should conduct these assessments regularly and include an analysis of relevant cultural and political factors.

Teachers and other education personnel can and should help promote a tolerant and respectful school culture in which diverse perspectives are respected. Communities should provide oversight and engage with schools to create holistic, protective learning environments (for more guidance, see *Supporting Integrated Child Protection and Education Programming in Humanitarian Action; Education in Emergencies - Child Protection Collaboration Framework; Minimum Standards for Child Protection, Standard 23*).

> See also Standard 2, Guidance Notes 2 and 4; Standard 4, Guidance Note 7; Standard 11, Guidance Note 3; Standard 14, Guidance Notes 2–3; Standard 15, Guidance Note 4

3. **Knowledge of referral pathways:** Any actors working with children and young people must have safeguarding mechanisms and referral pathways in place to address child protection concerns or MHPSS needs. If protection violations occur in and around the learning environment, or if learners show signs of experiencing neglect, abuse, or violence in the home, teachers must be able to report, follow up, and safely refer children to other specialized services. Children who are facing immediate risk should be referred immediately. Relevant actions to address child protection concerns in the learning environment may include the following:

- Establishing referral pathways to specialized services
- Training teachers, other education personnel, caregivers, and community leaders how to recognize signs of physical or psychosocial distress and other protection concerns
- Training teachers and other education personnel how to use the correct channels to report suspected child protection cases
- Clarifying where teachers and other education personnel can refer children who are facing imminent risks
- Making learners aware of their rights and how they can report violations of those rights
- Displaying reporting mechanisms openly in the classroom and community

Education and child protection actors should collaborate on training teachers. They also should promote awareness in the community and among learners about how to report safety violations. Learners who have experienced or are at risk of protection violations must be given support, and any response should be documented. This may include referral to health, protection, or psychosocial service providers. Education and child protection actors must maintain confidentiality in all cases. Education actors and teachers should be aware of situations where children and young people are at heightened risk of violence or psychological and social difficulties. This may occur in the home or in digital spaces, or when education is disrupted (for more guidance, see *Supporting Integrated Child Protection and Education Programming in Humanitarian Action*).

Q See also Standard 1, Guidance Note 7; Standard 10, Guidance Note 9; Standard 14, Guidance Note 2

4. **Positive classroom management:** SDG 4 addresses quality education and sets the goal of everyone having access to a safe and nonviolent learning environment. The teacher is responsible for creating a supportive atmosphere in the learning environment so that children can thrive and learn, and they should encourage mutual understanding, peace, and tolerance. Teachers should use positive reinforcement and positive discipline strategies and never corporal punishment, verbal abuse, humiliation, or intimidation. Intimidation includes mental stress, violence, abuse, and discrimination. Education stakeholders and school leaders should make sure that teachers are trained in positive classroom management and the prevention of bullying. This will enable them to teach learners how to prevent violence and conflict. Teacher codes of conduct can establish the importance of positive discipline, which can be addressed in teacher training, mentoring, and supervision activities. Breaches of the code of conduct, such as corporal punishment or abuse, should be reported and followed up on. Teachers also should receive support to include MHPSS and SEL activities in their teaching practices.

Q See also Standard 8, Guidance Note 2; Standard 13, Guidance Note 2; Standard 14, Guidance Note 2; Standard 16, Guidance Note 4

5. **Prevention of school-related gender-based violence:** SRGBV, particularly sexual violence, is a serious, life-threatening protection issue. Women, girls, gender diverse people, and people who are LGBTQIA+ are at greatest risk of experiencing SRGBV, but it can also be a threat to men and boys. Children with intersecting vulnerabilities are at heightened risk, especially those with disabilities.

Learners and teachers and other education personnel can be both perpetrators and victims of SRGBV, including sexual exploitation and abuse. Education stakeholders and school leaders should make sure that teachers and other education personnel and any volunteers in the classroom are trained to know what SRGBV is, how to prevent it, and, if it happens, how to respond and report it. They in turn should teach learners about gender equality and rights. Teacher training should include how to manage an SRGBV disclosure from a learner in a compassionate way. Education programs should monitor and respond to harassment and sexual exploitation. Parents and caregivers, learners, and teachers and other education personnel should agree on ways to reduce risks to children and young people within the learning environment, and while going to and from school. This can include:

- Jointly developing and publicly posting clear rules against sexual harassment, exploitation, abuse, and other types of gender-based violence
- Consistently enforcing consequences when those rules are violated
- Including these rules in the code of conduct for teachers and other education personnel, and training all parties in the code of conduct
- Increasing the number of adult women in the learning environment to help protect and reassure female learners; if this is not possible, women from the community can be asked to help in the classroom and offered training on protective measures
- Teaching evidence-based and age-appropriate sexual and reproductive health and rights education for all genders so that learners have appropriate knowledge about their rights, giving consent, and healthy relationships

Have a safe reporting, complaint, and response system in place to deal with gender-based violence if it does occur. The school may get assistance from the relevant national authorities or from a suitable independent organization to set up this system. Survivors of gender-based violence need health support, MHPSS, and protection from a well-organized referral system. In some cases this may also include referrals to law enforcement. The Child Protection Area of Responsibility under the Protection Cluster, protection working groups, United Nations Population Fund, and other specialized organizations may also be able to advise (for more guidance, see *INEE Guidance Note on Gender*).

> See also Standard 1, Guidance Note 6; Standard 2, Guidance Note 2; Standard 11, Guidance Notes 2–3; Standard 13, Guidance Note 2; Standard 14, Guidance Note 2; Standard 16, Guidance Note 4; Standard 18, Guidance Note 1

6. **Community participation in protection:** Communities should play a leading role in creating, protecting, and overseeing the learning environment. In environments where violence and other threats are common, it is important to involve families and communities in promoting safety in the home, school, and community, which can include:

- Involving the community in mapping protection risks and developing school safety plans or policies
- Raising awareness among parents and caregivers about positive methods of raising children and young people, including positive discipline
- Raising awareness of protection concerns in the community with recognized security forces
- Working with communities and authorities to manage protection concerns by, for example, organizing walking groups with safety escorts or providing transportation for learners going to and from school
- Training community members to assess and respond to protection issues
- Raising community awareness about harmful practices, such as forced marriage, honor killings, and female genital cutting, and about the risks of SRGBV

Representatives of all marginalized groups should be involved in designing protection programs in the learning environment, including girls, women, persons with disabilities, and ethnic minorities. They should be involved in ways that are culturally appropriate, such as providing women-only consultations. A community education committee can be a useful forum to strengthen the community's ownership of protecting the learning environment (for more guidance, see *Minimum Standards for Child Protection*, Standard 17).

See also Standard 1, Guidance Note 1; Standard 2, Guidance Note 2

7. **Risk reduction in insecure areas or situations:** During a crisis, being at or traveling to and from school might expose learners and teachers and other education personnel to a number of risks. As the primary duty bearer, the government is responsible for putting in place systems and plans to ensure that schools are safe. Education actors, protection actors, and communities should collaborate with the authorities to identify and reduce risks.

In insecure situations, the community should decide if they want learners to attend school in person. If the usual learning sites are not safe or available, alternative safe sites or alternative methods of delivery can be arranged to limit any disruption of learning. This may include home schooling or distance education. Education actors should plan distance education carefully so that all learners are able to access it. This may require providing both digital and non-digital options. When distance education is used, it is important to ensure that learners' protection and wellbeing needs continue to be addressed. This may include self-care MHPSS interventions to help learners deal with the stressors related to the crisis or the disruption to their learning. Learners need protection from the unauthorized use of their personal data, and from online harassment, bullying, and abuse.

All learners and teachers and other education personnel must have safe and secure routes to and from school. Communities, including girls, boys, gender diverse children and young people, and children with disabilities, should find out if there are threats and agree on how to manage them. When learners must walk to the learning environment along poorly lit roads, providing adult escorts or using reflectors or reflective tape on clothing and bags can improve safety. Walking groups supervised by adults or a learner buddy system can enable learners to walk together safely to and from school. Mobility aids or transportation can help learners with disabilities travel between home and learning sites. Working with other sectors, such as protection, shelter, and camp management, can help determine which schools and school routes are safe.

> See also Standard 2, Guidance Note 2; Standard 18, Guidance Note 4

8. **Proximity of learning sites:** The maximum distance between learners and learning sites should be in line with local and national standards and should take the learners' ages and abilities into consideration. It also is important to consider any nearby security, safety, and accessibility concerns, like soldiers' quarters, landmines, and dense bush. Curfews may restrict access to education, especially when imposed on young people. In such situations, education actors should ask learners, parents and caregivers, and other community members to help find alternative learning spaces and to identify possible dangers in those areas. If the distance some learners must travel to school makes it difficult to reach, it can be helpful to hold satellite or "feeder" classes in learning spaces nearer to their homes. Schools that offer boarding must manage protection risks carefully, including gender-based violence. Education actors and the community must create mechanisms to protect learners of all genders.

9. **Prevention of military use and attacks:** During conflict, military attacks may occur frequently and soldiers often will occupy education sites. Attacks on education include violence against education facilities, learners, and teachers and other education personnel. Attacks on education can cause injury, death, and severe distress, and often lead to school closures. Armed forces and non-state armed groups also may use schools for military purposes, such as barracks or detention centers. Armed forces also may attack education institutions during environmental crises.

Military use of schools can put learners and teachers and other education personnel at serious risk of forced recruitment, as well as sexual exploitation and abuse. It also undermines children's and young people's right to education and makes attacks on education more likely. Attacks against civilians and civilian objects, including schools, is generally considered a violation of international humanitarian law.

Attacks on schools and hospitals are one of the six grave violations monitored and reported on under UN Security Council Resolution 1612 (2005). This resolution established the Monitoring and Reporting Mechanism on children in armed conflict and is the subject of an annual report by the UN Secretary General. When an attack occurs, it should be reported through the UN Monitoring and Reporting Mechanism. Governments that endorse the Safe Schools Declaration, which is "an intergovernmental political commitment to protect learners, teachers, schools, and universities from the worst effects of armed conflict," commit to ensuring that education will continue during violent conflict. They also agree to collect data on attacks on education, to help all victims in a non-discriminatory way, and to follow the *Guidelines for Protecting Schools and Universities from Military Use during Armed Conflict*, issued in 2014 by the Global Coalition to Protection Education from Attack.

Collaboration between child protection, human rights, and education actors can strengthen the advocacy, analysis, and implementation of interventions to prevent and reduce attacks on education. Depending on the context, actions to prevent and reduce risks may include:

- Encouraging negotiations with the parties involved in the conflict to protect education institutions
- Campaigning for governments to endorse and adhere to the Safe Schools Declaration
- Advocating and coordinating with the military to discourage military use of schools, including, when appropriate, using the *Guidelines for Protecting Schools and Universities from Military Use during Armed Conflict* as practical guidance for armed actors
- Working with governments and military judicial systems, armed forces, and armed groups to increase their awareness of the rules of international humanitarian law and strengthening their capacity to apply them to the protection of education
- Encouraging armed forces and armed groups to refrain from locating military objectives (e.g., combatants, weapons depots) near education facilities to reduce the risk of damaging them
- Adding safety messages, MHPSS, education on human rights, conflict resolution, peacebuilding, social cohesion, humanitarian law, and/or the fundamental principles of humanitarian action to the curriculum as appropriate for the learning level and context
- Providing landmine awareness programs and demining where relevant
- Raising public awareness of the meaning and use of the Geneva Conventions and the Additional Protocols, and of the Rome Statute of the International Criminal Court, which prohibit attacks against civilians (including learners and teachers) and education buildings in times of war
- Reinforcing school buildings or perimeter walls and using security guards, either paid or community volunteers
- Providing alternative ways to deliver education, such as home- and community-based schools and distance education
- Moving endangered learners and teachers and other education personnel to safe locations

Depending on the security situation, the community may be able to help protect education (for more guidance, see *Supporting Integrated Child Protection and Education Programming in Humanitarian Action; The Role of Communities in Protecting Education from Attack: Lessons Learned*)

> See also Standard 6, Guidance Note 2; Standard 18, Guidance Note 3; Standard 19, Guidance Note 5

10. **Disaster and climate risk management:** Education authorities and other education actors should empower learners, teachers and other education personnel, and communities to support disaster prevention and risk management activities. These can include:

- Assessing risks using existing data from national authorities and early warning systems
- Mapping risks in and around schools
- Conducting annual school safety self-assessments including identifying relevant hazards, assessing the conditions of buildings and infrastructure, implementing school-based risk reduction activities, learning skills for disaster response, and maintaining response provisions
- Reducing risks with measures such as maintaining buildings in good repair and keeping exit pathways and evacuation routes clear
- Learning and practicing Standard Operating Procedures for safe building evacuation and safe assembly, evacuation to a safe haven, shelter-in-place, lockdown, and safe family reunification, and when to use each one
- Learning and practicing hazard specific protective actions such as Drop, Cover, and Hold during earthquakes, Drop, Cover, Hold and Count in tsunami-prone zones, and Stop, Drop, and Roll if on fire
- Developing and using emergency preparedness and DRR plans at the school level
- Teaching about landmine awareness in school surroundings and agricultural areas
- Including DRR awareness in the curriculum

Community members or school safety committees may need help integrating school safety into their school-based management or improvement plans. Education and disaster risk management stakeholders should help communities or school committees to assess and prioritize risks, carry out physical and environmental protection strategies, and develop response preparedness procedures and skills. Community and indigenous knowledge should be used in developing or adapting DRR and resilience plans and response preparedness strategies.

School-based disaster and climate risk management plans should be linked to the national and community-based disaster management system. School-level preparedness plans also should be connected with local and national contingency plans developed as part of the ESP or TEP.

Education authorities at the national, sub-national, and local level should review their risk assessment, risk reduction, and emergency response preparedness annually. These stakeholders should ensure that persons with disabilities participate in the planning process. They should communicate plans to the whole school community in ways that are accessible to all, including people with low levels of literacy and learners with disabilities (for more guidance see *Comprehensive School Safety Framework*).

> See also Standard 1, Guidance Note 6; Standard 2, Guidance Note 4; Standard 4, Guidance Note 8; Standard 11, Guidance Note 2; Standard 14, Guidance Note 4; Standard 18, Guidance Note 5; Standard 19, Guidance Note 2

References and further reading

Links to these and additional resources are available on the INEE website.

- *A Whole School Approach To Prevent School Related Gender-Based Violence: Minimum Standards and Monitoring Framework*, UNGEI, 2019
- *Comprehensive School Safety Framework*, GADRRRES, 2022
- *Education in Emergencies: Child Protection Collaboration Framework*, Child Protection Area of Responsibility and GEC, 2020
- *Environmental Emergencies Centre (EEC) Resource Center* [Website]
- *Global Guidance on Addressing School-Related Gender-Based Violence*, UNESCO and UN Women, 2016
- *Guidelines for Integrating Gender-Based Violence Interventions in Humanitarian Action*, Inter-agency Standing Committee, 2015
- *Guidelines for Protecting Schools and Universities from Military Use during Armed Conflict*, GCPEA, 2014
- *Helping Adolescents Thrive Toolkit*, UNICEF and WHO, 2021
- *IASC Guidelines on Mental Health and Psychosocial Support in Emergency Settings*, IASC, 2007
- *INEE Guidance Note on Psychosocial Support*, INEE, 2018
- *INEE Guidance Note on Teacher Wellbeing in Emergency Settings*, INEE, 2022
- *Minimum Standards for Child Protection in Humanitarian Action*, Alliance for Child Protection in Humanitarian Action, 2019
- *Operational Guidance for Child Friendly Spaces in Humanitarian Settings*, IFRC, 2018.

- *PSS-SEL Toolbox*, Harvard EASEL Lab and INEE, 2022
- *Risk-Informed Education Programming for Resilience: Guidance Note*, UNICEF, 2019
- *Safe Schools Declaration*, GCPEA, 2015
- *Supporting Integrated Child Protection and Education Programming in Humanitarian Action*, Alliance for Child Protection in Humanitarian Action and INEE, 2022
- *The Role of Communities in Protecting Education from Attack: Lessons Learned*, GCPEA, 2014

STANDARD 10: FACILITIES AND SERVICES

Education facilities promote the safety and wellbeing of learners and teachers and other education personnel, and are linked to health, nutrition, psychosocial, and protection services.

Key actions
(please read with guidance notes)

1. **Safe and inclusive sites:** Build, reconstruct, improve, or relocate education facilities to sites that promote inclusion and equity and ensure the safety of learners and of teachers and other education personnel.

2. **Solid structure, design, and construction:** Design and build education structures so they are safe, disaster resilient, and cost-effective.

3. **The climate crisis and disaster risks:** Address environmental sustainability in the planning, design, construction, and maintenance of education facilities.

4. **Promotion of learning and interaction:** Design education structures so that they promote participatory learning and interaction in inclusive, culturally appropriate, and age-appropriate ways.

5. **Regular maintenance and repair:** Regularly repair, retrofit, or replace temporary and permanent learning environments with disaster-resilient design and construction.

6. **Inclusive of persons with disabilities:** Design learning environments and education structures so that they are accessible to learners with disabilities.

7. **WASH promotion:** Provide enough safe water and sanitation facilities in the learning environment to allow good personal hygiene and protect all learners.

8. **Evidence-based school health and nutrition:** Provide evidence-based school health and nutrition programs to address hunger and other barriers to learning, and to foster learners' wellbeing and development.

9. **Multi-sectoral referral mechanisms:** Create links between schools and other learning environments and other relevant sectors such as child protection, health, and nutrition, and social and MHPSS services and referrals.

🗒 Guidance notes

1. **Safe and inclusive sites:** Education authorities and other education stakeholders should ensure that education facilities are in spaces that encourage inclusion and equity and guarantee safety from risks. Sites should have enough space for classes, administration, recreation, and WASH facilities.

Education actors should determine whether sites used before the emergency can be reused or if the learning environment should be moved to a safer and more appropriate location. If education facilities were not built in sites that promoted safety, inclusion, and equity, rebuilding physical structures in the same locations may continue discrimination against certain groups within the community or put learners at risk. Reconstruction plans should ensure that going to school will not expose learners or teachers and other education personnel to avoidable risks. If a school is damaged beyond repair or in an unsuitable location, education planners should determine whether any community buildings can be used for education purposes, such as community halls or sports facilities. Using alternative spaces can limit the disruption of education. If no existing structure is available or additional infrastructure must be added, it may be necessary to construct temporary learning spaces, such as tents.

When deciding where to locate a temporary or permanent learning structure, planners should do the following:

- Carry out protection, conflict, and disaster risk assessments
- Consult with a range of community members, especially those from marginalized or vulnerable groups, such as persons with disabilities, girls, gender diverse children and young people, and ethnic and religious minorities
- Consult with teachers and learners on the best arrangement and form for educational spaces to ensure that they meet their learning and pedagogical needs during emergencies
- Collaborate with the authorities responsible for regulating school infrastructure and make sure to secure land tenure
- Ensure that new sites have adequate escape routes so that everyone can leave safely in an emergency
- Choose sites large enough to accommodate classes and other learning spaces, administration, recreation, and WASH facilities
- When possible, include space for extra classrooms so that multiple shifts will not be necessary if more learners enroll, especially in situations of ongoing displacement
- Work with other sectors, such as camp coordination and camp management, shelter, protection, and health, to advocate for adequate space for education purposes and to make sure that schools and education facilities are close to learners' homes and other services

(For more guidance, see *Comprehensive School Safety Framework; Construction Good Practice Standards*.)

See also Standard 1, Guidance Note 1; Standard 4, Guidance Notes 7–8 and 10; Standard 8, Guidance Note 7; Standard 18, Guidance Note 4; Standard 19, Guidance Note 4

2. **Solid structure, design, and construction:** Education structures should be safe, disaster resilient, and cost-effective to operate. To limit the damage hazards and risks of all kinds do to education, including natural and climate-induced hazards, those who design and build temporary and permanent education facilities should consider the following:

- **Structural safety:** Qualified professionals should assess the structural safety of damaged buildings and prioritize which buildings are suitable for re-occupancy, repair, retrofitting, or replacement, based on need and cost.

- **Building to accepted standards:** Temporary and permanent learning structures should be in line with accepted international planning and building standards, or with national and local codes when they are of a higher standard.

- **Disaster-resilient design and construction:** Education facilities should be resilient to known hazards and risks, such as fires, floods, storms, earthquakes, and landslides. Communities can suggest suitable design options and draw from indigenous knowledge.

- **Participatory design and community engagement:** Education planners should involve teachers, learners, and community members in designing schools and other education facilities to ensure that they meet everyone's needs and to increase the community's sense of ownership. The facilities should provide the resources teachers need to do their jobs and space to store education equipment.

- **Good lighting and ventilation:** The design and construction of education facilities should include the appropriate use of materials to provide adequate lighting, cross-ventilation, and comfortable internal temperatures. It is important to create a teaching and learning environment that supports the health and wellbeing of learners and of teachers and other education personnel.

- **Safety:** Learning spaces should be protected by marked boundaries or fencing and clear signage. All schools need first aid kits, fire extinguishers, and emergency escapes on all floors. In some contexts, bomb shelters should be established or made available.

- **Costs:** Structures should be cost-effective and durable. Communities and education planners can help establish a budget and determine possible current and long-term uses. When possible, infrastructure managers should use local and environmentally friendly materials and labor to build the structure. This will enable authorities and communities to maintain the structure at an affordable cost.

- **Local livelihoods:** Education planners and infrastructure managers should use local building materials and labor as much as possible. This will help support the community and enable local laborers to develop their skills and capacities. They should promote market-based solutions (including the use of cash transfers or cash-for-work transfers) that support the local economy and community decision-making, and plan for the costs associated with maintaining facilities and early response.

Education structures may be temporary, semi-permanent, permanent, an extension to an existing building, or a mobile structure. Involving different groups from the affected community in joint activities, such as constructing and maintaining education facilities, may promote social cohesion and mitigate conflict. People involved in the construction and rehabilitation of education facilities must be trained in child protection, prevention of sexual abuse and exploitation, and child safeguarding and adhere to safeguarding policies (for more guidance, see *Sphere Handbook*, Shelter and Settlement Standards; *Minimum Standards for Child Protection*, Standards 23 and Standard 27; *Construction Good Practice Standards*).

> See also Standard 2, Guidance Note 4; Standard 4, Guidance Note 8; Standard 17, Guidance Note 1; Standard 18, Guidance Note 4

3. **The climate crisis and disaster risks:** There is an increasing need to design and construct infrastructure that is resilient to the effects of expected hazards, environmentally responsible, and helps to mitigate the impact of the climate crisis on the safety and accessibility of learning environments. The construction and reconstruction of education facilities should aim to be safer and greener by, for example, adhering to global standards for performance during earthquake shaking, strong winds, and heavy rains, reducing the carbon footprint, and using renewable resources.

Environmental sustainability should be a focus throughout the site selection, planning, design, construction, and maintenance of education facilities, including the following actions:

- Conducting an environmental assessment, such as NEAT+
- Analyzing how to mitigate risks before facilities are built and during the lifespan of the emergency education facilities, such as using nature-based solutions (for more guidance, see *Nature-based Solutions for Climate Resilience in Humanitarian Action*)
- Using reusable supplies when possible, especially for temporary learning spaces
- Using locally sourced materials or, when possible, reusing materials from damaged school facilities
- Using renewable energy, for example, solar and wind sources
- Raising awareness in the community on the climate crisis and how they can help mitigate it, such as helping to plant trees and creating school gardens

- Providing WASH facilities that are sensitive to the climate crisis, for example, by avoiding unnecessary water loss, using renewable energy to pump water, or maintaining a proper waste management system
- Engaging local authorities, families, the community, and schools in using water and energy resources efficiently and reducing carbon footprint

> 🔍 See also Standard 2, Guidance Notes 1 and 4; Standard 4, Guidance Note 8

4. **Promotion of learning and interaction:** Education planners should design education structures to promote participatory learning and interaction in an inclusive, culturally and age-appropriate way. Spaces need to suit the gender, age, physical ability, and culture of all users. To promote participatory methodologies and learner-centered approaches, learning spaces and seating arrangements should have the appropriate space for each learner and a reasonable teacher-learner ratio. Other design considerations include:

- Who uses the learning space and how, including what type and level of education the space is used for (e.g., ECD, tertiary education, specific subjects)
- Creating learning spaces that allow interactive learning by having multi-purpose spaces, movable furniture, and spaces for doing projects and group work
- Having age-appropriate learning spaces so that younger children have room to play, including outdoors, and furniture of a suitable size, perhaps with protective cushioning for younger learners
- Providing separate learning spaces and teachers of the same gender for girls and boys in contexts where interaction between boys and girls is restricted, or where mixed-gender classes can lead to exclusion
- Maintaining a maximum class size that still allows students to learn and is realistic for the circumstances

> 🔍 See also Standard 12, Guidance Note 1

5. **Regular maintenance and repair:** The building and furniture, including desks, chairs, and chalkboards, need regular maintenance. Members of the community and the community education committee can volunteer their time or materials, and young people can help them maintain the learning environment. Education planners should make sure that the infrastructure aligns with local market and labor conditions so that local authorities and the community will be able to maintain the structure affordably over the long-term and plan better for the associated costs.

> 🔍 See also Standard 2, Guidance Note 1; Standard 4, Guidance Note 8

6. **Inclusive of persons with disabilities:** Education planners should provide education facilities that are in line with the principles of universal design. This means that, as much as possible, education services are accessible to all people without having to make special adjustments. This will enable learners with disabilities to access education as readily as others in their community, as outlined in Article 3 of the Convention on the Rights of Persons with Disabilities.

    Education actors can take steps to help reduce or eliminate the barriers that learners with disabilities face in the classroom, including the following:

    - When choosing sites, designing, and re/building education facilities, consulting with OPDs, parents and caregivers of children with disabilities, and children and young persons with disabilities
    - Creating accessible structures (including WASH facilities) with entrances and exits that can accommodate people who use wheelchairs or other assisted-mobility devices
    - Ensuring that the furniture is suitable for the needs of learners with disabilities
    - Making sure that classrooms have good lighting, as poor lighting can make learning difficult for children with visual impairments
    - Maintaining a reasonable noise level in the classrooms, as loud noise and poor acoustics can make learning difficult for children with hearing impairments
    - Ensuring that learners with disabilities can access distance education, for example by providing taped recordings of lessons for those who may not be able to attend online

    Temporary structures, such as tents, prefabricated buildings, or buildings originally designed for other purposes, may create extra challenges. For example, they may not be soundproof or the lighting may be poor (for more guidance, see *INEE Pocket Guide to Supporting Learners with Disabilities*).

    > See also Standard 1, Guidance Note 1; Standard 8, Guidance Note 2; Standard 12, Guidance Note 3

7. **WASH promotion:** Learning environments must have water and sanitation facilities and make hygiene education and practices part of the curriculum. It is essential to ensure that learners of all ages and genders and those with disabilities have equitable access to these facilities and participation in WASH activities. It is important for education actors to collaborate with the WASH and protection sectors to ensure that the facilities and curriculum meet accepted standards. For more information about the key components of WASH, see the *Sphere Handbook*, Water Supply, Sanitation and Hygiene Promotion Standards.

Education stakeholders should consult learners, parents and caregivers, teachers, and other community members about the construction of sanitation facilities. This will ensure that children and young people are able to express their own sanitation needs. Including them in planning or improving the WASH facilities will make sure that they are appropriate for all learners' age, gender, ability, and culture. The following are things to consider in planning WASH facilities:

- WASH facilities must protect the privacy, dignity, and safety of all who use them.
- Toilets should be in or close to the learning environment. If they are not on the learning site, measures must be in place to protect learners, such as safety escorts.
- Toilet doors should lock from the inside.
- Separate toilets must be provided for boys/men and girls/women in safe, convenient, and easily accessible places. This will help to prevent sexual harassment or abuse. Where possible, gender neutral toilets can be provided for non-binary learners.
- Sphere guidelines call for one school toilet for every 30 girls and one for every 60 boys.
- Learners should be taught to wash their hands to prevent disease transmission.
- Facilities should be located so that people wash their hands before they touch food after using the toilet.
- Menstrual hygiene management facilities and supplies should be available in girls' facilities, including disposal containers and space to wash hands and menstrual materials.
- Toilets must be safe and accessible for persons with disabilities, and should be adapted, if necessary, to meet their needs.
- Teachers and other education personnel should have toilets that are separate from those for learners.

Learners and teachers and other education personnel of menstruating age should have access to hygiene products and WASH facilities that protect their dignity and wellbeing during menstruation and enable them to participate fully in teaching and learning. It is important to:

- Understand the practices, social norms, and stigma related to menstruation and adapt hygiene facilities and supplies to suit local practices
- Provide menstrual products in discrete locations to protect girls' and women's dignity and reduce stigma
- Provide culturally appropriate methods for disposing of sanitary materials
- Work with local women's rights organizations to procure locally produced, reusable sanitary supplies, if relevant

- Teach about menstruation and puberty in consultation with health, gender, or protection specialists, where possible
- Demonstrate the proper use of unfamiliar sanitary items

(For more guidance, see *INEE Guidance Note on Gender*; *Sphere Handbook*, Water Supply, Sanitation and Hygiene Promotion Standards, Standard 1.3.)

Providing a safe water source, potable water, and soap is an essential component of safe, protective learning environments and helps to prevent or reduce the spread of contagious diseases, such as cholera and COVID-19. Sphere guidelines for minimum water quantities in schools call for three liters of water per student per day for drinking and hand washing. Social, political, legal, or environmental factors that affect the control of water sources might be contentious, especially during a crisis. It is important that WASH services in education facilities are designed and implemented according to conflict sensitive and do no harm principles so that they do not increase tensions or contribute to conflict.

> See also Standard 4, Guidance Note 10; Standard 5, Guidance Note 3; Standard 11, Guidance Note 2; Standard 16, Guidance Note 1; Standard 19, Guidance Note 4

8. **Evidence-based school health and nutrition:** School-based health and nutrition programs are critical to support learners' health, wellbeing, and development. These programs connect education to resources in the health, nutrition, and WASH sectors. They can contribute to removing barriers to learning and to promoting healthy development. Programs can include:

- Education on health and nutrition, mental health and wellbeing, including self-care, and sexual and reproductive health and rights
- School meals
- School health services
- MHPSS services
- Communicable disease prevention programs, such as for measles, diarrhea, COVID-19, HIV/AIDS
- MHPSS services
- Identifying and supporting learners with disabilities

During a health crisis, schools can help protect children, young people, and communities by providing safeguards, such as physical infrastructure, water and sanitation, and training in healthy behaviors. Communities can play an important role in creating sustainable, manageable support systems for school meal programs, such as collaborating with local farmers. These programs should follow such guidelines as the *World Food Program's Guidelines on School Feeding*. Assessments of school-based health and nutrition interventions should be conducted in collaboration with the relevant national authorities, and with coordination systems like the health or food security clusters. Interventions may be directly supported by other sectors, but it is important that all services are coordinated at the school, local, and national levels (for more guidance, see *Sphere Handbook*, Food Security and Nutrition Standards).

See also Standard 4, Guidance Note 10; Standard 19, Guidance Note 4

9. Multi-sectoral referral mechanisms: Education actors should establish links between the learning environment and other relevant sectors, such as child protection, health, nutrition, and MHPSS. Referrals can be made when a learner needs assistance that teachers and other education personnel cannot provide. Learners or their families can be referred as needed; teachers and other education personnel may also benefit from referrals.

Referrals to specialized services may include standard legal and health services or services established to respond to crisis-specific needs, such as:

- Health services, including MHPSS
- Health services for victims of violence, including domestic and SRGBV
- Paramedical services for learners who have disabilities
- Sexual and reproductive health services, including youth-friendly health services for adolescents and young people
- Tracing and reunification for children who are unaccompanied or have been separated from their families
- Legal services, such as supporting civil registration
- Food, CVA, or livelihood support for families at risk of engaging their children in child labor

Communities may have limited access to specialized services, especially during a crisis. Education actors should identify the specialized services available in a community or in a camp setting that are relevant to learners. This may include engaging with stakeholders from different sectors and with representatives from the community and government to identify how service gaps can be addressed. They also can work out what role humanitarian actors can play in providing targeted and temporary specialized services.

If multi-sectoral referral mechanisms are to be effective, they should be established at the school level, and learners, communities, and teachers and other education personnel should learn how to use them. Policy-makers are responsible for establishing links between sectors within policy frameworks and should budget for multi-sectoral collaboration. In crisis situations, clusters and working groups can support cross-sectoral, inter-agency collaboration (for more guidance, see *Supporting Integrated Child Protection and Education Programming in Humanitarian Action*).

See also Standard 3, Guidance Note 4; Standard 4, Guidance Note 10; Standard 9, Guidance Note 3; Standard 11, Guidance Note 3; Standard 14, Guidance Note 1; Standard 17, Guidance Note 5; Standard 19, Guidance Note 4

References and further reading

Links to these and additional resources are available on the INEE website.

- *A Toolkit for Integrating Menstrual Hygiene Management (MHM) into Humanitarian Response*, Columbia University and International Rescue Committee, 2017
- *Comprehensive School Safety Framework*, GADRRRES, 2022
- *Construction Good Practice Standards*, Global Shelter Cluster, 2021
- *From the School Gate to Children's Plate: Golden Rules for Safer School Meals - Guidelines*, World Food Program, 2019
- *Guidelines for Integrating Gender-Based Violence Interventions in Humanitarian Action*, Inter-agency Standing Committee, 2015
- *Humanitarian inclusion standards for older people and people with disabilities*, ADCAP, 2018
- *INEE Guidance Note on Gender*, INEE, 2019
- *INEE Guidance Notes on Safer School Construction*, INEE, 2009
- *INEE Pocket Guide to Supporting Learners with Disabilities*, INEE, 2010
- *Nature-based Solutions for Climate Resilience in Humanitarian Action*, Sphere, FEBA, IUCN, PEDRR, EHAN, and IFRC, 2023
- *Nexus Environmental Assessment Tool (NEAT+)*, UNEP/OCHA Joint Environment Unit
- *Risk-Informed Education Programming for Resilience: Guidance Note*, UNICEF, 2019
- *Supporting Integrated Child Protection and Education Programming in Humanitarian Action*, Alliance for Child Protection in Humanitarian Action and INEE, 2022
- *The Sphere Handbook: Humanitarian Charter and Minimum Standards in Humanitarian Response*, Sphere, 2018
- *Towards Safe School Construction: A Community-Based Approach*, GADRRRES, 2015

For resources to help you with the implementation of the standards in Domain 2, visit inee.org/minimum-standards.

Teaching and Learning

Foundational Standards for a Quality Response: Community Participation, Coordination, Analysis

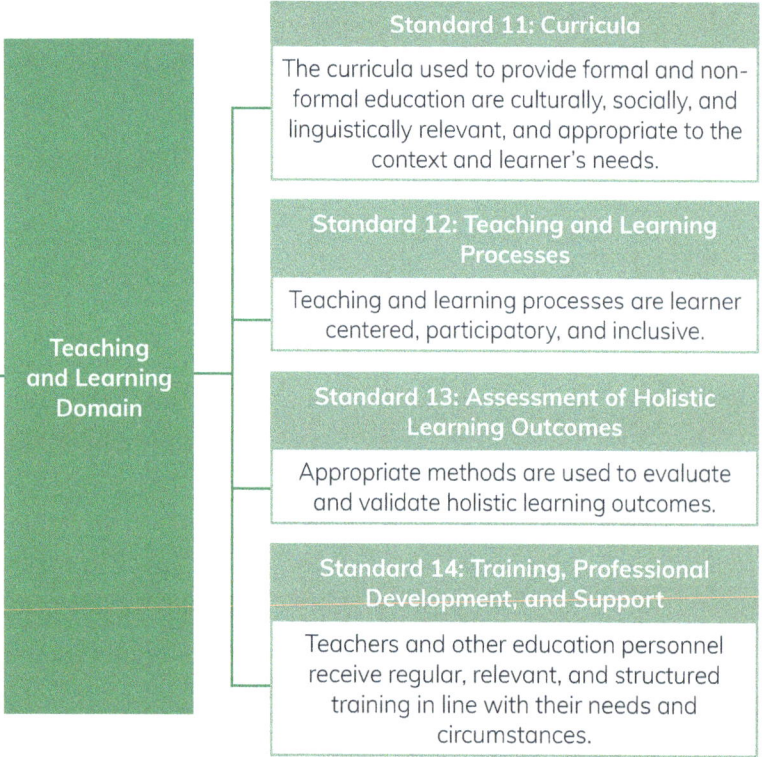

Teaching and Learning Domain

Standard 11: Curricula

The curricula used to provide formal and non-formal education are culturally, socially, and linguistically relevant, and appropriate to the context and learner's needs.

Standard 12: Teaching and Learning Processes

Teaching and learning processes are learner centered, participatory, and inclusive.

Standard 13: Assessment of Holistic Learning Outcomes

Appropriate methods are used to evaluate and validate holistic learning outcomes.

Standard 14: Training, Professional Development, and Support

Teachers and other education personnel receive regular, relevant, and structured training in line with their needs and circumstances.

Overview of Domain 3

The standards in this domain emphasize that equitable access to education must be accompanied by quality teaching and learning, and attention to children's and young people's emotional, physical, and cognitive wellbeing. This means that learners require a relevant and inclusive curriculum, along with teaching and learning approaches that promote their social and emotional development. Emergencies can offer the opportunity to improve many aspects of education, including the curriculum, teaching methodology, access to MHPSS, learner assessments, and teachers' professional development. It is important to seize these opportunities.

This domain has four standards: Curricula, Teaching and Learning Processes, Assessment of Holistic Learning Outcomes, and Training, Professional Development, and Support, which are discussed below.

> The key actions in this domain involve actors who support teaching and learning initiatives, such as:
>
> * National, sub-national, and local education authorities
> * School leaders and teachers and other education personnel
> * National curriculum bodies
> * Teacher training institutes/colleges
> * Communities affected by crisis
> * Stakeholders involved in the education response, including local and national CSOs and NGOs, faith-based organizations, humanitarian and development partners, donors, and private sector actors

Curriculum matters

What children and young people learn at school matters, and a country's national curriculum stipulates what this will be. It can help learners gain the knowledge, skills, and values they will need to thrive as individuals and to contribute to society. In keeping with global policy frameworks, refugee learners should follow the host country curriculum. This will enable them to progress through the education system, earn certifications, and move toward social integration, or have learning officially recognized if they return home or resettle in a third country. The curriculum also can play an important role in raising learners' awareness of human rights, climate change and environmental sustainability, peacebuilding, and citizenship.

The curriculum in formal and non-formal education programs can be further defined by four key components: intended curriculum, implemented curriculum, learned curriculum, and hidden curriculum. The "intended" curriculum includes the substance of the curriculum framework, syllabus, and learning materials. The "implemented" curriculum includes what teachers deliver. The "learned" curriculum refers to the knowledge and skills that learners learn in class. The "hidden" curriculum is formed from the teachers' and learners' values and beliefs which may reinforce or contradict the prescribed curriculum. Potential for bias exists in all of these. A curriculum reflects the country's social and political agenda and is the responsibility of the education authorities. It can promote peace, unity, and social inclusion. On the other hand, it can purposely or accidentally promote hatred, prejudice, and oppression, and even contribute to conflict. Teachers and other education personnel should be trained to recognize their own implicit bias and explicit bias in teaching and learning materials, and to address it by encouraging learners to discuss and consider the perspectives of others. Education stakeholders should work to raise community awareness and understanding of the importance of recognizing and addressing bias in the curriculum.

For learners who have crossed borders, the language of instruction may differ from their own. Thus, they may need extra support to be able to learn effectively in that language. For reasons of academic progression and social cohesion, global commitments and policies recommend that learning occur in the language(s) used in host country schools. Learning in a new language will be challenging for learners and for their teachers, and they will need extra support to help them make the transition (see also Domain 2: Access and Learning Environment).

Teaching to support learning and wellbeing

It is important that teachers can support the learning and wellbeing of a diverse group of learners. This is particularly relevant during a crisis, as the size and make-up of classes may change. Learners may be diverse in terms of age, developmental stage, life experience, and social and emotional needs. Teachers will need solid knowledge and understanding of the substance of the curriculum and the competence to adjust how they deliver it. It is essential that education authorities and EiE actors have a commitment to inclusion and to reducing learning barriers, and that they help teachers gain the skills and competencies needed to create a supportive and protective learning environment during crises. The way a teacher teaches and how they organize the learning environment, which may include opportunities for learners to work collaboratively, to succeed, and to enjoy what they are doing, all have an impact on learners' wellbeing.

Using alternative education approaches

Teaching and learning during emergencies may not take place through the usual face-to-face approach. Crises resulting in school closures can cause a significant loss of learning and have a negative impact on the wellbeing of learners, teachers and other education personnel, and communities. This was clearly highlighted by the COVID-19 pandemic. Alternative education can be used to address both short and longer-term disruptions of in-person learning. Digital approaches may be a viable option during a health pandemic, when it may not be possible to print and distribute learning materials. However, digital learning can also present challenges for learners, particularly for girls who may face social restrictions or limitations on access to devices and for children and young people with disabilities. Learners also may have limited access to technical devices, internet connectivity, and electricity. Many learners and teachers also may lack confidence in using technology. Education stakeholders will need to consider these factors carefully before planning any tech-enabled interventions and address any potential barriers to access during their implementation.

Whether distance education is delivered through high-, low-, or no-tech approaches, learners may need support when studying alone. This will depend on their age, developmental level, and experience. Self-study may be more challenging for learners who are used to a more didactic approach. All learners, including those in higher education, will require some support when learning from a distance. Younger children will need a lot of support. A blended learning approach that combines face-to-face and distance education can be a positive solution. Distance education can be used for practice work on key concepts, whereas face-to-face approaches are best used to teach new concepts and provide individual support to learners. Parents and caregivers who are involved in their children's education should receive the support they need, especially if in-person teaching has stopped.

Because TVET can be very practical, distance education might not seem a feasible choice for TVET learners. However, although they do need hands-on experience at various stages, distance education is also a workable choice. For the non-practical parts of a course, TVET learners can engage in self-study using books or online materials. They can combine this with online demonstrations of practical activities (for more guidance, see *INEE Background Paper on Distance Education in Emergencies*).

Online, digital, or blended tertiary education programs can help expand access to higher education for learners who have been displaced or whose studies have been interrupted by crisis. Education actors should work to ensure that these programs are certified and recognized in the country in which the learner lives.

Assessing learners is important

Student assessments are an integral part of the learning process. They give learners and teachers feedback and enable teachers to make adjustments or offer learners more support. An assessment should lead to meaningful outcomes that enable learners to move forward. The assessments teachers or classroom assistants carry out day-to-day are called formative assessments or assessments for learning. Teachers observe, ask questions, and look at the learners' work. If distance education approaches are being used, teachers will need to monitor learners' progress and use the time they have with learners face-to-face to assess their understanding and challenges further. Both approaches should enable teachers to provide targeted support.

The more formal assessments used for evaluation, progression, or certification are called summative, or assessments of learning. National assessments are designed to provide information on how an education system is performing. This is usually done in relation to a set of standards or learning goals to guide education policy and practice. Examples include large-scale assessments like the Early Grade Reading Assessment or Early Grade Math Assessment. Summative assessments should measure not just what is easy to assess or monitor what parts of the curriculum have been taught. They also should measure targeted skills and outcomes, with the goal of ensuring meaningful learning.

All forms of assessment should measure holistic learning outcomes, including literacy, numeracy, and social and emotional skills development.

Supporting teachers throughout a crisis

If teachers are to be competent and confident in managing all the new demands discussed above, it is important for them to be fully qualified, have clear and reasonable terms of employment, accredited professional development, and good support networks. During emergencies, however, untrained or under-qualified teachers may be called on, and a rapid assessment should be done of their knowledge, skills, and attitudes. This is further explored in Domain 4: Teachers and Other Education Personnel.

In emergency contexts, practicing teachers should be reminded of what they already know and what new things they may need to learn. The principles of inclusive and equitable quality education remain the same. Providing MHPSS and SEL is even more important during crises, and teachers may need to adapt their teaching approaches to respond to their learners' needs in these areas. Teachers should be aware of how their teaching practices can support learners' psychosocial wellbeing and know how to recognize learners who may be in distress and in need of additional support. Teachers also will need technical support in using distance education approaches. It is important that there is no bias or prejudice in their teaching approaches or in the learning materials, which may include new topics related to the emergency response, such as DRR, hazard awareness, conflict sensitivity, climate change, and human rights education.

Teachers often are living and working in the same emergency environment as their learners and experiencing similar adverse events and stressors. Despite this, they are expected to provide continuity and a sense of normalcy for their learners. Teachers may experience psychological and social difficulties and need access to informal support networks, as well as knowledge of where they can find formal support. Education personnel other than teachers, including head teachers, also need support and training so that they can support teachers and protect their own wellbeing.

If they receive quality training, mentoring, and support, teachers will be more effective in the learning environment and confident in using a range of teaching approaches and resources, including during emergencies. They will be able to support individual learners, be inclusive in their teaching, and do their best to keep discrimination and bias out of the learning environment. Effective teachers will adapt how they use technology as they consider the challenges learners may face. Training and support for teachers and other education personnel is discussed further in Domain 4: Teachers and Other Education Personnel.

STANDARD 11: CURRICULA

The curricula used to provide formal and non-formal education are culturally, socially, and linguistically relevant, and appropriate to the context and learner's needs.

Key actions
(please read with guidance notes)

1. **Appropriate curriculum:** Ensure that the curriculum is appropriate for learners' context, age, developmental level, capacities, and needs.

2. **Core competencies and skills:** Ensure that the curriculum, textbooks, and supplementary learning materials cover the core competencies of basic education.

3. **Mental health and psychosocial support, wellbeing, and protection:** Ensure that the curriculum addresses learners' social, emotional, and protection needs.

4. **Curriculum for diversity:** Ensure that the curriculum recognizes diversity and is responsive to the factors causing marginalization.

5. **Curriculum review and development:** Recognize and support the responsibility of education authorities to lead any development, review, or adaptation of the formal curriculum.

6. **Sourcing learning resources:** Promptly provide sufficient, locally-sourced teaching and learning resources.

Guidance notes

1. **Appropriate curriculum:** The curriculum should be age appropriate. This means that it is compatible with learners' reading levels and that the texts, examples, and illustrations align with their developmental levels. Developmental level usually refers to the cognitive, but it also includes life experience and psychosocial and physical development. The curriculum should reflect the learners' day-to-day environment, promote gender equity and inclusiveness of persons with disabilities, and avoid prejudicing or frightening learners. It also should give learners a constructive understanding of the key issues of climate change and environmental sustainability.

> **Differentiated learning:** This is a teaching approach that involves offering several different learning experiences. It proactively addresses students' varied needs to maximize learning opportunities for each student in the classroom. It requires teachers to be flexible in their approach and to adjust the curriculum and presentation of information for learners of different abilities. (see Annex 1: Glossary)

Learners of the same age will have different developmental levels. Even with an age-appropriate curriculum, this means that the materials and approaches need to be differentiated. This need may increase when classes change during emergencies. For example, they may increase in size due to newly-arrived refugee or displaced learners or serve multi-age learners. Teachers will require support to adapt their teaching to the learners' varying needs and levels. If different education delivery models are to be used, such as accelerated or non-formal education, an analysis of the curriculum will need to be undertaken to identify key concepts for each developmental level.

Learners who are being introduced to a new language will need additional support. In situations where learners have crossed borders and are to be integrated immediately into the host country education system, this support will have to be part of the classroom practice or provided in afterschool sessions. If a transition period is planned, education stakeholders can implement language support or bridging programs to help learners gain familiarity with the new language. Meanwhile, teachers from the same community can teach them in their mother tongue. Bilingual or multilingual education approaches, wherein learners' mother tongue is taught at the same time they are introduced to a second language, can help to improve learners' performance in the second language and in other subjects. Research and evidence has found that young children learn most effectively in a language they understand. To ensure that children develop strong foundational literacy and numeracy skills, their early education should be in their mother tongue as much as possible.

> See also Standard 1, Guidance Note 6; Standard 8, Guidance Notes 5 and 7; Standard 12, Guidance Note 2; Standard 14, Guidance Note 2; Standard 15, Guidance Note 2

2. **Core competencies and skills:** Education authorities and other education actors should identify the core competencies and skills that need to be taught to different age groups before developing any learning materials. National authorities may have established competency frameworks for age and level of education. International frameworks also exist. During emergencies, it will be necessary to determine whether the frameworks include the competencies and skills needed to build and support essential, crisis-specific needs.

Early childhood is a crucial time for helping learners build a strong foundation of competence and skill development. These foundational competencies provide a base on which learners will develop additional skills as they grow older and advance through leveled programs. Initial core competencies include functional literacy and numeracy, and social and emotional skills. However, to address the healthy development of the whole child, early childhood development may focus on a broader range of skills. Subject knowledge may be expanded and deepened across learning levels. This will help provide children and young people with the skills they need to build healthy relationships with peers and others, including communication skills. In an emergency context, it may be necessary to focus on additional knowledge, competencies, and skills. Depending on the context, this could include health and hygiene, sexual and reproductive health and rights, HIV/AIDs and other diseases, climate change, and human rights education, such as citizenship and democracy, peacebuilding, and humanitarian law.

Because there is an increased need to protect learners during emergencies and through to recovery, less time may be spent on instruction. This may create the need to prioritize competencies and skills by age and learning level. A prioritization process may be coordinated by national education authorities and supported by the relevant inter-agency coordination mechanism, or be addressed at the organization and program level. If a full curriculum is inappropriate or impossible to implement, the relevant decision-makers will need to determine whether programs should focus on specific competencies and skills. Core competencies and skills that are part of the curriculum design may need to be scaffolded so the initial focus can be on learners' wellbeing and essential skills. Scaffolding competencies and skills, including SEL, will depend on the crisis. For example, during a health crisis or pandemic, the focus will be on providing targeted health and safety content and skills-development opportunities. These may be part of an essential package that also includes MHPSS, SEL, and foundational literacy and numeracy.

Stakeholders should make every effort to coordinate their adaptations across learning levels, from ECD through tertiary and across formal and non-formal programs. This will ensure that learners have options and opportunities to progress in their learning during an emergency and through to recovery.

The key skills learners need are determined by the context and can include:

- **Social and emotional skills:** These are the skills needed to question, solve problems, collaborate, make decisions, and communicate with empathy, creativity, and self-awareness.
- **DRR and life-saving skills and behaviors:** These skills include gender-specific protection, education on landmines and unexploded ordnance, and safe practices during a pandemic.
- **Creative and sports skills:** These skills include music, dance, drama, and the visual arts, and various individual and team sports and games.

TVET courses and programs should offer different types of courses and different levels of certification that reflect current and future market needs, as affected by the crisis. Gender stereotyping should be avoided so that all learners receive information and advice on the courses available. TVET learners will also need certain competencies and social and emotional skills to succeed when later employed. TVET teaching and learning processes can emphasize these skills. This may include providing practical experiences, such as work placements and apprenticeships, that enable learners to apply new skills. TVET course options and recruitment should reflect an awareness of potential gender stereotyping so it can be avoided (for more guidance, see *Minimum Economic Recovery Standards*, Employment Standards and Enterprise and Market Systems Development Standards).

See also Standard 8, Guidance Note 6; Standard 9, Guidance Notes 1, 5, and 10; Standard 10, Guidance Note 7; Standard 14, Guidance Note 2

3. **Mental health and psychosocial support, wellbeing, and protection:** The curriculum should address learners' wellbeing and need for MHPSS and protection. Teachers and other education personnel need clear guidance on teaching approaches and classroom activities that will help them provide MHPSS. Education authorities and technical experts will need to establish learning objectives and benchmarks that outline what learners need to know to build their SEL and other aspects of wellbeing, along with knowledge and behaviors that enable them to protect themselves and seek assistance when needed. Those learning objectives may require a specific curriculum or teaching and learning resources. They may also require orientation and support for teachers and other education personnel on a variety of teaching methods. This may include contextualized play-based learning, which can help learners build confidence and self-esteem and support their wellbeing (see Annex 1: Glossary for a definition of play).

Teachers need to be able to recognize signs of distress in learners and know how to respond. This includes knowing when to refer learners to specialized services, where this is feasible. If these services are not available, education authorities and supporting organizations will need to provide guidance for teachers and schools on how to offer support, within reason. Teachers should not be expected, for example, to provide counselling services they are not qualified for, as this may cause more distress (for more guidance, see *Supporting Integrated Child Protection and Education Programming in Humanitarian Action; Minimum Standards for Child Protection*, Standard 23).

It can be difficult for teachers to follow a curriculum that does not meet their learners' needs, which can affect their wellbeing. It is important for education authorities and other education actors to review all curricula to ensure that they promote teachers' and learners' mental health and psychosocial wellbeing, including developing social and emotional skills. Curricula, textbooks, and other materials should address the potential stigma and discrimination related to MHPSS (for more guidance, see the *INEE Guidance Note on Teacher Wellbeing in Emergency Settings*).

> See also Standard 9, Guidance Notes 1, 2, and 5; Standard 10, Guidance Note 9; Standard 14, Guidance Note 2

4. **Curriculum for diversity:** It is important to consider diversity while developing and carrying out all educational activities at every stage of the emergency and through to recovery. Diversity relates to gender, sexuality, age, ethnicity, nationality, race, religion, language, displacement status, abilities and disabilities, and socioeconomic background. Diversity should be reflected in the content, examples, and illustrations of the learning materials used. Teachers should adopt inclusive approaches that recognize the success and achievements of all learners. Education stakeholders should develop formal and non-formal curricula in a way that respects local and indigenous ways of producing knowledge. The curricula should include learning materials and activities that reflect the knowledge, skills, values, and experiences of local and

indigenous communities. The learning environment should also reflect the diversity of the community, with people of different ages, genders, abilities, and ethnicities in displays or notice boards. Teachers and other education personnel should model and promote respect for diversity and all people in the learning environment.

Teachers and other education personnel should be given training that makes them aware of how the curriculum can contribute to exclusion, along with strategies to promote inclusivity, respect, and nonviolence (for more guidance, see *INEE Guidance Note on Gender*).

> See also Standard 8, Guidance Note 2; Standard 14, Guidance Note 2; Standard 18, Guidance Note 2

5. **Curriculum review and development:** Developing the curriculum is a sovereign issue, and adaptations or changes should come from a country's education authorities. If there is a need to develop learning materials, the curriculum from the country of origin or other EiE curriculum approved by the host country can be used. Partner organizations, such as UN agencies or NGOs, can offer guidance on curricula for EiE settings and help teachers create additional learning materials, as needed. This applies to both content and language. It should be clearly understood by education authorities and their partners that this material has been added, and that it is not an adaptation of the host curriculum but a temporary measure. Teachers can use stories and play activities to introduce new subject areas, such as climate change and human rights education, and should be supported in so doing. The curriculum for young children should provide plenty of play opportunities, both free and structured, that include hands-on experience and collaboration with other children.

In crisis-affected contexts, any curriculum reform should follow crisis and conflict sensitive principles, especially when examining a curriculum for any potential issues of inequity, prejudice, or bias. The reform should be gradual, participatory, and informed by a crisis analysis (for more guidance, see *INEE Guidance Note on Conflict Sensitive Education*).

> See also Standard 18, Guidance Note 2

6. **Sourcing learning resources:** At the beginning of an emergency, education stakeholders should assess what resources are available to support learning and learners. For refugees, this may include materials from their country of origin, which will help them transition to the host country curriculum. For higher education, this may include locally constructed knowledge, research methods that prioritize local ways of knowing, and research activities that comply with national or sub-national standards for ethics approval and research licenses. Stakeholders should evaluate materials to ensure that they are accessible to learners in terms of print size, page layout, illustrations, etc., and that they include a balance between input and tasks. It

is important to analyze these materials from a perspective of inclusion and to ensure that there is no gender, cultural, or religious bias. The materials should be approved by the education authorities.

Learning materials should be distributed through existing systems, such as those used for supplies or exam papers. Partner agencies can also help distribute materials along with other emergency items, such as food or blankets. When deciding how to distribute the materials during a health emergency, stakeholders should consider issues of health and safety.

> See also Standard 2, Guidance Note 1; Standard 4, Guidance Note 2; Standard 8, Guidance Note 11; Standard 17, Guidance Note 1; Standard 19, Guidance Note 3

References and further reading

Links to these and additional resources are available on the INEE website.

- *COVID-19 Pathways for the Return to Learning: Guidance on Condensing a Curriculum,* AEWG, 2021
- *INEE Background Paper on Distance Education in Emergencies,* INEE, 2022
- *INEE Guidance Note on Conflict Sensitive Education,* INEE, 2013
- *INEE Guidance Note on Gender,* INEE, 2019
- *INEE Guidance Note on Psychosocial Support,* INEE, 2018
- *INEE Guidance Note on Teacher Wellbeing in Emergency Settings,* INEE, 2022
- *Minimum Economic Recovery Standards,* SEEP Network, 2017
- *Minimum Standards for Child Protection in Humanitarian Action,* Alliance for Child Protection in Humanitarian Action, 2019
- *PSS-SEL Toolbox,* Harvard EASEL Lab and INEE, 2022
- *Supporting Integrated Child Protection and Education Programming in Humanitarian Action,* Alliance for Child Protection in Humanitarian Action and INEE, 2022
- *Teaching about refugees,* UNHCR, 2023

STANDARD 12: TEACHING AND LEARNING PROCESSES

Teaching and learning processes are learner centered, participatory, and inclusive.

Key actions
(please read with guidance notes)

1. **Appropriate teaching approaches:** Promote teaching approaches that are appropriate to the age, developmental level, language, culture, capacities, and needs of learners.

2. **Lesson content and teaching skills:** Confirm that teachers are able to understand the lesson content and have strong teaching skills when they interact with learners.

3. **Barriers to learning:** Promote inclusive teaching and learning and reduce learning barriers in order to fulfill the needs of all learners.

4. **Community endorsement:** Engage with parents and community leaders so they will be able to understand and support the learning content and teaching methods used.

Guidance notes

1. **Appropriate teaching approaches:** Teaching approaches should encourage all learners to be active and to feel safe and confident enough to participate fully. Teaching methods should emphasize inclusivity and work to identify and address any potential bias and prejudice in the learning environment. If teachers are expected to develop or select teaching materials, they should be trained to recognize bias and to ensure that the materials they choose are inclusive and age appropriate. Teachers can create opportunities for learners to work in different ways, both independently and collaboratively in groups of different sizes. Using varied approaches can help support learners' academically and will promote their development of social and emotional skills, such as communication, collaboration, self-awareness, and empathy. Teachers can explore play-based learning, as young children can benefit from hands-on learning experiences (see Annex 1: Glossary for a definition of play). If distance education is used, teachers will need training in how to support remote learners.

Teachers may find new methods difficult to implement, especially during an emergency. They will need ongoing support from their peers, mentors, and teacher trainers. Teaching methods used for higher education or TVET will also need to be adapted to the crisis context. Peer support groups, self-study, or distance education approaches may be helpful adaptations to support these learners. TVET learners will still need hands-on experience with practical tasks, so their teachers may need to use videos to demonstrate these skills. Higher education learners may be better able to adapt to distance education than those who are younger, but they may face other challenges, such as access to technology, internet, and electricity. They will need support from their peers, teachers and other education personnel, and tutors.

Local education authorities should approve, organize, and support changes in teaching methods in formal and non-formal education. It is also important that the community, parents and caregivers, and learners understand and support the changes.

> See also Standard 10, Guidance Note 4; Standard 14, Guidance Note 2

2. **Lesson content and teaching skills:** Emergencies may result in the loss of essential teaching and learning resources that teachers rely on in their classes. When textbooks have been damaged or destroyed, were lacking prior to the emergency, or are no longer relevant, the national education authorities may need to find replacements or develop new materials that include new content or revisions of problematic content. This often takes time and funding, so a short-term response that is locally produced or co-created with teachers may be needed. Teachers may also rely on their memory and knowledge of content and pedagogy. Education authorities should take the lead in the development and dissemination of teaching and learning resources. They may coordinate efforts with the inter-agency coordination mechanism, where it is present. Training and professional development should be guided by the resources available. Where resources are limited, education stakeholders can help teachers draw from other forms of knowledge and co-create content with their peers. It is important for teachers who have no previous experience to have strong role models or mentors, and adequate guidance to ensure that the foundations of teaching are applied in their classrooms.

Teachers may need to rely on what teaching and learning materials are available, including textbooks. Textbooks often include teacher notes and guidance on teaching specific content, which suggest teaching approaches and can help teachers understand the content. The guidance may encourage teachers to have learners engage in group work, to ask learners open questions, and to provide space and opportunity for learners to ask their own questions.

Teachers and other education personnel should structure lessons so that the learning objectives are stated clearly at the beginning of the lesson, repeated throughout, and summarized at the end. Learners can contribute to this process with help from their teacher, who can help them structure and scaffold their thinking, give constructive feedback, and encourage other learners to ask and respond to questions.

The content of non-formal education depends on who the learners are, their stage of development, the program objectives, the nature of the crisis, and the social, political, and economic environment. The knowledge and skills non-formal education teachers need will depend on what knowledge, skills, and attitudes their learners will need when they later transition to formal educational institutions, seek employment, and participate in the community. This might include literacy and numeracy, social and emotional skills, livelihood training, or knowledge of safety and security measures. As in formal education, the training and support of non-formal education teachers, volunteers, facilitators, and caregivers should model varied approaches that are inclusive and confidence building.

Teacher training and professional development should establish benchmarks for understanding and applying knowledge and teaching content. Additional systems should be in place to continually monitor teachers to ensure that they have the skills and knowledge to teach the content effectively. Support can be provided as needed.

See also Standard 11; Standard 14, Guidance Note 2; Standard 17, Guidance Note 4

3. **Barriers to learning:** Taking an inclusive approach is key to reducing barriers to learning. This means that teachers should embrace diversity, create a sense of belonging, and meet the needs of all learners.

Learners with disabilities, both hidden and visible, should have ongoing access to education during an emergency. These learners must not be excluded because of perceived challenges in providing access, or because education authorities, teachers and other education personnel, or even family members or caregivers do not prioritize their needs. Education officials, community leaders, and other stakeholders can advocate and communicate with parents and caregivers, and the wider community, about the importance of inclusion for learners with disabilities. When needed, specialized organizations and associations, such as OPDs can provide additional support for these children and young people. It is important to ensure that learners with disabilities, which may include sensory, physical, mental, cognitive, and developmental disability, have access to assistive devices and technologies. This can include low-tech or no-tech options, like communication boards, which may have been lost during an emergency.

Young women and girls face compounding barriers to learning, such as SRGBV, increased risk of early marriage and early pregnancy, increased burden of unpaid care work and domestic labor, and in some contexts, cultural norms that may prioritize educating boys over girls. Many of these barriers are made worse by crises. Education authorities, community leaders, and other stakeholders should work with parents and caregivers, and the wider community, to raise awareness about the importance of education continuity for young women and girls and to ensure that they have enough time and resources to learn. When needed, women's rights organizations and feminist and youth organizations can provide additional support.

Learning materials will address diversity and inclusion in various ways. Teachers other education personnel should receive professional development, including training on disability-inclusive and gender-responsive pedagogy, to help them teach inclusively and to manage any discrimination or bias that emerges in the learning environment (for more guidance, see *INEE Guidance Note on Gender; INEE Pocket Guide to Supporting Learners with Disabilities*).

> See also Standard 10, Guidance Note 6; Standard 14, Guidance Note 2; Standard 18, Guidance Note 2

4. **Community endorsement:** Emergencies may create opportunities to introduce teaching content that responds to the impact of the crisis or seeks to address its underlying causes. Examples include teaching environmental stewardship in response to climate-related crises, and conflict resolution and peacebuilding skills during a conflict. Teachers may acquire and apply new skills and knowledge in their teaching, such as learner-centered approaches to supporting learners' overall wellbeing, and their academic and social and emotional development.

These new approaches may be unfamiliar to parents and caregivers and the community. Therefore, education actors should find opportunities to inform caregivers and communities of new content and methodologies, and work with them to identify additional gaps in the content or other methodologies that draw from local and indigenous methods. They also should raise awareness of the intended impact of new content and methodologies and strengthen their relevance by creating connections between learning in class and learning at home. Efforts to raise awareness may also encourage the community to increase support for and become more engaged in education.

> See also Standard 1, Guidance Note 5; Standard 14, Guidance Note 2

References and further reading

Links to these and additional resources are available on the INEE website.

- *INEE Guidance Note on Conflict Sensitive Education*, INEE, 2013
- *INEE Guidance Note on Gender*, INEE, 2019
- *INEE Guidance Note on Psychosocial Support*, INEE, 2018
- *INEE Guidance Note on Teacher Wellbeing in Emergency Settings*, INEE, 2022
- *INEE Guidance Notes on Teaching and Learning*, INEE, 2010
- *INEE Pocket Guide to Supporting Learners with Disabilities*, INEE, 2010
- *Minimum Standards for Child Protection in Humanitarian Action*, Alliance for Child Protection in Humanitarian Action, 2019
- *Positive Discipline in the Inclusive, Learning-Friendly Classroom: A Guide for Teachers and Teacher Educators*, UNESCO, 2010
- *Supporting Integrated Child Protection and Education Programming in Humanitarian Action*, Alliance for Child Protection in Humanitarian Action and INEE, 2022
- *UNESCO Quality and Learning Indicators* [Website]

STANDARD 13: ASSESSMENT OF HOLISTIC LEARNING OUTCOMES

> Appropriate methods are used to evaluate and validate holistic learning outcomes.

Key actions
(please read with guidance notes)

1. **Continuous assessment and evaluation:** Conduct continual assessments and evaluations of learners' holistic outcomes and use them to guide teaching and learning.

2. **Fair, reliable, and non-threatening assessments:** Ensure that assessments are fair, reliable, and non-threatening to learners.

3. **Relevant assessments:** Design assessments so that they are relevant to learners' future educational, economic, and social needs.

4. **Tertiary education:** Conduct formal and informal assessments of technical and vocational learners and higher education learners.

5. **Recognition of learners' achievements and progress:** Recognize learners' achievements and progress, including awarding credits or documentation for prior learning and course completion.

Guidance notes

1. **Continuous assessment and evaluation:** Effective assessment and evaluation methods and measures should be in place during emergencies. Learners need to be part of the process and should understand what will be measured and for what reason. They should be guided in reflecting on their progress, including what they have learned and what they have found challenging. Learners should be encouraged to discuss their reflections with their peers, their parents and caregivers, and their teachers. Ongoing formative assessment is particularly important in times of crisis. It may be the most effective way to understand the effect an emergency has had on the learners' psychosocial wellbeing, the impact of any disruption of learning or irregular attendance caused by the emergency, and the effectiveness of different teaching modalities, including distance education. When conducting assessments of any nature, education actors have an ethical duty to be sensitive to the needs and experiences of learners affected by conflict and crises.

With MHPSS assessments, specific questions, the duration of a measure, or even the fact of being assessed can cause children additional and undue stress.

When conducting assessments, it is important for education actors to consider the following:

- **Relevance:** Tests and examinations should be appropriate to the learning context and age of children and young people.
- **Consistency:** All teachers should know and apply evaluation methods in similar ways at all locations.
- **Opportunity:** Absent learners should get another chance to be assessed.
- **Timing:** Formative assessment is ongoing and allows for real-time adaptation and support; summative assessment, which evaluates progress against established objectives, happens at the end of a term, semester, or school year.
- **Frequency:** Learners may be assessed less often during an emergency.
- **Safe setting:** Teachers and other education personnel should conduct summative assessments in a safe place and ensure that results are confidential.
- **Transparency:** Teachers should share and discuss results with learners and parents and caregivers, with the aim of improving future learning.
- **Accommodating learners with disabilities:** Education stakeholders must provide learners with disabilities with specific accommodations based on their needs, including having more time to complete assignments. These learners should be allowed to demonstrate their skills and understanding in ways that are appropriate to their needs (for more guidance, see *INEE Pocket Guide to Supporting Learners with Disabilities*).
- **Mode of assessment:** If it is not possible to bring learners together for face-to-face exams, the tests may be delayed or be replaced by a teacher assessment.
- **Use of assessment and evaluation results:** Teachers should be trained to carry out assessments and evaluations in the ways described above and be supported in so doing. Their training should include how to understand and use test results to support learners' progress and improve their own teaching.

See also Standard 6, Guidance Note 5; Standard 9, Guidance Note 1; Standard 17, Guidance Note 6

2. **Fair, reliable, and non-threatening assessments:** Assessments and evaluations should be fair, enable all learners to do their best, and not discourage learners who are returning to education after an absence. Assessments provide an opportunity to show learners what they can do, as well as what they are struggling with. Like the curriculum, assessment examples and tools should not show any bias. They should not favor one type of learning over another, such as memorization over application. Assessments should be fair; the way they are presented should not create barriers for learners, and learners should have adequate time to complete them. The tools and instruments used to assess learners should not be so complicated that the learner focuses on the tool rather than on what is being measured. The assessment tools, timetable, and application should accommodate the specific needs of learners with disabilities, which may mean using assistive devices and technologies, such as communication boards or large print. These learners may be allowed more time or be placed in a separate, quiet space to complete the assessment.

To ensure that assessment and evaluation are not used to threaten, harass, or coerce learners, teachers must be trained in child safeguarding measures and reporting mechanisms. Girls are particularly vulnerable to sexual harassment, coercion, and exploitation related to assessment. Codes of conduct, ethical guidelines, and contractual agreements for teachers and other education personnel should indicate that any threatening behavior will lead to immediate and strong disciplinary procedures. Head teachers, education personnel, and community members will need to monitor adherence to the codes and take immediate action if they believe a learner is at risk. All learners need to know how they can express their concerns about harassment or coercion, and that they can do so confidentially (for more guidance, see *Supporting Integrated Child Protection and Education Programming in Humanitarian Action*).

> See also Standard 9, Guidance Notes 4–5; Standard 14, Guidance Note 2; Standard 16, Guidance Note 4

3. **Relevant assessments:** Assessments should relate to what learners have been taught. Education stakeholders and teachers should identify learning objectives and benchmarks and modify assessments to reflect what was taught, as the curriculum covered during emergencies may be less than under normal circumstances. Assessment also should be in the language learners were taught in. Younger learners will need to be able to respond to assessment using hands-on activities. The purpose of the assessment also should be relevant; for example, to determine which grade learners who have missed school should enter or whether a learner needs additional support. Assessments can take place before an education cycle, at the end of studying a certain concept or skill, or at the end of a term, semester, or year. Community members can help assess the quality of learning and the effectiveness of the teaching.

4. **Tertiary education:** The progress and achievements of learners in tertiary education programs, including TVET, higher education, and adult education programs, should lead to certification. Systems should be in place to ensure these programs are accredited. For TVET, this will apply to achievements in learning practical, theoretical, and social and emotional skills. TVET providers should adhere to any national standards that are in place for pre-placement assessment, certification, and course completion, and should allow participants to complete national assessments.

Assessments of higher education learners will vary, depending on the course of study, and they will likely be ongoing formal and summative assessments. Both may include practical and oral tasks. An informal assessment may involve a teacher giving learners regular feedback on their progress and encouraging self-reflection, which will provide useful insights into the relevance and quality of their learning programs. If distance education or blended learning approaches are being used, assessments may be conducted online or by audio or video.

See also Standard 18, Guidance Note 1

5. **Recognition of learners' achievements and progress:** Recognizing learners' achievements is important for their future educational, economic, and individual needs. It is the role and responsibility of national authorities to establish and enforce accreditation for all education programs within the national system. During emergencies, when systems and staff members are under pressure or services are disrupted, opportunities may arise to strengthen certain aspects of national systems, including recognizing the participation and progress of displaced and refugee learners.

Recognizing learners' achievements and progress may be done informally by giving them and their parents and caregivers regular feedback. It may also be formal, such as awarding credits and providing documentation of completion of a level or course. During emergencies, recognition of learners' achievements and progress may emphasize softer skills, such as the ability to work collaboratively with others, to show empathy and respect, and to demonstrate peacebuilding and conflict resolution skills. Formal assessments and evaluations are designed to determine whether a learner is ready to continue on to the next level or to leave a study program with a certification or diploma. To receive recognition for successfully completing higher education, learners will likely need to take formal exams. In emergency situations, education stakeholders should administer exams as soon as it is safe and feasible, to lessen learning loss and to facilitate a smooth transition to employment or other post-graduation opportunities.

In addition to the established systems of recognition in formal education, it is essential that non-formal programs have similar systems and tools to acknowledge learners' progress, such as when they are ready to progress through curriculum levels or to complete a course. These programs should be coordinated with the national education authorities so that learners will have the opportunity to transition into formal programs or receive formal recognition. Clear and transparent policies and protocols should guide all programs and be shared with learners and their communities.

Issuing certificates, endorsing certificates and progress, and maintaining and safeguarding records in national or organizational systems are important parts of a strong education program and system. During emergencies, especially when people are displaced, it may be challenging or impossible to access learners' previous records. This can affect learners of all ages, in all types of programs by preventing or delaying progression to a new level, integration into the host country education system, or presentation of education completion records to potential employers. It may be necessary to create a new system to replace damaged, destroyed, or missing records, or to establish an assessment system that can indicate learning levels and allow quick integration into the appropriate learning program at the correct level. When possible, this should be facilitated by or done in coordination with local and national authorities to ensure broader and system-level recognition of learners' abilities. Issuing paper certificates and maintaining digital records are both important to the recognition process. Paper certificates have great value to the individual, as they demonstrate their recognized academic progress and are a source of pride.

For refugee learners, recognition of prior learning and qualifications from different countries can be a complex process. When enrolling primary and secondary learners in schools, education stakeholders should make efforts to recognize the learning and years of education completed before displacement. Many countries have frameworks in place for recognizing and equating grade completion, however, refugee learners and their families may need support and assistance to access these processes. Regional and inter-agency stakeholders should continue to emphasize the importance of recognizing the educational achievements of displaced learners. Advances have been made in this area in higher education, in particular the Global Convention on the Recognition of Qualifications concerning Higher Education, ratified in 2023. The Convention aims to facilitate mobility for refugee and displaced learners through the strengthening of certification, equivalence, and recognition procedures. The procedures may vary depending on whether a refugee student's learning was interrupted before completing a qualification program or if they had already received the qualification. The UNESCO Qualifications Passport aims to support this process by providing systems strengthening to national tertiary and higher education authorities and institutions to integrate the Qualifications Passport assessment procedures for evaluating refugee and displaced learners' academic, professional, and vocational qualifications. Regional qualifications frameworks are important tools for supporting the recognition of prior learning and qualifications within and across borders, and promoting learning at all levels, from ECD to tertiary.

See also Standard 6, Guidance Note 4; Standard 8, Guidance Notes 5–6 and 8; Standard 18, Guidance Notes 1–2

References and further reading

Links to these and additional resources are available on the INEE website

- *Early Grade Math Assessment (EGMA) Toolkit*, RTI International, 2014
- *Early Grade Reading Assessment (EGRA) Toolkit: Second Edition*, RTI International, 2016
- *INEE Guidance Notes on Teaching and Learning*, INEE, 2010
- *INEE Measurement Library* [Website]
- *INEE Pocket Guide to Supporting Learners with Disabilities*, INEE, 2010
- *INEE Technical Note on Measurement for Education during the COVID-19 Pandemic*, INEE, 2020
- *PSS-SEL Toolbox*, Harvard EASEL Lab and INEE, 2022
- *Remote Assessment of Learning (ReAL) Toolkit*, Save the Children, 2021
- *Supporting Integrated Child Protection and Education Programming in Humanitarian Action*, Alliance for Child Protection in Humanitarian Action and INEE, 2022
- *The International Development and Early Learning Assessment (IDELA)*, Save the Children
- *UNESCO Qualifications Passport* [Website]

STANDARD 14: TRAINING, PROFESSIONAL DEVELOPMENT, AND SUPPORT

Teachers and other education personnel receive regular, relevant, and structured training in line with their needs and circumstances.

Key actions
(please read with guidance notes)

1. **Opportunities for training and professional development:** Provide all teachers with access to training and professional development opportunities in accordance with their needs.

2. **Appropriate training:** Design training and professional development so that it is appropriate to the context and reflects the learning content and objectives.

3. **Training in risk prevention and mitigation:** Provide teachers in both formal and non-formal education with training and professional development that includes hazard awareness and DRR.

4. **Qualified trainers:** Use qualified trainers or senior school staff members to carry out training courses and ongoing school-based professional development for teachers and other education personnel.

5. **Training recognition and accreditation:** Ensure that teacher training and certified professional development is recognized and approved by education authorities.

6. **Professional development in using digital approaches:** Provide teachers with professional development to give them more confidence in using digital resources, particularly for distance education.

7. **Ongoing professional support:** Promote teacher collaboration to ensure that teachers are supported by their peers and their head teachers, in addition to an integrated support system outside the immediate learning environment.

Guidance notes

1. **Opportunities for training and professional development:** Emergencies may require teachers to learn new content and teaching methodologies. If a crisis has created a demand for additional teachers, such as in situations of displacement, a condensed and targeted teacher training program might be needed. National authorities have the ultimate responsibility for training and professional development standards, policies, and services for teachers engaged in the national education system. The implementing agencies and communities that directly engage teachers should align their support with national standards as much as possible. Training and professional development opportunities should be available to all teachers and other education personnel, regardless of gender, ethnicity, religion, age, or contractual or legal status.

   The need for teacher training may be significant during an emergency. Education actors should consider the following when assessing the need, planning, and support for training and professional development:

   - **Coordination and collaboration:** When possible, national authorities should lead training and professional development efforts, in collaboration with the inter-agency coordination mechanism. All implementing agencies should coordinate training opportunities to ensure greater consistency. Assessments carried out by various stakeholders should be coordinated to guide training needs.
   - **Prioritize training participants:** All teachers will require training to ensure that they have the skills needed to respond to learners' changing needs. Training plans should be created as soon as possible after a crisis for the teachers with the greatest need, such as those on the front lines, new teachers, and teachers welcoming refugee learners. Plans should be based on an understanding of teachers' needs in different situations, such as new and inexperienced teachers and those with previous training or experience. Plans also should reflect the learners' changing needs in a new learning environment, such as MHPSS, working with larger or mixed groups, and learning in a new language.
   - **Inclusive opportunities are essential:** Professional development opportunities should be flexible enough to accommodate the teachers and other education personnel who may need additional support to attend training sessions. This may include female teachers in contexts where women have historically been excluded from education and teachers with disabilities. Examples of targeted support may include providing flexible training schedules, child care, and safe transportation to and from training sites.
   - **Training and professional development modalities:** Pre-service and in-service training opportunities are important in emergencies. Condensing pre-service training can speed up the preparation of the new teachers needed to respond to the specific needs of an emergency. In-service

training is more often provided during the early stages of an emergency response to orient teachers to the specific content. Training opportunities should account for different factors, such as teachers' safety and ability to travel to learning sites, and the available technology. In-person, online, individual, and group teacher training options may all be appropriate. Teacher training during emergencies should be part of longer-term support, and one-off training with no follow up or continued support should be avoided.

- **Supporting teachers after training:** Head teachers should play a key role in their teachers' professional development. This should include providing opportunities for school-based training and drawing from the expertise of school staff members, those from a nearby school, or from the community. The creative use of mentors, peer learning, and support programs can provide another layer of sustained support (for more guidance, see *Teachers in Crisis Contexts Training for Primary School Teachers; INEE Guidance Notes on Teaching and Learning*).

> See also Standard 3, Guidance Note 4; Standard 5, Guidance Note 7; Standard 8, Guidance Note 8; Standard 10, Guidance Note 9; Standard 17, Guidance Note 2

2. **Appropriate training:** Teaching during emergencies requires specific skills and knowledge. Education authorities are responsible for developing and delivering formal training curriculum and content, while their partners, such as UN agencies, NGOs, and the private sector, can offer support. Stakeholders may need to review and adapt curricula for pre-service programs to ensure that current and future training prepares teachers to meet the specific needs of learners in emergencies. Special concerns may include MHPSS, SEL, health, and protection related content, and issues related to DRR and climate change.

It is particularly important to make sure that training addresses diversity and discrimination. Teachers should be helped to identify and address stereotypes, bias, or prejudice in the curriculum and to promote inclusivity, respect, and nonviolence. Teachers should be confident and competent in discussing these issues with learners, as well as concepts, principles, and practices related to human rights. Those working with teachers to address bias in the curriculum should recognize that some issues may be challenging for the teachers themselves. They should allow time for discussion and emphasize the important role teachers play in promoting diversity and inclusion. Teachers of all genders should be trained to use disability-inclusive and gender-responsive teaching practices. The approaches used in training can model practices and strategies for addressing gender-based discrimination directly, for example, identifying and addressing harmful gender norms and stereotypes (for more guidance, see *INEE Guidance Note on Conflict Sensitive Education; INEE Guidance Note on Gender*).

Other areas for teacher professional development can include:

- **Pedagogy and subject matter**
  - Literacy, numeracy, and subject area
  - Formative and summative learner assessment
  - Teaching methods and approaches, including inclusive and diverse approaches and classroom management
  - Teaching for specific age and developmental groups, including early and older learners

- **Creating and supporting an inclusive classroom**
  - Identifying and addressing curriculum bias and discrimination
  - Supporting learners with disabilities
  - Using content and methodologies that acknowledge and celebrate diversity
  - Teaching the conflict-resolution and peacebuilding skills needed to navigate challenges in the classroom and to teach learners those same skills

- **Skills and knowledge to mitigate and prevent abuse or provide protection**
  - Positive discipline and reporting mechanisms for violence against children and young people
  - MHPSS and SEL, including health and safety education
  - Understanding and effectively using school-based referral systems, including referral mechanisms for sexual harassment, coercion, bullying, and mental health or other issues (for more guidance, see *Supporting Integrated Child Protection and Education Programming in Humanitarian Action; Minimum Standards for Child Protection*, Standard 23)
  - DRR and conflict prevention
  - Human rights principles and perspectives, and humanitarian law
  - Codes of conduct for teachers and other education personnel, and their adherence to them

- **Supporting learners beyond the classroom**
  - Engaging parents and caregivers and the community in the learning process
  - Providing specific training for school leaders related to professional support for school staff and quality assurance

---

See also Standard 8, Guidance Note 7; Standard 9, Guidance Notes 1–5; Standard 11, Guidance Notes 1–4; Standard 12; Standard 13, Guidance Note 2; Standard 17, Guidance Note 2

3. **Training in risk prevention and mitigation:** Teachers should receive training to develop the knowledge and skills they will need to reduce the risks that learners and the community may face. Head teachers and teachers and other education personnel can play an important role in making learners aware of hazards and risks at school and beyond and in teaching them safe practices for dealing with what they encounter. Teachers should have information that helps them to identify, prevent, and deal with potential hazards and risks they and their learners might face (for more guidance, see *Comprehensive School Safety Framework*; *Supporting Integrated Child Protection and Education Programming in Humanitarian Action*).

> See also Standard 4, Guidance Note 7; Standard 5, Guidance Note 6; Standard 9, Guidance Notes 2 and 10

4. **Qualified trainers:** Education stakeholders should identify qualified trainers from the context to help develop and implement appropriate training for teachers and other education personnel. Qualified local trainers and external stakeholders can engage in capacity sharing activities to create a mutual understanding of the challenges to teaching and learning at all stages of an emergency, from preparedness through to recovery. Stakeholders should make the effort to identify and engage a diverse group of qualified trainers. They should be aware of potential gender and cultural sensitivities and group trainers with teachers accordingly. Trainers' demographics should reflect those of the teachers they are working with.

5. **Training recognition and accreditation:** It is important that education authorities recognize and approve the teacher training and certified professional development provided during emergencies. Their approval and accreditation should ensure the quality of all teacher training. Education authorities in the host or home country should make sure that training for refugee teachers is relevant and adapted to the teachers' and the learners' needs. Regional qualifications frameworks, such as the Djibouti Declaration on Refugee Education adopted by the Intergovernmental Authority on Development in 2017, are important tools for supporting the equivalency of qualifications within and across borders. They can help to promote the inclusion of refugee teachers in national education systems and support the recognition of their professional development and certifications.

> See also Standard 8, Guidance Note 8; Standard 18, Guidance Notes 1–2

6. **Professional development in using digital approaches:** Teachers and other education personnel will likely need professional development and training in using digital and technology-based teaching and learning approaches. Teachers will need guidance on using technology to support children's learning in crisis contexts, whether they use distance, face-to-face, or hybrid delivery. Education stakeholders can engage expert trainers, where they are available, to help teachers with less

digital competence or confidence. Confident users of technology can be paired or grouped, virtually and in person, with those who are less confident. Training should highlight how resources can vary, from low-tech (print, audio, television) to high-tech (mobile phones, online, interactive), and how to use each technology effectively. Most learners, even in higher education, will need support in using digital approaches, especially if engaged in distance education. Parents and caregivers and older siblings can be important sources of support in any distance education model, but the amount of support they are expected to provide should be reasonable. Parents and caregivers should be given clear guidance on their roles and responsibilities.

Education actors should carefully consider how to deliver distance education so that all children and young people will have access to learning during emergencies. It is important to weigh the benefits and challenges of using digital approaches, and education stakeholders must ensure that these approaches protect learners' and teachers' digital safety and promote their wellbeing (for more guidance, see INEE Background Paper on Distance Education in Emergencies).

> See also Standard 8, Guidance Note 5; Standard 17, Guidance Note 1

7. **Ongoing professional support:** Teachers and other education personnel should have ongoing and relevant professional support. Within the immediate learning environment, support should be provided by peers, senior teachers, and head teachers. Head teachers can make teachers aware of the value of communities of practice, teacher learning circles, peer support groups, and other forms of teacher collaboration that can supplement the existing formal support.

Having professional development and ongoing professional support will make a difference to teachers' overall wellbeing in emergency settings. Although most teachers are resourceful and resilient and often can support their own wellbeing, they also are often exposed to the same adverse events and stressors as their learners. This makes support from their peers and managers especially important. Stakeholders managing teachers should provide opportunities for teachers to meet informally and share what they are doing, how they are feeling, and what strategies they use to stay resilient and resourceful. If a teacher does become distressed and feels unable to cope, especially if it is affecting their teaching, the head teacher, professional support staff, and other local partners should make sure the teacher receives the help they need, including MHPSS services (for more guidance, see INEE Guidance Note on Teacher Wellbeing in Emergency Settings).

During emergencies, teachers need a strong, cohesive system of professional support beyond the immediate learning environment. It is important that the various stakeholders who fund and manage teachers work together to ensure the provision of consistent professional support. The roles, responsibilities, and line management of key education personnel should be clear and complementary. A regular needs analysis should take place and guide planning for teacher professional development support (for more guidance, see *INEE Teachers in Crisis Contexts Peer Coaching Pack*).

> 🔍 See also Standard 9, Guidance Note 1; Standard 17, Guidance Notes 3 and 5

References and further reading

Links to these and additional resources are available on the INEE website.

- Comprehensive School Safety Framework, GADRRRES, 2022
- EiE-GenKit: a core resource package on gender and education in emergencies, ECW, INEE, and UNGEI, 2021
- Exploring Humanitarian Law (EHL) Guide: A Legal Manual for EHL Teachers, International Committee of the Red Cross, 2020
- Inclusive Distance Education Toolkit, INEE, 2023
- INEE Background Paper on Distance Education in Emergencies, INEE, 2022
- INEE Guidance Note on Teacher Wellbeing in Emergency Settings, INEE, 2022
- INEE Guidance Note on Conflict Sensitive Education, INEE, 2013
- INEE Guidance Note on Gender, INEE, 2019
- INEE Guidance Note on Psychosocial Support, INEE, 2018
- INEE Guidance Notes on Teaching and Learning, INEE, 2010
- Minimum Standards for Child Protection in Humanitarian Action, Alliance for Child Protection in Humanitarian Action, 2019
- Supporting Integrated Child Protection and Education Programming in Humanitarian Action, The Alliance for Child Protection in Humanitarian Action and INEE, 2022
- Teachers in Crisis Contexts Peer Coaching Pack, INEE, 2018
- Teachers in Crisis Contexts Training for Primary School Teachers, INEE, 2016

> For resources to help you with the implementation of the standards in Domain 3, visit inee.org/minimum-standards.

Teachers and Other Education Personnel

Foundational Standards for a Quality Response:
Community Participation, Coordination, Analysis

Teachers and Other Education Personnel Domain

Standard 15: Recruitment and Selection

A sufficient number of appropriately qualified teachers and other education personnel are recruited through a transparent and fair process, based on selection criteria that reflect diversity and equity.

Standard 16: Conditions of Work

Teachers and other education personnel have clearly defined conditions of work and receive appropriate compensation.

Standard 17: Support and Supervision

The support and supervision mechanisms in place for teachers and other education personnel function effectively.

Overview of Domain 4

The standards in this domain focus on managing, administering, and supporting human resources in education, particularly teachers and other education personnel. They establish the importance of teacher recruitment and selection, conditions of work, professional support, and overall management. They also address the meaningful participation of teachers and other education personnel in these areas, from emergency preparedness and through to recovery. Teachers are key to achieving inclusive and equitable quality education. This means that their qualifications, skills and aptitudes, professional training, the ongoing support they receive, and the terms and conditions of their employment are also key. Professional development is also discussed in Domain 3: Teaching and Learning.

> The key actions in this domain involve actors who support and manage teachers and other education personnel, such as:
> - National, sub-national, and local education authorities
> - Teacher training institutes/colleges
> - Teachers unions and associations
> - School leaders and teachers and other education personnel
> - Communities affected by crisis
> - Stakeholders involved in the education response, including local and national CSOs and NGOs, faith-based organizations, humanitarian and development partners, donors, and private sector actors
> - Actors from protection, MHPSS, livelihood, and other relevant sectors

Teachers are directly involved in learners' learning

Teachers and other education personnel provide for the education needs of children and young people during emergencies and through to recovery. Their professional status may vary, from state employees to volunteers to community-based educators, and their education levels may range from having a university degree to little formal education. The term "teacher" generally refers to someone directly responsible for the learning of children, young people, and adults. They may be:

- Classroom teachers
- Early childhood or pre-school teachers
- Higher education faculty
- Special education teachers
- Subject specialists and vocational trainers
- Religious educators
- Head teachers
- Volunteers teachers from the community

"Education personnel" refers to pedagogical, administrative, and support personnel involved in planning, delivering, monitoring, evaluating, and quality assurance of education and teaching practices at all levels. This includes school principals, ECD and tertiary personnel, deputies, advisors, supervisors, counselors, mentors , paraprofessionals, and classroom specialists and assistants, including those who support the learning of persons with disabilities. Many of these personnel will have been teachers. The primary responsibility for employing teachers and education personnel lies with the education authorities.

Recruiting and compensating teachers

Whether teachers and other education personnel are recruited by education authorities or by humanitarian and development partners, the process of identifying, recruiting, and selecting these personnel should be done in accordance with clear professional criteria. Identification and selection should determine how suitable applicants are, and each person recruited will need to have the right experience, aptitudes, and skills for their role. The process should be non-discriminatory. Special measures may be needed in some cases to proactively identify and recruit teachers from marginalized groups to ensure that the teaching workforce is representative of the community in which they are teaching.

Teachers and other education personnel should be fairly compensated, including their salaries and stipends or incentives, as non-competitive compensation can contribute to teacher turnover and attrition. Compensation should be regular and transparent so that teachers are able to rely on a single, predictable source of compensation and thus be free to focus fully on their professional work. Teachers and other education personnel should have the freedom to join or form a trade union and to exchange information about their working conditions, including salaries and stipends or incentives. Refugee teachers may face specific challenges, such as not being granted the right to work legally as a teacher in a host country and having their professional credentials from their home country recognized. In the host country, policy changes may be needed at the national level to address these challenges (see Domain 5: Education Policy). There may be opportunities for refugee teachers to help integrate refugee learners into a host country education system. They also might be engaged to teach learners who are unable to access or transition into a local system. Education stakeholders who employ refugee teachers should work to ensure that their compensation is coordinated and equitable and that they have fair and equal working terms and conditions.

Using the UNESCO/ILO recommendations for teachers

Two key instruments from UNESCO and the International Labour Organization (ILO) are related to the rights, roles, and responsibilities of the teaching profession. These include the UNESCO/ILO Recommendation concerning the Status of Teachers (1966) and the UNESCO Recommendation concerning the Status of Higher-Education Teaching Personnel (1997). Both describe the responsibilities and rights of teachers and other education personnel and provide guidelines for dialogue among education authorities, teachers, and their associations. They provide an international frame of reference for a variety of topics relating to teaching conditions. Their implementation is monitored through the Committee of Experts on the Application of the Recommendations concerning Teaching Personnel (CEART). Stakeholders can also use the recommendations to develop codes of conduct.

Contracts are important

The rights, roles, responsibilities, working conditions, and compensation of teachers and other education personnel should be clearly stated in their employment contracts. A contract is a legally binding document, and having one gives an employee some degree of security. It also is a recognition of the professional role teachers and other education personnel play in the learning environment and the community. The professional details of all teachers and other education personnel should be recorded in a database; this should include a background check for anyone working with children and young people. To prevent learners from being harmed by teachers or other education personnel, including volunteers, safeguarding procedures should be in place when recruiting, selecting, and managing teachers. Employment contracts should reflect teachers' responsibility for safeguarding children and young people and state that any suspected violation will result in the immediate suspension and investigation of the person in question and, depending on the outcome, possible loss of job.

Professional support for teachers

Teachers need strong professional support, including regular in-service training, mentoring, and peer support. This exists in many countries, with support mechanisms working at many levels, from the national education authority to the schools. The role of each should be clear so that actors at the various levels complement each other and facilitate professional support that is meaningful, harmonized, and timely. Head teachers should also have access to professional development so they are able to take the lead in providing quality teaching and learning in their school and ongoing support to teachers.

Teacher wellbeing is crucial

Teachers' wellbeing is crucial to the learning process. Teachers play a key role in creating a sense of normalcy and continuity in the learning environment during a crisis. However, teachers and other education personnel will also be dealing with the crisis themselves, and though many are resilient, some will need support to maintain their own wellbeing. Teachers with mental health conditions and psychosocial challenges will need MHPSS services that fit their needs and circumstances. When they are able to take better care of themselves, they will be more able to create a positive learning environment, manage stress, and prevent burnout.

If a key standard in this domain is not being met—for example, clear teacher selection criteria are not followed, compensation is insufficient and paid irregularly, or no training or professional support is provided—teacher wellbeing will be negatively affected. This could cause teacher attrition and result in having fewer teachers, all of which could lead to a general decline in the status of teachers and negatively affect the quality of education.

Every effort must be made to ensure that all teachers and other education personnel and learners feel safe from external and internal threats. Teachers need to feel that they and their pupils are safe, so clear measures should be in place to protect them from risks. Education and protection stakeholders should work together to establish and/or maintain mechanisms to address any threats effectively and immediately.

STANDARD 15: RECRUITMENT AND SELECTION

A sufficient number of appropriately qualified teachers and other education personnel are recruited through a transparent and fair process, based on selection criteria that reflect diversity and equity.

Key actions
(please read with guidance notes)

1. **Clear job descriptions:** Develop clear, appropriate, non-discriminatory job descriptions and guidelines before any recruitment process begins.

2. **Clear and transparent recruitment criteria:** Establish clear and detailed criteria for recruiting and employing teachers and other education personnel.

3. **Appropriate number of teachers and staff:** Ensure that the number of teachers and other education personnel recruited reflects current needs and finances.

4. **Safety and security of teachers and learners:** Prioritize the security and safety of teachers and other education personnel and learners during the recruitment process, including conducting background checks on teachers.

Guidance notes

1. **Clear job descriptions:** Job descriptions for teachers and other education personnel, including volunteers, must not discriminate based on gender, ethnicity, religion, disability, or any other personal characteristics. Job descriptions at a minimum should include roles and responsibilities, rights, compensation and pay, terms and conditions, working environment, a code of conduct, clear lines of support and reporting, and contract duration. These conditions should be harmonized among all stakeholders who employ teachers and other education personnel. Education jobs should be clearly advertised in the community.

> See also Standard 16, Guidance Note 2; Standard 17, Guidance Note 4

2. **Clear and transparent recruitment criteria and process:** Education actors should establish equitable recruitment and selection processes that are non-discriminatory and sensitive to the crisis or conflict. These processes should consider and address the challenges and opportunities teachers' experience because of their gender, ethnicity, employment status, and displacement or refugee status.

If a crisis brings an influx of displaced persons, including refugees, systems should be put in place to screen potential teachers with clear criteria, including their qualifications, skills, and aptitudes and what experience is required. If qualified teachers do not have access to their professional certificates or documentation because of the emergency situation, or if there is an insufficient number of qualified teachers, it will be necessary to implement a transparent and impartial assessment process. This process should include a recruitment committee involving community members, education authorities, and existing education personnel. Such an assessment should determine whether applicants have the necessary teaching skills, including language of instruction, knowledge of relevant subjects, pedagogy, and others relevant to the learners' situation and ages. Assessment of the skills, attitudes, and aptitudes of all candidates, whether they are trained or untrained teachers, is crucial. The minimum age for teachers and other education personnel should adhere to national labor laws and regulations, and to international labor and human rights instruments. It may be necessary to recruit younger people to serve as facilitators, assistants, or tutors (for more guidance, see *INEE Guidance Note on Teacher Wellbeing in Emergency Settings*).

Teachers play a critical role in creating protective learning environments, so their attitudes on child protection issues and the rights of children should be assessed during the recruitment process. Questions on attitudes about gender, corporal punishment, and child abuse will be integral to child safeguarding procedures. Teachers must ensure that the learning environment is inclusive for all learners, regardless of disability, gender, ethnicity, religion, nationality, language, or socioeconomic background. Teachers in a crisis context also will need to be aware of their learners' psychosocial needs. Education stakeholders should work together to establish coherent and harmonized selection criteria for teachers, which will be important to ensure that teacher selection is fair and not biased by influential people in the community.

A gender-responsive recruitment process can help work towards a more gender equitable workforce. To support more equitable recruitment, recruitment committees should include women and men, and selection criteria should be transparent and consider the barriers faced by marginalized groups such as women and persons with disabilities. Evaluating gender gaps in the teaching staff will help to determine whether special measures are needed to proactively identify and recruit female or male teachers. These might include adjusting entry qualifications, providing ongoing training and additional support, or organizing safe transportation, and accommodation and child care for female teachers, especially those living in remote or underserved areas. Education stakeholders should engage with the community to promote awareness of the value of having both women and men as teachers at every level of education (for more guidance, see *INEE Guidance Note on Gender*).

It is critical that teachers can communicate clearly in languages learners will understand and that they can communicate with caregivers and community members. Where possible, it may be necessary to recruit teachers who speak both the local languages and those of a displaced population, including refugees. Additional language facilitators may be needed in some situations to help learners participate or transition into host community schools.

Another important consideration is community acceptance. Teachers and other education personnel should be able to interact easily and effectively with the community. When possible, they should be members of the affected community so they understand the social, economic, political, and cultural issues that affect daily life. However, a balance should be achieved between hiring from the local and other communities to ensure that there is no discrimination, for example between host and displaced communities or ethnic minorities.

See also Standard 1, Guidance Note 6; Standard 11, Guidance Note 1

3. **Appropriate number of teachers and staff:** Education stakeholders should determine what is a locally appropriate and realistic number of teachers and other education personnel. Important factors to consider include:

- How many learners the available learning spaces can safely accommodate
- The teacher-student ratio
- The need for female teachers and/or support staff at all levels
- The subject areas that will be taught and teachers' qualifications
- National and local standards for class size and teacher-student ratios
- The ratio of support staff to teachers and counselors to learners
- The ages of children, as younger learners will benefit from smaller classes and direct time with teachers

The ILO/UNESCO Recommendation concerning the Status of Teachers recommends that class size should allow the teacher to give learners individual attention. Crises and displacement may contribute to higher student-teacher ratios. Education stakeholders should ensure that teachers and other education personnel receive support to manage larger classes, especially in contexts where displacement is in flux and class size may grow significantly (for more guidance, see *INEE Guidance Notes on Teaching and Learning*).

A critical aspect of the education response is to support collective efforts to mobilize the funding needed to plan for, recruit, and maintain a consistent cadre of teachers. Supporting a larger cadre for the duration of an emergency and ensuring a sustained and appropriate teacher-student ratio into recovery is likely to require substantial funds. Efforts to secure funding should be led by the national authorities and relevant coordination mechanisms. Gaps in funding will make it necessary to establish priorities across the learning continuum (ECD, primary, secondary, tertiary), learning approaches (formal, non-formal), and length of service (for more guidance, see *INEE Guidance Notes on Teacher Compensation*).

> See also Standard 3, Guidance Note 5; Standard 5, Guidance Note 5; Standard 8, Guidance Note, 11; Standard 18, Guidance Note 5; Standard 19, Guidance Note 3

4. **Safety and security of learners and teachers:** It is important that recruitment processes consider the potential risks teachers and other educational personnel, including volunteers, and learners may face. If qualified teachers do not have their certificates or other documentation because of the emergency and obtaining them poses a risk because of the security situation, education stakeholders should consider alternate ways to assess their skills and qualifications. They also should conduct a safety assessment of the learning environment and establish systems for evacuation or other responses. This should be done in coordination with those responsible for external safety and security, school management committees, and the education authorities.

To ensure the safety of learners, education authorities and other relevant stakeholders should conduct background checks and obtain references for teachers and other education personnel, as much as the situation allows. Local authorities or other respected members of the community should provide this information. Background checks and references should be in keeping with the policies and protocols of the child protection and education authorities (for more guidance, see *Minimum Standards for Child Protection*, Standard 23).

Teachers also need to be safe from discrimination or harassment by their peers, supervisors, or learners. This includes discrimination or harassment based on disability, age, gender, sexual orientation, class, caste, ethnicity, socioeconomic background, or any other characteristic. The recruitment of teachers and other education personnel should be based on clear criteria that consider the circumstances they will be working in, including any risk to individuals or groups. When aiming for diversity, particularly gender parity, it is important to consider the safety of teachers and the principle of do no harm, which will help to minimize risks. When placing teachers and other educational personnel, it is important to have mechanisms in place for reporting harassment and discrimination. It is important that teachers know how to use these mechanisms and are safe when they do so (for more guidance, see *INEE Guidance Note on Teacher Wellbeing in Emergency Settings; INEE Guidance Note on Gender*).

> See also Standard 9, Guidance Note 2; Standard 16, Guidance Note 1; Standard 18, Guidance Note 4

References and further reading

Links to these and additional resources are available on the INEE website.

- *Crisis-Sensitive Teacher Policy and Planning: Module on the Teacher Policy Development Guide*, International Task Force on Teachers for Education 2030, 2022
- *Global Framework of Professional Teaching Standards*, Education International and UNESCO, 2022
- *INEE Guidance Note on Gender*, INEE, 2019
- *INEE Guidance Notes on Teacher Compensation*, INEE, 2009
- *INEE Guidance Notes on Teaching and Learning*, INEE, 2010
- *INEE Guidance Note on Teacher Wellbeing in Emergency Settings*, INEE, 2022
- *Minimum Standards for Child Protection in Humanitarian Action*, Alliance for Child Protection in Humanitarian Action, 2019
- *Recommendation concerning the Status of Higher-Education Teaching Personnel*, UNESCO, 1997
- *Recommendation concerning the Status of Teachers*, ILO/UNESCO, 1966
- *Supporting Integrated Child Protection and Education Programming in Humanitarian Action*, Alliance for Child Protection in Humanitarian Action and INEE, 2022

STANDARD 16: CONDITIONS OF WORK

Teachers and other education personnel have clearly defined conditions of work and receive appropriate compensation.

Key actions
(please read with guidance notes)

1. **Coordination of compensation and conditions of work:** Coordinate compensation systems and conditions of work for all teachers and other education personnel.

2. **Contracts in place:** Establish compensation and working conditions in contracts, and ensure that staff members are compensated regularly.

3. **Right to organize:** Allow teachers and other education personnel to organize to negotiate the terms and conditions of their employment.

4. **Codes of conduct:** Include clear implementation guidelines in teachers' codes of conduct and ensure that they are adhered to by all.

Guidance notes

1. **Coordination of compensation and conditions of work:** In situations of crisis or displacement, systems for compensating teachers and other education personnel may be disrupted. Payroll systems may break down or become ineffective, teachers displaced within their home country may be unable to get their wages, and refugee teachers and schools may not be formally recognized by the host country education authorities and thus will be ineligible for payment. It is important for education stakeholders to work together to develop an appropriate, equitable, and sustainable system for identifying and compensating teachers.

   Primary responsibility for employing and compensating teachers and other education personnel lies with education authorities. If education authorities are unable to fulfill this role, other stakeholders may take it on temporarily. They can do it directly or by supporting national or sub-national education authorities. If teachers are employed by a range of stakeholders, such as communities, UN agencies, donors, NGOs, and other agencies, they will need to work together to establish a fair level of compensation that is in line with national policies and frameworks, is sustainable, and based on an exit strategy. This will pave the way for future sustainable compensation policies and practices.

Compensation can be monetary (salaries and stipends or incentives) or non-monetary (in-kind payment such as food, shelter, health care, and transportation). Whatever form it takes, compensation should enable teachers and other education personnel to focus on teaching without taking on additional employment and reflect their qualifications, experience, and responsibilities. This will help avoid conflicts of interest, such as teachers privately charging students fees for teaching and tutoring. Teacher compensation during an emergency should be based on demand, the cost of living, and wages paid to similar professionals, such as those in health care, in the private sector, or working across borders (for more guidance see, *Minimum Economic Recovery Standards, Employment Standards*).

Stipends and incentives are a form of payment usually associated with training or on-the-job learning prior to full qualification, for example teaching assistants or unqualified teachers. They are often lower than permanent salary levels for similar work by qualified individuals and are complemented by other benefits, such as training, food, and accommodation allowances.

Teachers and other education personnel should be compensated regularly and should not have to travel any great distance to collect their pay. In some cases, CVA may be used to support education services by providing teacher incentives. If CVA is being used in this way, stakeholders should be aware of the risks involved in implementing cash-based assistance and take steps to mitigate them. Dispute mechanisms should be in place to address grievances that arise if contractual obligations are ignored, or if compensation is withheld or frequently delayed (for more guidance, see *INEE Guidance Notes on Teacher Compensation*).

In some contexts, refugees may face legal restrictions to work, and thus it may be necessary to advocate and collaborate with policy-makers to address these restrictions. Education stakeholders should work together to establish a clear pathway for career progression that acknowledges teachers' professional growth and promotes their job satisfaction and retention. This may require collaboration with teacher unions, education authorities, and other stakeholders to ensure that refugee teachers' rights are upheld and their contributions are recognized.

The conditions of work for teachers and other education personnel are also important. The ILO defines this as a broad issue that includes compensation, manageable class size, professional education and development, and supervision and support. It also addresses teachers' involvement in the reform of education policies and programs; the provision of basic facilities in classrooms; adequate equipment, learning materials, and supplies; and the maintenance of school buildings. Conditions of work for teachers must include access to safe and appropriate sanitation and hygiene facilities and access to safe drinking water. Teachers from vulnerable groups may need specific WASH, transportation, and protection support. Education stakeholders should coordinate with the relevant sectors to provide this holistic support.

There should be no discrimination in compensation or working conditions. Measures should be in place to prevent harassment or discrimination, and mechanisms must be in place to report any abuse. It is important that teachers know how to use these mechanisms and are safe when doing so. Education stakeholders should collaborate to ensure that conditions of work are harmonized between the different actors that employ teachers and that they reflect the practices of the education authorities (for more guidance, see *INEE Guidance Note on Gender*).

> See also Standard 1, Guidance Note 6; Standard 2, Guidance Note 1; Standard 3, Guidance Note 4; Standard 4, Guidance Note 3; Standard 5, Guidance Note 7; Standard 10, Guidance Note 7; Standard 15, Guidance Note 4

2. **Contracts in place:** In most contexts, a contract gives teachers and other education personnel a legally binding document that provides some employment security and helps to professionalize their role in the schools and in the community. Contracts should include a job description and list teachers' key roles and responsibilities, conditions of employment, attendance requirements, working hours, contract length, the code of conduct, support and management systems, and dispute resolution systems. Teacher safety should always be an important consideration in a contract, which also should establish what compensation teachers will receive, both monetary and non-monetary, and include salary review mechanisms. If teachers and other education personnel have to change their location, those who employ them should consider offering extra compensation, such as accommodation and transportation costs. If it is not possible to issue a contract in a given operating context, employers can explore what written documentation they can provide in place of a contract, such as a letter of commitment.

> See also Standard 15, Guidance Note 1

3. **Right to organize:** Two UNESCO/ILO recommendations related to teaching and education (see domain introduction) express the rights of teachers and other education personnel to the freedom of association, to organize, and to negotiate their terms and conditions of employment. The ILO refers to any type of negotiation, consultation, or exchange of information between government representatives, employers, and workers as social dialogue. Teachers and other education personnel, like all other public workers, should be involved in any such social dialogue, in keeping with national traditions and context.

> See also Standard 19, Guidance Note 5

4. **Codes of conduct:** A code of conduct sets clear standards of behavior for teachers and other education personnel. The standards set out in a code should apply to the learning environment and to education-related events and activities. There should be clear consequences for people who do not adhere to them. It is important that teachers and other education personnel receive training in the code of conduct. This should take place before a contract is signed to ensure that the potential employee understands and agrees to follow the code. The code should be reviewed every year to make sure it is still pertinent. A code of conduct includes a commitment to do the following:

- Respect, protect, and fulfill the education rights of learners
- Maintain high standards of conduct and ethical behavior
- Remove barriers to education and create a non-discriminatory environment for all learners
- Maintain a safe, protective, and inclusive environment free from sexual, gender-based and other forms of violence, harassment, exploitation, intimidation, violence, and discrimination
- Promote the physical and psychosocial wellbeing of learners and all education personnel
- Reflect and support learners' diversity in teaching approaches and classroom interactions
- Avoid teaching or encouraging knowledge or actions that contradict human rights or non-discrimination principles
- Participate in professional development
- Safeguard children and young people and report any concerns in this regard (for more guidance, see *Minimum Standards for Child Protection*, Standard 23)
- Work collaboratively with other teachers and education personnel
- Establish and maintain professional relationships with learners' parents and caregivers
- Maintain regular attendance and punctuality

An example of a code of conduct is given in the *Teachers in Crisis Contexts Training for Primary School Teachers*.

See also Standard 9, Guidance Notes 4–5; Standard 13, Guidance Note 2; Standard 17, Guidance Note 4

References and further reading

Links to these and additional resources are available on the INEE website.

- *Crisis-Sensitive Teacher Policy and Planning: Module on the Teacher Policy Development Guide*, International Task Force on Teachers for Education 2030, 2022
- *Global Framework of Professional Teaching Standards*, Education International and UNESCO, 2022
- *INEE Guidance Note on Gender*, INEE, 2019
- *INEE Guidance Notes on Teacher Compensation*, INEE, 2009
- *INEE Guidance Note on Teacher Wellbeing in Emergency Settings*, INEE, 2022
- *Minimum Economic Recovery Standards*, SEEP Network, 2017
- *Recommendation concerning the Status of Higher-Education Teaching Personnel*, UNESCO, 1997
- *Recommendation concerning the Status of Teachers*, ILO/UNESCO, 1966
- *School Code of Conduct Teacher Training Manual: How to Create a Positive Learning Environment*, Save the Children, 2017
- *Teachers in Crisis Contexts Training for Primary School Teachers*, INEE, 2016

STANDARD 17: SUPPORT AND SUPERVISION

The support and supervision mechanisms in place for teachers and other education personnel function effectively.

Key actions
(please read with guidance notes)

1. **Adequate and appropriate resources:** Provide enough teaching and learning resources to allow teachers to manage their students' learning.

2. **Ongoing professional development:** Provide teachers and other education personnel with ongoing professional development.

3. **Transparent and effective support mechanisms:** Establish and maintain transparent, accountable management and support mechanisms that make it possible to regularly appraise, monitor, and support teachers and other education personnel.

4. **Performance appraisals in place:** Ensure that performance appraisals for teachers and other education personnel are a meaningful process.

5. **Mental health and psychosocial support:** Ensure that teachers and other education personnel have access to appropriate and practical MHPSS.

6. **Learner feedback:** Create regular opportunities for learners to give feedback on teaching and learning and other aspects of their education experience.

Guidance notes

1. **Adequate and appropriate resources:** Teachers and other education personnel need adequate and appropriate resources to allow them to teach and work effectively. When these resources are not available, teachers may experience more stress and job burnout. Under such conditions, teachers may be able to draw from their own knowledge, or training can be organized on how to adapt materials that are readily available in the environment in a creative and safe way. If a digital approach will be used in a distance education model, a needs assessment will be needed to determine what access learners have to mobile technologies and whether they have electricity, internet connectivity, and the skills to use digital devices. The needs assessment should target parents and caregivers, teachers, and learners and

should include questions on any social or cultural sensitivities around access to technology, particularly for women and girls. Learners' ages and developmental levels will need to be considered when designing both print and digital learning materials to ensure that they are relevant and inclusive (for more guidance, see *INEE Background Paper on Distance Education in Emergencies*).

> See also Standard 2, Guidance Note 1; Standard 8, Guidance Note 11; Standard 11, Guidance Note 6; Standard 14, Guidance Note 6; Standard 18, Guidance Note 5; Standard 19, Guidance Note 3

2. **Ongoing professional development:** Receiving ongoing professional development is key for teachers, as it can improve their ability to deliver quality, safe, and inclusive education. It also can increase their motivation, confidence, and overall wellbeing. Professional development needs to start at the teachers' level of training and experience. It should be relevant to their needs, delivered by qualified trainers, and inclusive and non-discriminatory. Professional development should include awareness raising and skills building on gender-responsive pedagogy, inclusive education practices, and how to support learners' psychosocial needs during times of crisis.

Teacher training should be feasible in terms of the logistics, such as venue, timing, frequency, and resources needed, including digital. Stakeholders can put in place a framework for teacher professional development that will help to achieve coherence, consistent quality, and efficient funding. This will help determine the training needs for teachers and other education personnel at different levels and maximize existing materials to support the training. Under-trained and under-qualified teachers should have access to training that pays special attention to the foundational concepts around pedagogy and children's and young people's learning and wellbeing. Professional development for these teachers should be followed up with regular training and support to build their skills. Teachers', head teachers', and other education personnel's thoughts and priorities about their own support needs should be at the center of any professional development planning (for more guidance, see *Teachers in Crisis Contexts Training for Primary School Teachers*).

> See also Standard 3, Guidance Note 4; Standard 5, Guidance Note 7; Standard 14

3. **Transparent and effective support mechanisms:** Effective management, supervision, and accountability are important to providing professional support and maintaining teacher motivation and teaching quality. Teachers require ongoing professional support which should be available at different levels, from the learning environment (peers, head teachers, senior teachers, etc.), to education authority support systems (advisors, education specialists, teacher training institutes, etc.). If management and support systems already exist, they should be built on and strengthened as needed. Support systems are likely to operate at different levels—

national, sub-national, and local. If no support mechanism systems are in place, education authorities, teachers unions, community members, relevant committees or associations, UN agencies, donors, and NGOs should work together to design and establish them. Higher education institutions may need to give special attention to ensuring that their standard support and supervision structures cover EiE programs and the faculty involved (full-time, part-time, contract-based, or short-term).

To ensure complementarity and avoid confusion or duplication of support systems, all those who provide support should have clear roles, responsibilities, and accountability. Support from peers and communities of practice can motivate teachers and other education personnel and help them improve their teaching practice. They can provide a safe space for teachers to reflect on their work, set goals, and discuss new practices. When face-to-face meetings are not possible, mobile technologies can be useful to promote teacher collaboration and set up professional discussion and support groups (for more guidance, see the *Teachers in Crisis Contexts Peer Coaching Pack*).

See also Standard 1, Guidance Note 6; Standard 3, Guidance Note 4; Standard 14, Guidance Note 7

4. **Performance appraisals in place:** During emergencies, well-designed and managed performance appraisals support good teacher performance and education quality. Education stakeholders should use existing education authority appraisal frameworks during emergencies when possible, and the appraisal criteria should be transparent and known to the teachers. If an appraisal framework must be developed, it should be clearly linked to the job description and code of conduct. It should include classroom observations of teachers to determine if their practices are inclusive and support the learning of all students. Performance appraisals also should be linked to key safeguarding procedures, including monitoring teachers' adherence to the code of conduct. After they are observed in the classroom, teachers should be given feedback and the opportunity to discuss what actions they can take to improve their teaching practice, set goals, and establish a time frame for working to reach them.

Assessment of other education personnel can be done by observing them as they carry out a key activity, through a review of their planning, and following up on meetings or classroom observations. A performance appraisal system for teachers and other education personnel should identify key areas to focus on and include self-evaluation.

See also Standard 12, Guidance Note 2; Standard 15, Guidance Note 1; Standard 16, Guidance Note 4

5. **Mental health and psychosocial support:** Any teacher or other education personnel can feel overwhelmed by a crisis. They and their families are likely to have concerns about their own security and safety and uncertainty about the future. How well teachers can support learners will depend on their own wellbeing and the support they receive. Having access to information on what emergency, protection, and safeguarding measures are in place can empower teachers and other education personnel. Holding peer group meetings to discuss and share concerns can also be helpful. Those who support and supervise teachers should be trained in protection and safeguarding, including the do no harm principle, and be familiar with the principles and tools for providing MHPSS. It is also important that non-specialized personnel are recruited and trained to provide individual and group support, and that specialists are on hand to offer MHPSS. Education stakeholders, teachers, and communities should work together to address stigma around mental health issues in culturally appropriate ways, such as sharing information, raising community awareness, and advocacy (for more guidance, see *Guidance Note on Teacher Wellbeing in Emergency Settings*).

> See also Standard 2, Guidance Note 1; Standard 9, Guidance Note 1; Standard 10, Guidance Note 9; Standard 14, Guidance Note 7

6. **Learner feedback:** It is important to include learners in the evaluation of teaching and learning and to get their feedback on their education experience. Their participation will help them understand the learning environment more fully and contribute to the quality and safety of education. Learner participation is particularly important in tertiary education to ensure that programs meet their current and future needs. Teachers and other education personnel should create a supportive learning environment that encourages learners to share their thoughts on their own learning, the teaching approaches their teacher uses, their own wellbeing, and issues of behavior, protection, safety, and security. Helping young learners share this feedback can be done both in the learning environment and at home using simple questionnaires. Stakeholders should make sure to use child-friendly strategies when engaging children for feedback (see Annex 1: Glossary for a definition of child-friendly). Engaging learners in the evaluation of teaching and learning will help build their confidence and enable them to understand their strengths, as well as what challenges they face. It will also help teachers reflect on their own practice and strengthen the links between home and the learning environment.

> See also Standard 1, Guidance Note 7; Standard 13, Guidance Note 1

References and further reading

Links to these and additional resources are available on the INEE website.

- *Crisis-Sensitive Teacher Policy and Planning: Module on the Teacher Policy Development Guide*, International Task Force on Teachers for Education 2030, 2022
- *Global Framework of Professional Teaching Standards*, Education International & and UNESCO, 2022
- *INEE Background Paper Distance Education in Emergencies*, INEE, 2022
- *INEE Guidance Note on Teacher Wellbeing in Emergency Settings*, INEE, 2022
- *Minimum Standards for Child Protection in Humanitarian Action*, Alliance for Child Protection in Humanitarian Action, 2019
- *Protecting Education Personnel from Targeted Attack in Conflict-Affected Countries*, GCPEA, 2014
- *Recommendation concerning the Status of Higher-Education Teaching Personnel*, UNESCO, 1997
- *Recommendation concerning the Status of Teachers*, ILO/UNESCO, 1966
- *Teachers in Crisis Contexts Peer Coaching Pack*, INEE, 2018
- *Teachers in Crisis Contexts Training for Primary School Teachers*, INEE, 2016

> For resources to help you with the implementation of the standards in Domain 4, visit inee.org/minimum-standards.

Education Policy

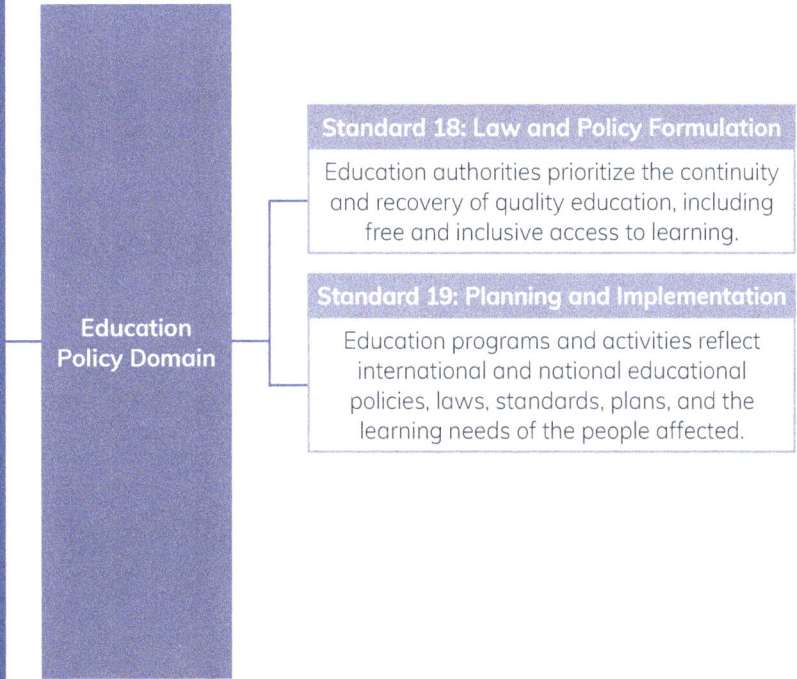

Foundational Standards for a Quality Response:
Community Participation, Coordination, Analysis

Education Policy Domain

Standard 18: Law and Policy Formulation
Education authorities prioritize the continuity and recovery of quality education, including free and inclusive access to learning.

Standard 19: Planning and Implementation
Education programs and activities reflect international and national educational policies, laws, standards, plans, and the learning needs of the people affected.

Overview of Domain 5

This domain highlights the importance of education policy in providing inclusive and equitable quality education during crises. There are two standards, the first relating to the formulation of law and policy, the second to planning and implementation. The main areas addressed in the key actions are discussed below.

The key actions in this domain involve actors such as:

- National, sub-national, and local education authorities
- Education policy-makers and planners at the global, national, sub-national, and local levels
- Authorities from child protection, WASH, shelter, MHPSS, health, nutrition, finance, disaster management, and other relevant sectors
- Stakeholders involved in the education response, including local and national CSOs and NGOs, faith-based organizations, humanitarian and development partners, donors, and private sector actors
- Communities affected by crisis

Education policy underpins all areas of education

Education policy is a set of ideas or values about what education as a social institution and set of practices should look like. This includes who is taught what and how, and how these practices are to be governed. The substance of education policy is the stated objectives and the actions taken to achieve those objectives. Education policy is also about the process of formulating policy and who participates, which influences the process of implementing policy.

Education policy provides a foundation for education planning, including in emergencies. It expresses the goals of an education system which are further set out in laws, regulations, budgets, and programs. In this sense, the Education Policy Domain underpins the other four domains. Education policy should establish and reflect the principles, practices, and services that will most effectively support the provision of inclusive and equitable quality education for all learners, even during crises. The humanitarian-development-peacebuilding nexus should also be reflected in education policy, including the process of developing policy, its key underlying principles, and its substance. This will result in education policy that provides a framework for meaningful links between education authorities and humanitarian, peacebuilding, and development actors who are working together.

Aligning national policies with global instruments

Education policy at the national level should have the principles of global instruments as their foundation. This includes UN standard-setting instruments, conventions, declarations, and recommendations, frameworks for action, and charters, all of which enshrine the right to education. The key international legal instruments and agreements make a commitment to promoting policies and laws that protect against all forms of discrimination in education. These include instruments and agreements such as:

- UN Convention on the Rights of the Child (1989)
- International Convention on the Elimination of all Forms of Racial Discrimination (1969) (Articles 5, 7)
- UN Convention on the Rights of Persons with Disabilities (2006) (Article 24)
- Convention on the Elimination of All Forms of Discrimination against Women (1979) (Article 10)
- Global Compact on Refugees (sections 68 and 69)

A comprehensive list is provided in Annex 3: Relevant Legal Instruments.

SDG 4 relates specifically to education at the global level. It highlights the importance of providing quality and equitable education for all: "Ensure inclusive and equitable quality education and promote lifelong learning opportunities for all." This goal builds on decades of work by many countries and the UN to develop and reaffirm the right to education. "Education for all" means creating education systems that are inclusive of all learners, regardless of gender, wealth, disability, ethnicity, language, location, migration, displacement, sexual orientation, gender identity and expression, sexual characteristics, religion, legal status, and other factors. No learner should face discrimination or exclusion from education systems, including those who were never in school, have dropped out, have disabilities, are pregnant, or are young mothers. These learners in particular need supportive policies to access or return to education.

The Education 2030: Incheon Declaration and Framework for Action was built on SDG 4, which also considers the impact crisis and conflict have on education and development and emphasizes the need for safe, violence-free, supportive, and secure learning environments.

Another key global framework of relevance to EiE is the Global Compact on Refugees. The Compact strongly advocates for the inclusion of refugees into national systems and recognizes the need for international cooperation to achieve this. As such, the Compact is a "framework for more predictable and equitable responsibility-sharing, recognizing that a sustainable solution to refugee situations cannot be achieved without international cooperation." It is a guide for governments, international organizations, and other stakeholders on how to ensure that refugee and host communities both get the support they need. The Compact emphasizes how providing access to inclusive and equitable quality education in national systems enables all refugee, asylum seeking, returnee, and stateless children and young people, and their hosting communities to learn, develop their potential, build individual and collective resilience, and contribute to their societies. It also advocates for aligning responses with national education laws, policies, and planning, and for supporting states to develop and implement national education plans that include refugees. Another key instrument is The Global Compact for Safe, Orderly and Regular Migration. The Global Compact for Migration addresses a wide range of issues that migrants often face in accessing education, vocational trainings, and facilitating mutual recognition of skills and qualifications.

National governments are responsible for providing education

As the main duty bearers, national governments are responsible for providing education and employing teachers. Duty bearers are state or non-state actors who must respect, protect, promote, and fulfill the human rights of the people (rights holders). Governments at the national level should adhere to the key global instruments and frameworks and ensure that the right to education is realized through national legislation. This includes education acts, education laws, and education policies, strategies, and programs. It is also important that education authorities and line ministries from other sectors collaborate on such issues as protection, WASH, health, MHPSS, shelter, and refugees' right to work and to freedom of movement. Formulating and implementing education policy should be a consultative process that includes stakeholders across the different levels of the education system in both the initial analysis and the detailed planning.

The key document at the national level is the education sector plan (ESP), which articulates the long-term overall vision for a country's education system. It establishes the country's education policies, strategies, program priorities, and plans over multiple years. The ESP should be holistic and be based on evidence and a careful analysis of the context. It is important that policy-makers consider existing and potential social and economic disparities affecting learners and that plans and budgets are created to address them. The ESP should include all levels of education, from ECD to tertiary. Policy-makers should establish indicators and baselines to measure and capture the results, outcomes, inputs, and outputs of policy within a national results-based framework. Governments lead the ESP development process, which also should involve the community, education stakeholders, CSOs, and development and humanitarian partners.

In crisis situations, when long-term planning and implementation are difficult, national or sub-national authorities can develop a transitional education plan (TEP) to help maintain the education sector's long-term vision while focusing on urgent issues and challenges. National education plans like the ESP and TEP should include emergency preparedness and contingency planning for education. Education authorities should lead the process of developing these plans and collaborate, when relevant, with inter-agency coordination mechanisms, education partners, and other stakeholders, including teachers and learners. All EiE plans and related actions should respect diversity, be fully inclusive, and protect against all forms of discrimination in education. They also should identify and address existing inequalities to improve equity and social justice.

National and subnational ESPs, TEPs, and other emergency plans provide a framework for all education partners in both normal and crisis situations. These plans should include links with other sectors, such as health, nutrition, WASH, child protection, MHPSS, shelter, and food security. The INEE MS specifically support this kind of meaningful and coordinated planning and response to emergencies.

The importance of advocacy and engaging stakeholders in policy-making

Advocacy is an important tool for advancing policies that protect the right to quality, safe, and relevant education for all during emergencies. Advocacy can be led by education stakeholders, communities, or CSOs, who must appeal to the decision-makers for policies, plans, and budgets that ensure access to education during crises. Advocacy efforts can take place through face-to-face meetings, leaflets, posters, the radio, television, or online. The INEE MS are a key advocacy tool to help education stakeholders negotiate humanitarian spaces and resources. They can help humanitarian actors to advance awareness of the importance of EiE and hold duty bearers accountable in providing it.

Policy-makers should meaningfully engage education stakeholders, communities, and children and young people throughout the policy-making process, from initial consultations to monitoring how policies are implemented. These stakeholders have direct experience of the successes and challenges in the learning environment and engaging them in policy-making will help develop more relevant and effective policies. It also will help promote their ownership of policies and programs, their understanding of how the policies affect them, and their role in implementing them. Engaging stakeholders also will ensure that policy-makers are accountable to the community about national and local policies and budgets related to EiE.

STANDARD 18: LAW AND POLICY FORMULATION

Education authorities prioritize the continuity and recovery of quality education, including free and inclusive access to learning.

Key actions
(please read with guidance notes)

1. **Right to education:** Respect, protect, and fulfill the right to education for all through national education laws, regulations, and policies.

2. **Non-discrimination:** Ensure that there is no discrimination in education access at any level.

3. **Protected status of education facilities, teachers, and learners:** Uphold the protected status of education facilities, learners, and teachers and other education personnel through national education laws, regulations, and policies, in keeping with international humanitarian and human rights law.

4. **Safe and secure education facilities:** Ensure that laws, regulations, and policies promote the selection of safe and secure locations for education facilities and the construction of disaster-resilient buildings.

5. **National action plans and budgets:** Support national education policies with action plans, laws, and budgets that allow a quick response in emergencies.

6. **Disaster preparedness:** Include education as an integral part of national disaster preparedness frameworks to ensure continuity of education.

7. **Context analysis:** Conduct a context analysis through an inclusive and participatory process and use the findings to guide laws, regulations, and policies.

8. **Evidence-based analysis, planning, monitoring, and evaluation:** Design policies and programs based on reliable and timely information.

9. **Support of UN and non-state actors**: Ensure that laws, regulations, and policies allow UN and non-state actors, such as NGOs, civil society, and the private sector, to support and supplement national education programs.

⬡ Guidance notes

1. **Right to education:** International human rights law guarantees the right to education, as expressed in key human rights documents, such as the UN Universal Declaration of Human Rights and the Convention on the Rights of the Child (see Introduction to the INEE MS). The right to education encompasses both rights and entitlements including:

   - the right to free and compulsory primary education
   - the right to available and accessible secondary education, including TVET (made progressively free)
   - the right to equal access to higher education on the basis of capacity (made progressively free)

   All individuals have the right to live life and to learn without barriers, to be independent, and to participate fully in the community. Education plays a critical role in learners' wellbeing and sense of normalcy. The right to education is also addressed in the 1951 Convention Relating to the Status of Refugees and the 2018 Global Compact on Refugees. The Compact emphasizes the need to include refugees in national education systems, and that partner states have an obligation to share the responsibility to protect and assist refugees and support host countries and communities. Education enables learners at all levels to develop their potential and individuality, makes them aware of their rights, teaches them to be respectful of the rights and cultures of others, and teaches them ways to protect the environment.

   The Convention of the Rights of the Child states that children have the right to be consulted on decisions that affect them, to be treated with respect and without discrimination, and to know their legal and human rights. Advocacy and information sharing on the right to education are important to strengthen duty bearers' understanding and recognition of these rights. These key rights, and the right to education during emergencies, are the focus of the 2010 UN General Assembly Resolution 64/290 on the Right to Education in Emergency Situations (see Annex 3 for a fuller list of the international legal instruments, soft law, and global frameworks related to the right of to education for all, including during emergencies).

> See also Standard 1, Guidance Note 7; Standard 8, Guidance Notes 1, 4, and 7–8; Standard 9, Guidance Note 5; Standard 13, Guidance Notes 4–5; Standard 14, Guidance Note 5

2. **Non-discrimination:** Education authorities should make sure that education reaches all learners in an equitable way, regardless of age, gender, sexuality, religion, ethnicity, language, socioeconomic background, location, displacement status, disability, or other factors. This may require policies and actions that actively address inequalities, disparities, and barriers to education access. Education policies should be responsive to the needs of all learners and prohibit discrimination and exclusion. The Global Compact on Refugees advocates for refugees to have equitable access to all levels of education.

> See also Standard 8, Guidance Notes 2, 4, and 7–8; Standard 11, Guidance Notes 4–5; Standard 12, Guidance Note 3; Standard 13, Guidance Note 5; Standard 14, Guidance Note 5

3. **Protected status of education facilities, teachers, and learners:** Under international humanitarian law that governs the conduct of hostilities, civilian learners and teachers and other education personnel are protected from attack, unless and for such time as they directly participate in hostilities. Schools and other learning environments are similarly considered civilian objects and thus protected against attack, unless they become military objectives. Even if they do become military objectives, all feasible precautions must be taken to avoid or at least minimize incidental harm to civilian learners, education personnel, and education facilities. Attacks expected to cause excessive harm to civilians or damage to civilian objects are prohibited. This protection is part of international humanitarian law and is binding on all parties to armed conflict, both government forces and non-state armed groups. UN Security Council Resolution 1612 (2005) outlines the six grave violations committed against children in times of armed conflict, which includes attacks on schools. The resolution is monitored annually through the UN-supported Monitoring and Reporting Mechanism.

National authorities and international stakeholders should support efforts to build this protected status into national law and practice, and to prevent the use of education facilities for military purposes. The Global Coalition to Protect Education from Attack, an inter-agency coalition established in 2010, monitors and profiles attacks made on schools through the Safe Schools Declaration, which was endorsed by well over one hundred states by 2023. It reflects states' commitment to:

- Ensure that education can continue during violent conflict
- Follow the *Guidelines for Protecting Schools and Universities from Military Use during Armed Conflict*
- Collect data on attacks on education facilities
- Help victims in a non-discriminatory way

The Safe Schools Declaration is "an intergovernmental political commitment to protect learners, teachers, schools, and universities from the worst effects of armed conflict and its implementation is monitored." In some cases, armed groups may target female teachers, learners, and girls' schools for attack and sexual harassment.

Endorsement and implementation of the Safe Schools Declaration can be a key step towards addressing violence in and around schools and protecting girls and young women and their access to education. Reporting mechanisms, such as the Monitoring and Reporting Mechanism, should systematically disaggregate reports of attacks on education by gender to better understand the gender dimension of these attacks at a global level.

When violence threatens education continuity and learner safety, advocacy to promote education, human rights, and adherence to international humanitarian law is a priority.

See also Standard 6, Guidance Note 2; Standard 9, Guidance Note 9

4. **Safety and security of education facilities:** Governments should guarantee safe access to education through policies and systems that aim to protect the safety, health, and wellbeing of all learners and ensure continuity of education. This includes ensuring that school grounds are free from weapons and explosives, that routes to and from school are safe, and that buildings are reinforced and protected. Safety measures for learners and teachers on their way to and from the learning environment should consider their different protection needs related to age, gender, and disability, and should reflect the realities of different groups in the community, particularly vulnerable and marginalized groups. It is important to take measures to protect physical infrastructure in the learning environment from hazards and risks. Education stakeholders should ensure that teachers and other education personnel receive training in how to identify, mitigate, and respond to risks. Education authorities and other duty bearers should lead in establishing school safety systems, policies, and plans. Linking local school safety and improvement plans to operational planning at the sub-national and national levels is a key step to ensure that these efforts are sustained and funded (for more guidance, see *Comprehensive School Safety Framework*).

When choosing locations for schools and education facilities, education authorities and other education stakeholders should consider national, regional, and local knowledge of hazards and risks. Learning environments should be designed and built to be disaster resilient so that learners and teachers and other education personnel are safe. Schools and education facilities should not be used as shelters or evacuation centers. Developing and/or maintaining emergency preparedness plans is a key step to minimizing the use of education facilities as shelters during emergencies. If national authorities are unable to identify temporary solutions for shelters other than schools, then it will be important for them to work with education stakeholders and the community to agree on timeframes, identify alternative locations for learning, and budget the necessary funds to ensure that education facilities are returned in a usable or improved state.

See also Standard 4, Guidance Note 8; Standard 5, Guidance Note 6; Standard 8, Guidance Note 10; Standard 9, Guidance Note 7; Standard 10, Guidance Notes 1–2; Standard 15, Guidance Note 4

5. **National action plans and budgets:** National laws and policies should have action plans and budgets that enable a quick response to emergencies and ensure continuity of education. If there is no national ESP, or none that includes plans for emergencies, including accommodations for refugee and IDP learners, authorities should review other national action plans and find opportunities to create links with them and to source budgets dedicated to emergency response.

Where there is no national plan, education authorities can develop a TEP. It is important that policy-makers gather information and data on the state of the education system before developing a sector plan (see Guidance Note 6 below). Education authorities and partners should identify opportunities for cross-sectoral collaboration with other line ministries and national agencies, where they exist, including when sourcing data and developing the plan. A TEP, or any other emergency education plan, should do the following:

- Consider the status and implementation of existing national laws, standards, and policies, as well as international frameworks and commitments
- Show a commitment to the right to education for all learners
- Respond to the learning needs and rights of people affected by crisis
- Include steps to ensure access to quality education for all, with specific provisions for women, girls, and learners with disabilities
- Recognize refugees' right to education
- Articulate the right to access lifelong learning opportunities, including ECD and post-secondary and higher education
- Integrate measures to protect the health, safety, and security of all learners
- Reflect the humanitarian-development-peacebuilding nexus, including longer-term measures to strengthen the education system, such as measures to adapt to climate change

Education authorities and partners can develop budgets and action plans in accordance with the TEP. Budgets and action plans should include an operational approach for programs linked to the TEP that outlines proposed activities, roles, responsibilities, costs, anticipated sources of funding, and a results framework. This helps to promote accountability among education authorities and partners in addressing the learning needs of people affected by crisis and meeting agreed-upon priorities.

> See also Standard 1, Guidance Note 6; Standard 3, Guidance Notes 4–5; Standard 5, Guidance Note 7; Standard 8, Guidance Note 11; Standard 15, Guidance Note 3; Standard 17, Guidance Note 1

6. **Disaster preparedness:** To ensure that key education services are continued during crises, national authorities should make sure that education is integrated into national disaster preparedness frameworks. National and sub-national authorities from education, disaster management, child protection, finance and other relevant sectors should lead in establishing crisis-sensitive policies and plans, including school safety plans. Advocacy that targets national authorities on the life-saving and life-sustaining role of EiE can help ensure that it is included in national preparedness frameworks and plans (for more guidance, see *Creating Change: Advocacy Toolkit for Education in Emergencies; Comprehensive School Safety Framework*).

    This is supported by the Sendai Framework for Disaster Risk Reduction 2015-2030, which highlights the importance of promoting and protecting all human rights while managing the risk of a disaster. The Sendai Framework recognizes that the state plays a central role in reducing disaster risk but that the responsibility should be shared with other stakeholders. The framework also emphasizes an all-of-society approach to ensure inclusive, accessible, and non-discriminatory participation, with special attention given to people disproportionately affected by disasters, particularly women, girls, and persons with disabilities. Preparedness frameworks should make explicit provisions for the participation of children, young people, and teachers and other education personnel in community response efforts.

    See also Standard 5, Guidance Note 6; Standard 9, Guidance Note 10

7. **Context analysis:** Education laws and policies, including a TEP or other emergency education plan, should be based on an analysis of the context. They should reflect a thorough understanding of the social, economic, security, environmental, and political dynamics of the emergency context. This might include the immediate and longer-term effects the crisis will have on education, or the possibility that existing education policies and curricula or the exclusion of marginalized groups could increase tensions and conflict. Context analyses may include assessments of the conflict, human rights, and risk and emergency preparedness.

    A context analysis should involve wide consultation with stakeholders at different levels of the education sector, including local and national actors, teachers unions, community leaders, and humanitarian and development partners. Education authorities and other education stakeholders should advocate for a context analysis as part of regular education sector reviews and reform processes.

    See also Standard 4, Guidance Note 7

8. **Evidence-based analysis, planning, monitoring, and evaluation:** It is important to develop laws, regulations, and policies based on reliable information. A national EMIS is central to this, as it makes it possible to store, aggregate, and analyze education data at all levels of an education system. The EMIS, which is usually managed by national education authorities, should be linked to information about areas and population groups that are vulnerable to particular types of emergencies, including displacement. An EMIS can be a useful entry point for strengthening the humanitarian-development-peacebuilding nexus and for promoting alignment, collaboration, and long-term planning. An EMIS that can be adapted to crises and risks should have the capability to track trends and collect comparable system-wide data that is useful for emergency preparedness, response, and recovery.

    Developing, adapting, or upgrading an EMIS should be a collaborative process between education authorities and partners, including jointly identifying needs and establishing clear roles and responsibilities at each level. This will help build ownership over the long term and make it possible to use the EMIS during planning, decision-making, policy formulation, analysis, monitoring, and management at all levels of the education system. When certain geographic areas are not accessible or EMIS coverage is incomplete, other entities may be able to help, such as a national or regional bureau for statistics or partner agencies. Although it can be difficult to develop, upgrade, or adapt an EMIS during an emergency, doing so may be an opportunity to improve the function of the EMIS and to build back better.

> See also Standard 3, Guidance Note 6; Standard 6, Guidance Note 4

9. **Support of UN and non-state actors:** Education provided by UN and non-state actors such as NGOs, civil society, and the private sector, can play an important role in supplementing the provision of education, especially for learners from marginalized and vulnerable groups (see Annex 1: Glossary for a definition of non-state actors). Support from non-state actors should align with the national ESP, and with other national plans, policies, strategies, and emergency preparedness or contingency plans. The host country is the main duty bearer and should ensure that non-state actors are able to set up agreed-to programs and facilities safely and quickly. This may include fast tracking visas or putting special customs arrangements in place for learning resources.

    Global humanitarian actors should acknowledge any power imbalances that exist among global, national, and local actors and shift decision-making power to local actors as much as possible to ensure that the education activities are sustainable and locally led. All actors involved in the provision of EiE should coordinate their efforts to harmonize the delivery of programs and activities, and to ensure that access to them is equitable.

Private sector actors should also work within existing systems and be regulated by education or other authorities. As with all partners, the private sector should emphasize:

- The principle of do no harm
- Community participation
- Transparency, equity, and coordination
- Making an ongoing commitment to strengthen public education

The Abidjan Principles outline governments' human rights obligations to regulate private involvement in education.

See also Standard 3, Guidance Note 5

References and further reading

Links to these and additional resources are available on the INEE website.

- *Comprehensive School Safety Framework*, GADRRRES, 2022
- *Creating Change: Advocacy Toolkit for Education in Emergencies*, INEE, 2022
- *Education 2030: A Strategy for Refugee Education*, UNHCR, 2019
- *Guidance Note on Developing a Crisis-Sensitive Teacher Policy*, International Task Force on Teachers for Education 2030, 2020
- *Guidelines for Protecting Schools and Universities from Military Use during Armed Conflict*, GCPEA, 2014
- *Guidelines for Transitional Education Plan Preparation*, Global Partnership for Education and UNESCO-IIEP, 2016
- *INEE Background Paper Distance Education in Emergencies*, INEE, 2022
- *INEE Guidance Note on Conflict Sensitive Education*, INEE, 2013
- *INEE Guidance Note on Gender*, INEE, 2019
- *INEE Guidance Note on Psychosocial Support*, INEE, 2018
- *INEE Guidance Notes on Teacher Compensation*, INEE, 2009
- *INEE Guidance Note on Teacher Wellbeing in Emergency Settings*, INEE, 2022

STANDARD 19: PLANNING AND IMPLEMENTATION

Education programs and activities reflect international and national educational policies, laws, standards, plans, and the learning needs of the people affected.

Key actions
(please read with guidance notes)

1. **National and international legal frameworks:** Ensure that formal and non-formal education programs reflect national and international legal frameworks.

2. **Planning for emergencies:** Develop and implement education plans that prepare for and respond to current and future crises.

3. **Sufficient resources:** Mobilize enough financial, technical, material, and human resources to develop and implement education plans and EiE programs effectively and transparently.

4. **Inter-sectoral links:** Integrate EiE planning and implementation with other emergency response sectors.

5. **Advocacy:** Advocate for EiE as part of education policy planning and implementation.

Guidance notes

1. **National and international legal frameworks:** Formal and non-formal education programs should be in line with national and international legal frameworks and policies and meet the needs of all learners. Programs should ensure that education access, the curriculum, and teaching and learning are inclusive and non-discriminatory.

> See also Standard 2, Guidance Note 2

2. **Planning for emergencies:** ESPs and other national and local education plans should prepare for and respond to future and current emergencies. They should include emergency preparedness plans and contingency plans. Contingency plans should be appropriate to the context and, where possible, include early warning systems for

natural hazards and conflicts. Emergency preparedness and contingency planning should be an inclusive process. Policy-makers and education stakeholders must identify the needs of vulnerable and marginalized groups and make sure they are reflected in these plans. Community participation in contingency or response planning is important so that the perspectives and needs of different groups in the community are addressed. This will also strengthen the community's sense of ownership, awareness, and commitment to EiE activities. Connections should be made with other sectors, including WASH, nutrition, health, child protection, and MHPSS.

Plans should include detailed explanation of how to respond to a crisis, including decision-making, coordination, and providing security and protection mechanisms for inter-sectoral coordination. The roles of key stakeholders, including learners, teachers and other education personnel, parents and caregivers, and the wider community, should be clearly defined. Plans should consider how to continue education if the education facilities are used as shelters, or if they become inaccessible or unusable due to natural hazards or conflict. Safety and security measures should be in place in each education facility, including evacuation plans. Plans need to be reviewed regularly to ensure that they are up to date. They also should be coordinated with longer-term plans to develop the education sector. Stakeholders who support national or local education programs should promote emergency preparedness and contingency planning as part of development activities.

> See also Standard 1, Guidance Notes 1 and 6; Standard 4, Guidance Notes 2 and 7; Standard 5, Guidance Notes 2 and 6; Standard 8, Guidance Note 5; Standard 9, Guidance Note 10

3. **Sufficient resources:** National authorities, humanitarian actors, donors, NGOs, communities, and other stakeholders should work together to ensure that there is adequate funding for EiE. National authorities should lead the coordination of the financial, technical, material, and human resources for a response, in cooperation with the inter-agency coordination mechanism. Meeting immediate resource needs should be a priority. Actors should consider the environmental impact when sourcing these needs and can use an environmental assessment tool, such as the NEAT+, to ensure that a response is sustainable. Education authorities and humanitarian partners should allocate resources for reporting attacks on education in a centralized and systematic way, and for collecting, analyzing, and sharing education data.

The private sector may also be well suited to support tech-enabled interventions and to provide important mobile technologies and other digital learning resources. Education authorities and the relevant partners should decide which digital learning platforms to use to make sure that they are suitable to the context and needs of the people affected. It is also important that resource allocation is balanced between physical resources, such as classrooms, textbooks, and other learning materials, and human resources, such as teachers, MHPSS, and teacher support. Schools, ECD centers, and tertiary education institutions also need resources to report attacks on education and the use of learning environments by the military and non-state armed groups.

Transparency and accountability are key when it comes to managing resources effectively. Confidential and culturally appropriate systems should be in place to monitor and manage issues relating to public policy or corruption. These systems should encourage people to report corruption, in both monetary and non-monetary forms, without fear of punishment. Sharing information about resources among the central and local authorities, communities, and other humanitarian stakeholders and having accountability mechanisms in place will make it possible to source and provide resources ethically and safely.

> Q See also Standard 2, Guidance Note 1; Standard 3, Guidance Notes 5 and 8; Standard 5, Guidance Note 2; Standard 6, Guidance Note 1; Standard 7, Guidance Note 3; Standard 8, Guidance Note 11; Standard 11, Guidance Note 6; Standard 15, Guidance Note 3; Standard 17, Guidance Note 1

4. **Inter-sectoral links:** The EiE response for all ages, from early childhood to tertiary, should be connected to activities in other sectors, such as WASH, nutrition, food security, shelter, health, livelihoods, urban planning, shelter, economic recovery, child protection, and MHPSS. This will help ensure that the EiE response addresses the diverse and multi-sectoral needs of crisis-affected learners. A multi-sector assessment is an important starting point for any emergency response. Emergency preparedness and contingency plans should include specific provisions for inter-sectoral coordination at the national and subnational levels. For example, collaboration between education authorities and other sectors or national agencies for disaster management can promote the integration of education into multi-sectoral rapid response efforts, strengthen referral pathways, and avoid the use of schools as temporary shelters.

> Q See also Standard 3, Guidance Note 4; Standard 4, Guidance Note 10; Standard 8, Guidance Notes 1–2; Standard 10, Guidance Notes 1 and 7–9

5. **Advocacy:** Advocacy can take place at a local, national, and global level. It targets those in positions of power, frequently governments, donors, and institutions. EiE advocacy focuses on ensuring access to quality, safe, and relevant education for all during a crisis. EiE advocacy can begin before an emergency. It can include, for example, efforts to advance policies that protect the right to education in the event of a crisis. It can also continue after a crisis and into recovery, such as negotiations for a safe return to school for learners affected by an emergency.

EiE advocacy can work toward the following:

- Influencing changes at the policy level to increase the reach and sustainability of education access
- Ensuring that duty bearers are held accountable for fulfilling their responsibilities and their commitment to ensure all individuals' right to education, as enshrined in international human rights law

- Ensuring that national authorities and humanitarian actors prioritize education in humanitarian responses and mobilize adequate resources
- Ensuring that policy-makers and decision-makers listen to and consider the voices, experiences, perspectives, and priorities of those affected by crises, including children, young people, teachers and other education personnel, and marginalized groups

EiE advocacy should be a key part of planning and implementing education policy. It should be carried out at all levels, but responsibility for advocacy will depend on what issues need attention. Policy-makers should engage communities and other key stakeholders, such as CSOs, in all stages of developing and implementing education policy. Communities may need to advocate for their own involvement, and CSOs can lead advocacy efforts if the policy process is not happening in an inclusive way. To ensure that there is a coherent and relevant approach to EiE advocacy, a strategy is needed to identify what to advocate for, how, and to whom. As highlighted in the introduction to this domain, advocacy can take place through different modalities, including face-to-face interaction or online. The INEE MS are a key tool to use in advocating for the provision of inclusive and equitable quality education for all in times of crisis (for more guidance, see *Creating Change: Advocacy Toolkit for Education in Emergencies*).

> See also Standard 1, Guidance Notes 1 and 5; Standard 2, Guidance Note 2; Standard 8; Standard 9, Guidance Note 9; Standard 16, Guidance Note 3

References and further reading

Links to these and additional resources are available on the INEE website.

- *Creating Change: Advocacy Toolkit for Education in Emergencies*, INEE, 2022
- *INEE Background Paper on Distance Education in Emergencies*, INEE, 2022
- *INEE Guidance Note on Conflict Sensitive Education*, INEE, 2013
- *INEE Guidance Note on Gender*, INEE, 2019
- *INEE Guidance Note on Psychosocial Support*, INEE, 2018
- *INEE Guidance Notes on Teacher Compensation*, INEE, 2009
- *INEE Guidance Note on Teacher Wellbeing in Emergency Settings*, INEE, 2022
- *Integrating Conflict and Disaster Risk Reduction into Education Sector Planning: Guidance Notes for Educational Planners*, UNESCO-IIEP and UNICEF, 2011
- *Risk-Informed Education Programming for Resilience: Guidance Note*, UNICEF, 2019

For resources to help you with the implementation of the standards in Domain 5, visit inee.org/minimum-standards.

ANNEX 1: GLOSSARY

See the INEE website for a full and up-to-date list of terms, their definitions, and sources.

A

Accelerated Education Program: A flexible, age-appropriate program that promotes access to education in an accelerated timeframe for disadvantaged groups and over-age and out-of-school children and young people who missed out or had their education interrupted due to poverty, marginalization, conflict, and crisis. The goal of AEP is to provide learners with equivalent certified competencies for basic education and learning approaches that match their level of cognitive maturity.

Access: An opportunity to enroll in, attend, and complete a formal or non-formal education program. When access is unrestricted, it means that there are no practical, financial, physical, security-related, structural, institutional, or socio-cultural obstacles to prevent learners from participating in and completing an education program.

Accessibility: Entails the removal or mitigation of barriers to people's meaningful participation. These barriers and the measures needed will vary according to disability, age, illness, literacy level, status of language, legal and/or social status, etc.

Accountability: The process of using power responsibly; taking account of and being held accountable by different stakeholders, primarily those who are affected by the exercise of such power.

Accreditation: A process of quality assurance through which accredited status is granted to a program of education or training, showing it has been approved by the relevant legislative or professional authorities by having met predetermined standards.

Adversity: A single event, such as a disaster associated with a natural hazard, an industrial accident, or an act of terrorism or sustained events, or severe losses, limited access to essential resources, chronic poverty, endemic community and gender-based violence, long-term civil conflict, or displacement.

Advocacy: The deliberate process, based on demonstrated evidence, to directly and indirectly influence decision-makers, stakeholders, and relevant audiences to support and implement actions that contribute to the fulfillment of human rights.

Age-appropriate: Age-appropriate activities, materials, or settings are those which are developmentally suitable for a particular age or age group.

All-hazards: Any and all of those dangerous processes, phenomena, substances, human activities, or conditions in and around schools that may cause: loss of life, injury, other health impacts, or harm to people; damage to learning facilities and environments, loss of education sector investments; or disrupt educational continuity. These include rapid, slow-onset, intensive, and extensive hazards.

Anti-racism: Anti-racism recognizes that racism has systemic and structural elements, and actively takes steps to combat them. This work often requires changing systems, policies, and practices and taking positive measures to correct for the disadvantages inflicted by racism. In essence, it is a practice that is used to disrupt racism.

Assessment: An investigation carried out before planning educational activities and intervening in an emergency to determine needs and gaps in the response and available resources; Within an education program, an assessment is a test of learners' progress and achievement. An 'assessment of learning outcomes' is a form of assessment determined by an education program.

Asset-based approach: An asset-based approach focuses on strengths. It views diversity in thought, culture, and traits as positive assets. Teachers and students alike are valued for what they bring to the classroom rather than being characterized by what they may need to work on or lack.

Assistive devices and technology: External products (devices, equipment, instruments, software), specially produced or generally available, that maintain or improve an individual's functioning and independence, participation, or overall well-being. They can also help prevent secondary impairments and health conditions. Examples of assistive devices and technologies include wheelchairs, prostheses, hearing aids, visual aids, and specialized computer software and hardware that improve mobility, hearing, vision, or the capacity to communicate.

Asylum seeker: An individual who is seeking international protection is an asylum seeker. In countries with individualized procedures, an asylum seeker is someone whose claim has not yet been finally decided on by the country in which the claim is submitted. Not every asylum seeker will ultimately be recognized as a refugee, but every refugee was initially an asylum seeker.

Attacks on education: Attacks on education are any intentional threat or use of force carried out by state or non-state armed groups for political, military, ideological, sectarian, ethnic, religious, or criminal reasons against students, educators, or education personnel while within, going to, or coming from an education institution or elsewhere because of their status as students or educators. Includes abduction, recruitment of child soldiers, forced labor, sexual violence, targeted killings, threats and harassment, and other violations. Actual and threatened looting, seizure, occupation, closure, and demolition of educational property by armed groups may displace educators and students, denying students access to education.

B

Baseline data: Baseline data often describes a situation that existed before an event, which can be defined in many ways, depending on the operational context. An event might be a drought or an incident of political upheaval, or it may simply be the first time the indicators were ever measured. Baseline data may help to interpret the impact of an event when compared to a subsequent assessment.

Best interests of the child: The right of the child to have his or her best interests assessed and taken as a primary consideration in reaching a decision. It refers to the wellbeing of a child and is determined by a variety of individual circumstances (age, level of maturity, the presence or absence of parents, the child's environment and experiences).

Blended learning: Any formal education program in which a student learns at least in part through online learning, with some element of student control over time, place, path, and/or pace.

Bridging program: A short-term, targeted preparation course that supports student's success, taking various forms such as language acquisition and/ or other existing differences between home and host education curricula and systems for entry into a different type of certified education.

C

Capacity: A combination of the strengths, attributes, and resources of individuals or available within a community, society, or organization that can be used to achieve agreed goals.

In a humanitarian response, the agreed goal should be to prevent or reduce human suffering. The capacity needed to do this work should be understood in relation to specific contexts and crises and not as a standard list of technical criteria. Some parts of capacity in humanitarian responses may include respect for humanitarian principles and the ability to prepare for, anticipate, and deliver quality humanitarian assistance, strengthen the resilience of affected people, and manage resources. Just as important, however, are understanding the context, meaningfully relating to affected people and other stakeholders, and the ability to bridge humanitarian and development activities, among others.

Capacity assessment: The identification of capacity assets (such as technical, financial, and institutional) and needs at national and local levels, equivalent to measuring baselines and the progress of (capacity) development indicators.

Capacity sharing: Use of the term "capacity" varies, and different actors in the humanitarian sector use it in different ways. Capacity sharing and related terms such as "capacity exchange," "capacity strengthening," "capacity building," and "capacity development" may be used interchangeably. Whatever term is used to describe the activity, it is essential that it promotes locally led humanitarian action. A "capacity sharing" approach does the following:

- Challenges ways of working that are based on the assumption that local capacity is lacking or needs to be built up
- Puts the diverse strengths and knowledge of local actors and the people affected at the center
- Acknowledges any power imbalance between international, national, and local actors and works to shift power to local actors and communities
- Reflects the principles of respect, mutual learning, and equitable partnerships

Achieving these things requires first defining how capacity is understood in a context, and the actions taken to address gaps must be a collective process led by communities.

Caregiver: An individual, community, or institution (including the State) with clear responsibility (by custom or by law) for the wellbeing of the child. It most often refers to a person with whom the child lives and who provides daily care to the child.

Cash and voucher assistance: All programs where cash transfers or vouchers for goods or services are directly provided to recipients. In the context of humanitarian assistance, the term is used to refer to the provision of cash transfers or vouchers given to individuals, households, or community recipients; not to governments or other state actors. This excludes remittances and microfinance in humanitarian interventions (although microfinance and money transfer institutions may be used for the actual delivery of cash). The terms "cash" or "cash assistance" should be used when referring specifically to cash transfers only (i.e., "cash" or "cash assistance" should not be used to mean "cash and voucher assistance"). This term has several synonyms, but cash and voucher assistance is the recommended term.

Catch-up program: A short-term transitional education program for children and young people who had been actively attending school prior to an educational disruption, which provides students with the opportunity to learn content missed because of the disruption and supports their re-entry to the formal system.

Certification: The process of provision of documentary proof of a learner's competency in and successful completion of an education program.

Child protection: Freedom from all forms of abuse, exploitation, neglect, and violence, including bullying; sexual exploitation; violence from peers, teachers, or other educational personnel; natural hazards; arms and ammunition; landmines and unexploded ordnance; armed personnel; crossfire locations; political and military threats; and recruitment into armed forces or armed groups.

Child safeguarding: The responsibility that organizations have to make sure their staff, operations, and programs do no harm to children. It includes policy, procedures, and practices to prevent children from being harmed by humanitarian organizations as well as steps to respond and investigate when harm occurs.

Child wellbeing: A dynamic, subjective, and objective state of physical, cognitive, emotional, spiritual, and social health in which children:

- Are safe from abuse, neglect, exploitation, and violence
- Have their basic needs, including survival and development, met
- Are connected to and cared for by primary caregivers
- Have the opportunity for supportive relationships with relatives, peers, teachers, community members, and society at large
- Have the opportunities and elements required to exercise their agency based on their evolving capacities

(see wellbeing)

Child-friendly: Working methods that do not discriminate against children and that take into account their age, evolving capacities, diversity, and capabilities. These methods promote children's confidence and ability to learn, speak out, share, and express their views. Sufficient time and appropriate information and materials are provided and communicated effectively to children. Staff and adults are approachable, respectful, and responsive.

Child-friendly spaces and schools: A supportive educational and community environment that is inclusive, healthy, friendly, protective, and rights-based. The Child-Friendly School model, developed by UNICEF, promotes inclusiveness, gender-sensitivity, tolerance, dignity, and personal empowerment.

Children: All people between 0 and 18 years of age. This category includes most adolescents (10–19 years). It overlaps with the category of young people (15–24 years) (see young people).

Children associated with armed forces and armed groups: Children may be abducted or recruited by force or may join the fighting forces "voluntarily." They do not always take up arms. They may be porters, spies, cooks, or victims of grave sexual violence. These children are deprived of the opportunity for education. During demobilization and reintegration processes, special attention must be given to their specific educational needs, including formal and non-formal education, accelerated learning, life skills, and vocational learning. Particular attention needs to be given to girls, who are often overlooked and omitted from rehabilitation programs.

Climate change: The Inter-governmental Panel on Climate Change (IPCC) defines climate change as: a change in the state of the climate that can be identified (e.g. by using statistical tests) by changes in the mean and/or the variability of its properties, and that persists for an extended period, typically decades or longer. Climate change may be due to natural internal processes or external forcings, or to persistent anthropogenic changes in the composition of the atmosphere or in land use. The United Nations Framework Convention on Climate Change (UNFCCC) defines climate change as a change of climate which is attributed directly or indirectly to human activity that alters the composition of the global atmosphere and which is in addition to natural climate variability observed over comparable time periods.

Climate change education: Education is an important element of the global response to climate change. Climate change education addresses the challenges of climate change and sustainable development, facing both developed and developing countries. It helps people understand and address the impacts of the climate crisis, empowering them with the knowledge, skills, values, and attitudes needed to act as agents of change. It also enhances the education system's preparedness for and responses to climate change, both in terms of mitigation and adaptation.

Code of conduct: A code of conduct is a statement of principles, rules, and values that establishes a set of expectations and standards for how an organization, school, government body, company, or affiliated individuals or group will behave, including minimal levels of compliance and disciplinary actions.

Cognitive: Skills and competencies required to manage and direct behavior towards a goal, including those related to executive function, self-regulation, decision-making, and problem-solving.

Colonialism: Some form of invasion, dispossession, and subjugation of a people. The invasion need not be military; it can begin—or continue—as geographical intrusion in the form of agricultural, urban, or industrial encroachments. The result of such incursion is the dispossession of vast amounts of land from the original inhabitants. This is often legalized after the fact. The long-term result of such massive dispossession is institutionalized inequality. The colonizer/colonized relationship is by nature an unequal one that benefits the colonizer at the expense of the colonized. Ongoing and legacy colonialism impact power relations in most of the world today.

Community education committee: An existing or new committee, which identifies and addresses the educational needs of a community. Members include representatives of parents and caregivers, teachers, learners, community organizations and leaders, marginalized groups, civil society associations, youth groups, and health workers.

Complex emergency: A multifaceted humanitarian crisis in a country, region, or society where there is a total or considerable breakdown of authority resulting from internal or external conflict which requires a multi-sectoral international response that goes beyond the mandate or capacity of any single agency and/or the ongoing United Nations country program.

Conflict: Violent fighting between two or more parties that threatens the safety and security of communities or of the general population. This includes situations of repression through coercion or fear backed by the threat of violence, as well as acts of violence up to and including the level of armed conflict.

According to international humanitarian law, the term "armed conflict" is used to refer to situations where hostilities reach a threshold synonymous with war. Although rarely questioned, when applied to conflicts between states, the term often comes under debate when used in relation to internal conflict. In essence, it involves armed parties at a higher and more sustained level of violence than "situations of internal disturbances and tensions, such as riots, isolated and sporadic acts of violence or other acts of a similar nature" (Article 8.2(d), Rome Statute of the International Criminal Court).

Conflict analysis: The critical first step in delivering conflict sensitive education programming. It is the systematic study of the background and history, root causes, actors, and dynamics of a conflict, which contribute to violent conflict and/or peace, and their interaction with the education program or policy.

Conflict mitigation: Actions and processes that 1) are sensitive to conflict and do not increase tensions or sources of violence; and 2) aim to address causes of conflict and change the way that those involved act and perceive the issues. Humanitarian, recovery, and development activities are reviewed for their effect on the conflict context in which they take place and their contribution to longer-term peace and stability. Conflict mitigation approaches can be used for conflict prevention and interventions in conflict and post-conflict situations.

Conflict sensitive education: Conflict sensitive education requires an organizational understanding of the interactions between a context of conflict and education programs and policies for the development, planning, and delivery of education services which act to minimize negative impacts and maximize positive impacts of education policies and programming on conflict (such as increased peace, social harmonization, social justice, etc.).

Contextualization: The process of interpreting or adapting the INEE MS to a context; the process of debating, determining, and agreeing upon the meaning of global guidance in a given local situation; "translating" the meaning and guidance of the INEE MS for the context of a country (or region) so as to make the content of the Standards appropriate and meaningful to the given circumstances.

Contingency planning: A management process that analyzes specific potential events or emerging situations that might threaten society or the environment and establishes arrangements in advance to enable timely, effective, and appropriate responses to such events and situations. Contingency planning results in organized and coordinated courses of action with clearly identified institutional roles and resources, information processes, and operational arrangements for specific actors at times of need. Based on scenarios of possible emergency conditions or disaster events, it allows key actors to envision, anticipate and solve problems that can arise during crises. Contingency planning is an important part of overall preparedness. Contingency plans need to be regularly updated and exercised.

Coordination: Involves assessing situations and needs, agreeing on common priorities, developing common strategies to address issues such as mobilizing funding and other resources, clarifying consistent public messaging, and monitoring progress. Humanitarian coordination involves bringing together humanitarian actors to ensure a coherent and principled response to emergencies. The aim is to assist people when they most need relief or protection. Humanitarian coordination seeks to improve the effectiveness of humanitarian response by ensuring greater predictability, accountability, and partnership.

Country-based Pooled Funds: Established by the UN Emergency Relief Coordinator when a new emergency occurs or when an existing humanitarian situation deteriorates. Contributions from donors are collected into single, unearmarked funds to support local humanitarian efforts.

Crisis: A serious disruption of the functioning of a community or a society involving widespread human, material, economic, or environmental losses and impacts that exceeds the ability of the affected community or society to cope using its own resources and therefore requires urgent action. Terms can refer to slow- and rapid-onset situations, rural and urban environments, and complex political emergencies in all countries. Related terms are "disaster", mostly referring to disasters associated with natural hazards, conflict, and emergency (see disaster).

Crisis-sensitive educational planning: Crisis-sensitive educational planning involves identifying and analyzing the risks to education posed by conflict and natural hazards. This means understanding (1) how these risks impact education systems and (2) how education systems can reduce their impact and occurrence.

D

Data: Information that can be analyzed or used to gain knowledge or make decisions; a set of values of qualitative or quantitative variables. Data can exist in a variety of forms - as numbers, words, sounds, or images.

Data collection: The process of gathering and measuring information on variables of interest in an established systematic fashion that enables one to answer stated research questions, test hypotheses, and evaluate outcomes.

Data responsibility: The safe, ethical, and effective management of personal and non-personal data for operational response, in accordance with established frameworks for personal data protection.

Decolonization: The active resistance against colonial powers, and a shifting of power towards political, economic, educational, cultural, psychic independence and power that originate from a colonized nation's own indigenous culture. This process occurs politically and also applies to personal and societal psychic, cultural, political, agricultural, and educational deconstruction of colonial oppression.

Decoloniality: A long-term process involving the bureaucratic, cultural, linguistic, and psychological divesting of colonial power.

Differentiated learning: An approach to teaching that involves offering several different learning experiences and proactively addressing students' varied needs to maximize learning opportunities for each student in the classroom. It requires teachers to be flexible in their approach and adjust the curriculum and presentation of information to learners of different abilities.

Disability: Disability is an evolving concept. It results from the interaction between persons with a physical, psychosocial or mental, developmental, or sensory impairment and barriers in the environment that hinder their full and effective participation in society on an equal basis with others.

Disability-inclusive education: Disability-inclusive education means ensuring that informational, environmental, physical, attitudinal, and financial barriers do not inhibit learners with disabilities from participating in education. Achieving quality disability-inclusive education in emergency and crisis-affected contexts depends on:

- Requiring all schools and facilities to meet minimum standards for accessibility, including in emergency settings
- Investing in teacher training that will equip all teachers to respond to diversity in the classroom and disability inclusion in particular

- Ensuring that teaching and learning materials/resources are available in accessible formats and are easily adaptable for specific types of disabilities
- Investing in assistive technology and devices for children with disabilities
- Ensuring the involvement of Organizations of Persons with Disabilities in education planning and monitoring

Disaggregated data: Statistical information that is separated into its component parts. For example, assessment data from a population or a sample can be analyzed by sex, age group, disability, and geographic area.

Disaster: see crisis.

Disaster risk management: The application of disaster risk reduction policies and strategies to prevent new disaster risk, reduce existing disaster risk, and manage residual risk, contributing to the strengthening of resilience and reduction of disaster losses.

Disaster risk reduction: The concept and practice of reducing risks through systematic efforts to analyze and manage the causal factors of disasters, including through reduced exposure to hazards, reduced vulnerability of people and property, wise management of land and the environment, and improved preparedness for adverse events.

Discrimination: Treating people differently leading to denial of access to facilities, services, opportunities, rights, or participation on the basis of gender, disability, nationality, race, religion, sexual orientation, age, ethnicity, HIV status, or other factors.

Distance education: An umbrella term encompassing a variety of education approaches that is applied when teachers and learners are separated by space and time, or both. Distance Education includes high-, low-, no-tech approaches and solutions; and formal and non-formal learning at multiple levels (pre-primary, primary, secondary, post-secondary, and all tertiary levels, including technical and vocational education and training). Terms like "distance learning," "online learning," "remote learning," and "e-learning," all of which identify technology-enabled education approaches that require digital devices and internet connectivity, are a critical subset of the wider distance education arena.

Distress: Refers to experiencing difficult emotions or feelings that are severe enough to affect day-to-day functioning and ability to participate in social interactions. Psychosocial distress can result in negative views of the environment, of others, and of the self. Sadness, anxiety, distraction, and disruption in relationships with others and some symptoms of mental illness are manifestations of psychological distress.

Diversity: The difference and/or variety in a group of people, in relation to ethnicity, ability/disability, gender, culture, religion, language, etc. Promoting diversity or diversity approaches necessitates responding positively to the differences between and within groups and taking a unified approach to tackling the causes and outcomes of discrimination.

Do no harm: An approach which helps to identify unintended negative or positive impacts of humanitarian and development interventions in settings where there is conflict or risk of conflict. It can be applied during planning, monitoring, and evaluation to ensure that the intervention does not worsen the conflict but rather contributes to improving it. Do no harm is considered an essential basis for the work of organizations operating in situations of conflict.

Duty bearer: Central to the idea of human rights is establishing and sustaining the relationship between the rights-holder (who has the right) and the duty bearer (who has the obligation to fulfill the right). A duty bearer is the person(s) or institution(s) which have obligations and responsibilities in relation to the realization of a right, such as the right to education. When a state has ratified a treaty that guarantees the right to education, it has the obligation to respect, protect, and fulfill this right. According to international law, other actors also have responsibilities in upholding the right to education: multilateral intergovernmental agencies in providing technical and financial assistance; international financial institutions in their policies, credit agreements, structural adjustment programs, and measures taken in response to the debt crisis; private businesses also have the responsibility to respect human rights and avoid infringing on the rights of others; civil society plays a crucial role in promoting the right to education and holding the State accountable for its obligations; and parents and caregivers have the responsibility to ensure that their children attend compulsory education.

E

Early childhood development: The processes through which young children, aged 0-8 years, develop their optimal physical health, mental alertness, emotional confidence, social competence, and readiness to learn. These processes are supported by social and financial policies and comprehensive programming that integrate health, nutrition, water, sanitation, hygiene, education, and child protection services. All children and families benefit from high-quality programs, but disadvantaged groups benefit the most.

Early childhood development in emergencies: A comprehensive approach that addresses the holistic needs and rights of children affected by all forms of emergencies and those of their families starting from preconception to age 8, including displaced children, children with disabilities, developmental delays, and other needs. It is a multi-sectoral, culturally relevant, and inclusive service and intervention that:

1. seeks to prevent and mitigate crises' negative effects
2. champions young children's holistic development by providing nurturing care, mental health and psychosocial support, and age and developmentally appropriate early learning, socialization, and play opportunities
3. supports parents, caregivers, and families in assuring protective, life-saving, accessible, and inclusive environments
4. recognizes primary caregivers as the first teachers and advocates in their children's lives - they possess the agency to support their children, provide responsive care, and advocate for their children's needs before, during, and after an emergency

Early warning system: An integrated system of hazard monitoring, forecasting and prediction, disaster risk assessment, communication, and preparedness activities systems and processes that enables individuals, communities, governments, businesses, and others to take timely action to reduce disaster risks in advance of hazardous events.

Education authorities: Governments with their associated ministries, departments, institutions, and agencies who are responsible for ensuring the right to education. They exercise authority over education provision at national, district, and local levels. In contexts where government authority is compromised, non-state actors, such as NGOs and UN agencies, can sometimes assume this responsibility.

Education Cluster: An inter-agency coordination mechanism for agencies and organizations with expertise and a mandate for humanitarian response within the education sector in situations of internal displacement. Established in 2007 through the IASC, the Education Cluster is led by UNICEF and Save the Children at the global level. At a country level, other agencies may lead and the national ministry of education is actively involved. UNHCR is the lead agency in refugee contexts. The Education Cluster is responsible for strengthening preparedness of technical capacity to respond to humanitarian emergencies. During humanitarian response, it should ensure predictable leadership and accountability in the education sector.

Education in emergencies: Quality learning opportunities for all ages in situations of crisis, including early childhood development, primary, secondary, non-formal, technical, vocational, higher, and adult education. EiE provides physical, psychosocial, and cognitive protection that can sustain and save lives.

Common situations of crisis in which education in emergencies is essential include conflicts, protracted crises, situations of violence, forced displacement, disasters, and public health emergencies. EiE is a wider concept than "emergency education response" which is an essential part of it.

Education management information system: A system for the collection, integration, processing, maintenance, and dissemination of data and information to support decision-making, policy-analysis and formulation, planning, monitoring, and management at all levels of an education system. It is a system of people, technology, models, methods, processes, procedures, rules, and regulations that function together to provide education leaders, decision-makers and managers at all levels with a comprehensive, integrated set of relevant, reliable, unambiguous, and timely data and information to support them in completion of their responsibilities.

Education policy: A set of ideas or values about what education as a social institution and set of practices should look like. This includes who is taught what and how, and how these practices are to be governed. The substance of education policy is the stated objectives and the actions taken to achieve those objectives. Education policy is also about the process of formulating policy and who participates, which influences the process of implementing policy.

Education response: The provision of education services to meet people's needs and rights to education during an emergency through to recovery.

Education sector plan: Outlines in detail the intended way to pursue the achievement of the goals, objectives, and targets for the education system. The plan is specific in terms of what to attain, by when, in what way, who is responsible, the resource inputs required, and the necessary resources to provide the required inputs and manage plan implementation. Different types of plans are designed by the time period covered and the degree of detail they contain, e.g. long-, medium-, and short-term plans.

Education system: Includes the full range of formal and nonformal learning opportunities available to children, young people, and adults in a given country or society—whether they are provided and/or financed by state or nonstate entities. An education system has several core policy domains that correspond to various system functions and together keep it running: primary and secondary schools, tertiary institutions, training institutes, and other private and nonformal learning programs, together with their teaching staff (e.g., teachers, trainers, and professors), nonacademic personnel, and administrators. An education system consists of all stakeholders who participate in the provision, financing, regulation, and use of learning services. Thus, in addition to national and local governments, participants include students and their families, communities, private providers, and nonstate organizations. This larger network of stakeholders makes up an education system in the broader sense.

Education technology: Any technology—including hardware, software, and digital content-designed or appropriated for (any) educational purpose. It may be a deliberately designed piece of educational software, such as an educational video platform, or a piece of technology designed for more general use but incorporated into the teaching and learning process, such as database software. The use of this technology may be at home, at an education institution, in an afterschool program, in a library, or at an informal learning center. Education technology may be used by teachers, school directors, or students.

Emergency: see crisis.

Enrollment: The official registration of individuals in a given formal or non-formal educational program, stage, or module thereof, regardless of age.

Environmental emergency: A sudden-onset disaster or accident resulting from natural, technological, or human-induced factors, or a combination of these, that cause or threaten to cause severe environmental damage as well as harm to human health and/or livelihoods. It includes emergencies caused by: water and wind (flood, tropical cyclone, windstorm, coastal erosion, tsunami, dam break, drought, water shortage, hailstorm, sandstorm, lightning); earth (earthquake, landslide, debris or mudflow, glacial lake outburst, volcanic eruption, avalanche; fire (wildfire, structural fire); or temperature (extreme cold, extreme heat).

Equality: A state of affairs or result whereby all members of a group enjoy the same inputs, outputs, or outcomes in terms of status, rights, and responsibilities.

Equity: Fairness and justice achieved through systematically assessing disparities in opportunities, outcomes, and representation and redressing those disparities through targeted actions.

Ethnicity: A social construct that divides people into smaller social groups based on characteristics such as shared sense of group membership, values, behavioral patterns, language, political and economic interests, history, and ancestral geographical base.

Evaluation: The comparison of actual intervention impacts against the agreed strategic plans. It looks at what the intervention set out to do (objectives), what has been accomplished (impacts), and how it was accomplished (processes). It can be used for an ongoing intervention or to draw lessons learned from a completed intervention.

In the context of teaching and learning, evaluation refers to the systematic process of judging learner performance, teaching instructions, and making evidence-informed decisions to enhance overall educational outcomes.

Evidence-based: Any concept or strategy that is derived from or informed by objective evidence; most commonly, educational research or metrics of school, teacher, and student performance. Among the most common applications are evidence-based decisions, evidence-based school improvement, and evidence-based instruction. While research and quantitative data are arguably the most common forms of evidence used in education and school reform, educators also use a wide variety of qualitative information to diagnose student learning needs or improve academic programming.

F

Facilities and services: A school's basic facilities and services include clean water, separate toilets, electricity, kitchen/canteen, telephone, and various other components, which are recorded and reported as data in the annual school census. Administrators at various levels of the education system can use this information to evaluate the environment and physical facilities of schools they oversee and then prioritize and plan the upgrade or improvement of facilities.

Feedback: The transmission of findings generated through the evaluation process to parties for whom it is relevant and useful to facilitate learning. This may involve the collection and dissemination of findings, conclusions, recommendations, and lessons from experience.

Forced displacement: Occurs when individuals and communities have been forced or obliged to flee or to leave their homes or places of habitual residence as a result of or in order to avoid the effects of events or situations such as armed conflict, generalized violence, human rights abuses, natural or man-made disasters, and/or development projects.

It includes situations where people have fled as well as situations where people have been forcibly removed from their homes, evicted, or relocated to another place not of their choosing, whether by state or non-state actors. The defining factor is the absence of will or consent.

Formal education: Education that is institutionalized, intentional, and planned through public organizations and recognized private bodies and – in their totality – constitute the formal education system of a country. Formal education programs are thus recognized as such by the relevant national education authorities or equivalent authorities, e.g., any other institution in cooperation with the national or sub-national education authorities. Vocational education, special needs education, and some parts of adult education are often recognized as being part of the formal education system.

Formal education is often organized in two tracks: traditional academic schooling, which includes education in literacy and language arts, numeracy and mathematics, social studies, science, physical education, and creative arts; and TVET, which involves skills-based training, work readiness, and employability skills.

Formal education programs are implemented and managed by national governments and lead to the accreditation of learning outcomes. Curricula are approved and teachers are recognized by the government.

G

Gender: The socially constructed roles, responsibilities, and identities for women, men, and gender diverse people and how these are valued in society. They are culture-specific and they change over time. Gender identities define how women and men are expected to think and act. These behaviors are learned from family, schools, religious teaching, and the media. Since gender roles, responsibilities, and identities are socially learned, they can also be changed.

Gender, together with age group, sexual orientation, gender identity and expression, and sexual characteristics, determines roles, responsibilities, power dynamics, and access to resources. This is also affected by other diversity factors such as disability, social class, race, caste, ethnic or religious background, economic wealth, marital status, migrant status, displacement situation, and urban or rural setting. Gender is different from sex, which refers to the physical and biological characteristics that distinguish females, males, and intersex individuals. Sex refers to a person's anatomy and physical attributes, such as external and internal reproductive sex organs.

Gender parity: An equal number of women and girls, men and boys in a given area, such as accessing education, in the workplace, or holding public office. Analyzing gender parity in education means comparing the participation of female and male learners in education. This can be analyzed in regard to a wide range of indicators and at each education level, including early childhood development programs, primary, secondary, tertiary, and non-formal education programs, as well as among teachers and other education personnel. While gender parity is important to ensure that the needs and interests of all genders are taken into account, parity does not necessarily translate to equal opportunities, participation, or outcomes.

Gender-responsive: Addressing the different situations, roles, needs, and interests of women, men, girls, and boys in the design and implementation of activities, policies, and programs. A program, policy, or activity that is gender-responsive addresses gender-based barriers, respects gender differences, enables structures, systems, and methodologies to be sensitive to gender, ensures gender parity is a wider strategy to advance gender equality, and evolves to close gaps and eradicate gender-based discrimination.

Gender transformative education: Gender transformative education moves beyond simply improving access to education for girls and women towards equipping and empowering stakeholders – students, teachers, communities, and pollicy-makers – to examine, challenge, and change harmful gender norms and imbalances of power that advantage boys and men over girls, women, and persons of other genders.

Gender-based violence: An umbrella term for any harmful act that is perpetrated against a person's will and that is based on socially ascribed (i.e. gender) differences between males and females. It includes acts that inflict physical, sexual, or mental harm or suffering, threats of such acts, coercion, and other deprivations of liberty. These acts can occur in public or in private. In many contexts, women, girls, and gender diverse people are at a higher risk because of their lower status in society, but men and boys may also experience gender-based violence. Examples of gender-based violence include:

- Sexual violence, including exploitation, abuse, and harassment
- Forced and early marriage
- Domestic and family violence, which may be physical, emotional, psychological, or sexual
- Harmful cultural and traditional practices, such as female genital mutilation/cutting, honor killings, and widow inheritance
- Denial of resources or opportunities, such as education

H

Hazard: A potentially damaging physical event, phenomenon, or human activity that may cause loss of life or injury, property damage, social and economic disruption, or environmental degradation. Hazards can have natural or human-made origins or a combination of these. The risk posed by a hazard depends on how likely it is, and where, how often, and with what intensity it takes place. For example, a small earthquake in a desert region that occurs once in 100 years poses a very low risk for people. An urban flood that occurs to a height of 3 meters within 48 hours once every 5 –10 years has a relatively high probability and requires mitigation measures.

Health emergency: An occurrence or imminent threat of an illness or health condition, caused by bioterrorism, epidemic (ex: gastrointestinal, malaria, Dengue, Zika) or pandemic disease (ex: flu, Avian Flu, Ebola), or (a) novel and highly fatal infectious agent or biological toxin, that poses a substantial risk of a significant number of human facilities or incidents or permanent or long-term disability. The declaration of a state of public health emergency permits the governing authorities to suspend state regulations and change the functions of state agencies.

Hidden curriculum: The way policymakers, school administrators, teachers, and learners interact with each other (and the community) teaches them the values and the existence of power structures and relationships. Hidden curriculum is closely linked to social norms and collective behavior and must be taken into account in any teaching and learning effort attempting to influence attitudes and behaviors. Hidden curriculum is what is taught outside the prescribed curriculum. It goes beyond the specific content of the subject matter, and can be expressed in the school environment, in the classroom climate and its furniture arrangement, in the pedagogical methods, in teacher student interactions, in the student-student interactions, and in many other invisible dynamics. Sometimes the hidden curriculum reinforces the prescribed curriculum, sometimes it contradicts it. For instance, the prescribed curriculum may promote a better understanding and value of democracy, but if the teacher (or the school climate) is highly authoritarian, the democratic lesson may become distorted.

Host community: A community that hosts large populations of refugees or internally displaced persons, whether in camps, integrated into households, or independently.

Higher Education: Encompasses all types of education (academic, professional, technical, artistic, pedagogical, distance education, etc.) provided by universities, technological institutes, teacher training colleges, etc., which are normally intended for students having completed a secondary education, and whose education objective is the acquisition of a title, a grade, certificate, or diploma of higher education.

Higher education is sometimes also referred to as tertiary education. However, there is a conceptual distinction. Tertiary education is an umbrella that encompasses all post-secondary education (see *tertiary education*). Therefore, within international human rights law, the term tertiary education is generally not used. Rather, the instruments refer to technical and vocational education and training and higher education. (See also *technical and vocational education and training*).

Human rights: A means to a life in dignity. Human rights are universal and inalienable: they cannot be given, nor taken away. In an emergency context, key human rights, such as non-discrimination, protection, and the right to life, take immediate priority, while the progressive realization of other rights may rely on available resources. As education is instrumental to protection, non-discrimination, and survival, it must be seen as a key human right. International human rights law is the body of international legal treaties and normative standards that govern states' obligations to respect, protect, and fulfill human rights at all times, including during emergencies. During conflict, international humanitarian law also applies. International humanitarian law is a set of rules that seek to limit the effects of armed conflict. It protects people who are not or are no longer participating in hostilities and restricts the means and methods of warfare, and place duties on both state parties to armed conflict, and non-state armed groups who are parties to armed conflict. International criminal law criminalizes serious violations of international humanitarian law (i.e., war crimes) and applies in situations outside of armed conflict, for example where it is established crimes against humanity or genocide have occured.

Human rights education: Promotes values, beliefs, and attitudes that encourage all individuals to uphold their own rights and those of others. It develops an understanding of everyone's common responsibility to make human rights a reality in each community.

Humanitarian action: The objectives of humanitarian action are to save lives, alleviate suffering, and maintain human dignity during and in the aftermath of human-made crises and disasters, as well as to prevent and strengthen preparedness for the occurrence of such situations. Humanitarian action has two inextricably linked dimensions: protecting people and providing assistance. It is rooted in humanitarian principles – humanity, impartiality, neutrality, and independence (see Humanitarian response).

Humanitarian actors: A wide range of authorities, communities, organizations, agencies, and inter-agency networks that all combine to enable humanitarian assistance to be channeled to the places and people in need of it. This includes UN agencies, the International Red Cross/Red Crescent Movement, local, national, and international non-governmental organizations (NGOs), local government institutions, and donor agencies. The actions of these organizations are guided by key humanitarian principles: humanity, impartiality, independence, and neutrality.

Humanitarian program cycle: A coordinated series of actions undertaken to help prepare for, manage, and deliver humanitarian response. It consists of five elements coordinated in a seamless manner, with one step logically building on the previous and leading to the next: 1) needs assessment and analysis, 2) strategic response planning, 3) resource mobilization, 4) implementation and monitoring, and 5) operational review and evaluation. Successful implementation of the humanitarian program cycle is dependent on effective emergency preparedness, effective coordination with national/local authorities and humanitarian actors, and information management.

Humanitarian response: One dimension of humanitarian action. It focuses on the provision of services and public assistance during or immediately after a specific emergency in order to save lives, reduce health impacts, ensure public safety, maintain human dignity, and meet the basic subsistence needs of the people affected. It should be governed by the key humanitarian principles.

Humanitarian-development coherence: A broad and complex topic that relates to many aspects of education, from policy and coordination to planning, financing, and programming. Coherence describes linkages between the two types of international assistance (humanitarian and development) in order to achieve more cost-effective, sustainable results for crisis-affected countries and populations. "Coherence" is an umbrella term that includes the humanitarian-development nexus, which refers more specifically to the meeting point of humanitarian and development approaches, and the triple nexus, which includes a peace-building dimension.

Humanitarian-development-peacebuilding nexus: Also referred to as "nexus," "HDP Nexus," "HDPN," and "Triple Nexus." Humanitarian-development-peacebuilding nexus is the term used to capture the interlinkages between the humanitarian, development and peace sectors. It specifically refers to attempts in these fields to work together to meet peoples' needs more effectively, mitigate risks and vulnerabilities, and move toward sustainable peace. This approach calls for a New Way of Working that transcends the humanitarian-development-peace divide, reinforces (not replaces) national and local systems, and anticipates crises by working toward (1) collective outcomes (2) over multi-year timeframes (3) based on leveraging comparative advantage.

Hybrid learning: An educational approach where some individuals participate in person, and some participate online. Instructors and facilitators teach remote and in-person learners at the same time using technology like video conferencing. With hybrid learning, the in-person learners and the online learners are different individuals.

I

Impairment: A personal characteristic that limits an individual's functional capacity. It can be temporary or permanent. An impairment can be developmental, physical, sensory, psychosocial or mental, or other.

Inclusion: Emphasizes equitable access and participation and responds positively to the individual needs and competencies of all people. Inclusive approaches work across all sectors and the wider community to ensure that every person, irrespective of gender, language, ability, religion, nationality, or other characteristics, is supported to meaningfully participate alongside their peers. Inclusive teaching fosters a classroom culture of inclusion.

Inclusion in national systems: In a refugee context, inclusion also refers to a gradual approach to ensure refugees and other people have access to national systems and services in law and practice and without discrimination, in accordance with international norms and standards.

Inclusive education: A process that protects the presence, participation, and achievement of all individuals in equitable learning opportunities. It ensures that education policies, practices, and facilities respect the diversity of all individuals in the classroom context. Exclusion from education can result from discrimination, or from a lack of support to remove barriers and avoid the use of languages, content, or teaching methods that do not benefit all learners. Persons with physical, sensory, psychosocial/ mental, and developmental disabilities are often among the most excluded from education. Inclusive education acknowledges that all individuals can learn and that everyone has unique characteristics, interests, abilities, and learning needs. Therefore, inclusive education means ensuring that the barriers to participation and learning are removed and that curricula, and teaching and learning materials are adapted, made accessible, and appropriate for all learners, in all their diversity to reach their full potential.

In relevant contexts, it can also be referred to as "inclusive education in emergencies."

Information management: Comprises assessment of needs, capacities, and coverage and the associated monitoring and evaluation, data storage, data analysis, and systems for sharing information. Information management tools and systems should help stakeholders decide which facts and data to collect, process, and share with whom, when, for what purpose, and how.

Information sharing protocol: A system-wide ISP serves as the primary document of reference governing data and information sharing in a response. It includes a context-specific Data and Information Sensitivity Classification outlining the sensitivity and related disclosure protocol for key data types.

Integration: The two-way process of mutual adaptation between migrants and the societies in which they live, whereby migrants are incorporated into the social, economic, cultural, and political life of the receiving community. It entails a set of joint responsibilities for migrants and communities and incorporates other related notions, such as social inclusion and social cohesion.

Note: Integration does not necessarily imply permanent residence. It does, however, imply consideration of the rights and obligations of migrants and societies of the countries of transit or destination, of access to different kinds of services and the labor market, and of identification and respect for a core set of values that bind migrants and receiving communities in a common purpose.

Integration also refers to the provision of education services for children and adolescents with disabilities in the same school but in separate classrooms, or in the same classrooms on the condition that the learner with disability adapts to and complies with the same school norms, standards, and requirements as their peers.

Inter-agency Standing Committee: An inter-agency forum for coordination, policy development, and decision-making within humanitarian assistance. The IASC was established in June 1992 in response to a UN General Assembly Resolution on the strengthening of humanitarian assistance. The IASC involves both key UN and non-UN humanitarian partners.

Inter-sectoral linkages: The interaction between two or more sectors, such as education, health, food security, nutrition, shelter, and protection. In the context of the education sector, these linkages are normally actions taken in partnership with other sectors outside the education sector. Examples are MHPSS in education (with child protection), the planning of a school in an IDP camp (with Camp Coordination and Camp Management), etc.

Internally displaced person: A person who has been forced to leave their home area to find a safe place inside his or her home country, rather than crossing an international border. IDPs often flee for similar reasons as refugees, such as armed conflict, disasters, generalized violence, or human rights violations. However, legally they remain under the protection of their own government, even though that government might be the cause of their flight. As citizens, they retain their rights, including protection, under both human rights law and international humanitarian law.

Institutional racism: The way that institutional policies and practices disadvantage different racial groups.

Intersectionality: Intersectionality recognizes that the many elements of individual identity such as disability, gender, ethnicity, race, age, language, class or caste, citizenship status, or religion, are not static or one-dimensional characteristics. They are dynamic and complex. They overlap and interact in ways that affect how individuals or groups may experience marginalization or exclusion from education.

K

Key informant: People with specific knowledge about certain aspects of the community, the site visited, the population, or the emergency, either because of their professional background, leadership responsibilities, or particular personal experience.

L

Learners: People, including children, young people, and adults, who participate in education programs. This includes students in formal schools, children in early learning opportunities or ECD programs, learners in higher education institutions, trainees in technical and vocational education and training programs, and participants in non-formal education, such as accelerated education, literacy and numeracy classes, social and emotional skills courses in the community, and peer-to-peer learning.

Learning environment: The diverse physical locations, contexts, and cultures in which students learn, such as outdoor environments, private homes, child care centers, pre-schools, temporary structures, and schools. The term also encompasses the culture of a school or class - its presiding ethos and characteristics, including how individuals interact with and treat one another - as well as the ways in which teachers may organize an educational setting to facilitate learning, for example, by conducting classes in relevant natural ecosystems, grouping desks in specific ways, decorating the walls with learning materials, or utilizing audio, visual, and digital technologies. School policies, governance structures, and other features may also be considered elements of a learning environment.

Learning outcomes: The knowledge, attitudes, skills, and abilities that students have attained as a result of taking part in a course or education program. Learning outcomes are usually described as what students should know and be able to do as a result of teaching and learning processes.

Learning sites: The location of learning environments.

Life-saving educational messages: Imparting information to strengthen critical survival skills and coping mechanisms. Examples include: information on how to avoid landmines, how to protect oneself from sexual abuse, how to avoid HIV infection, and how to access health care and food.

Literacy: The ability to identify, understand, interpret, create, communicate, and compute, using printed and written materials associated with varying contexts. Literacy involves a continuum of learning in enabling individuals to achieve their goals, develop their knowledge and potential, and participate fully in their community and wider society.

Livelihood: The capabilities, assets, opportunities, and activities required for a means of living. Assets include financial, natural, physical, social, and human resources. Examples include stores, land, and access to markets or transport systems. A livelihood is sustainable when it can cope with and recover from stress and shocks, maintain or enhance its capabilities and assets, and provide sustainable livelihood opportunities for the next generation.

Local and indigenous knowledge systems: The understandings, skills, and philosophies developed by societies with long histories of interaction with their natural surroundings. For rural and Indigenous peoples, local knowledge informs decision-making about fundamental aspects of day-to-day life. This knowledge is integral to a cultural complex that also encompasses language, systems of classification, resource use practices, social interactions, rituals, and spirituality. These unique ways of knowing are important components of the world's cultural diversity and contribute to the achievement of Agenda 2030 and the Paris Agreement.

Local and national actors: Local and national actors are of two types:

1. Local and national non-state actors are organizations engaged in relief that are headquartered and operating in their own aid recipient country and which are not affiliated to an international NGO. A local actor is not considered to be affiliated merely because it is part of a network, confederation, or alliance wherein it maintains independent fundraising and governance systems. Local and national non-state actors include:
   - National NGOs/civil society organizations (CSOs);
   - Local NGOs/CSOs;
   - Red Cross/Red Crescent National Societies;
   - Local and national private sector organizations

2. National and sub-national state actors are state authorities of the affected aid recipient country engaged in relief, whether at the local or national level. This includes national and local governments.

Localization: A process of recognizing, respecting, and strengthening the independence of leadership and decision-making by local and national actors in humanitarian action in order to better address the needs of people affected by crises.

Locally led humanitarian action: see *localization*.

M

Marginalization: A form of acute and persistent disadvantage rooted in various factors, including discrimination, prejudice, unequal power dynamics, and systemic inequalities.

Marginalized groups: Groups in any given culture or context where they are at risk of being excluded and discriminated against because of their personal and group characteristics. Such groups may encounter barriers that limit their access to resources, opportunities, and decision-making processes.

Mental health: A state of mental wellbeing that enables people to cope with the stresses of life, realize their abilities, learn well and work well, and contribute to their community. Mental health is more than the absence of mental disorders. It exists on a complex continuum, which is experienced differently from one person to the next, with varying degrees of difficulty and distress and potentially very different social and clinical outcomes.

Mental health conditions include mental disorders and psychosocial disabilities as well as other mental states associated with significant distress, impairment in functioning, or risk of self-harm.

Mental health and psychosocial support: MHPSS is a composite term used across different sectors and aims to help individuals recover after a crisis has disrupted their lives and to enhance their ability to return to normality after experiencing adverse events. MHPSS can be both local or outside support that is:

- Promotive – promotes wellbeing
- Preventative – decreases the risk of mental health problems
- Curative – helps overcome psychosocial/mental health problems. *The term "curative" should be used with caution as it is suggestive of a medical term. MHPSS is a "support," not a "cure."

Monitoring: The ongoing process by which stakeholders obtain regular feedback on the progress being made towards achieving their goals and objectives. In the more limited approach, monitoring may focus on tracking projects and the use of the agency's resources. In the broader approach, monitoring also involves tracking strategies and actions being taken by partners and non-partners, and figuring out what new strategies and actions need to be taken to ensure progress towards the most important results.

N

Natural hazard: A natural process or phenomenon that may cause loss of life, injury, or other health impacts; property damage, and loss of livelihoods and services; social and economic disruption; or environmental damage.

Needs assessment: An investigation carried out before planning educational activities and intervening in an emergency to determine needs, gaps in the response, and available resources. Assessment tools should always be adapted to reflect information needed in a specific context or environment.

Non-state actors: A broad, catch-all term describing individuals and organizations involved not only in education provision, but also in education financing and influencing the state's direction in its obligation to fulfill the right to education. This term can be in reference to:

- Individuals who benefit from and/or pay for education, provide education, and express views on its content, modality, and delivery
- Private corporations
- Philanthropic foundations
- Non-governmental, civil society, trade union and faith-based organizations, and others

Non-formal education: The overarching term that refers to planned, structured, and organized education programming that is outside the formal education system. Some types of NFE lead to equivalent certified competencies, while others do not. NFE programs are characterized by their variety, flexibility, and ability to respond quickly to the new educational needs of learners in a given context, as well as their holistic, learner-centered pedagogy.

O

Organizations of Persons with Disabilities: Organizations and associations that are led, directed, and governed by persons with disabilities; that are committed to the Convention on the Rights of Persons with Disabilities (CRPD); and that fully respect the principles and rights affirmed therein. They also include organizations for the families and relatives of persons with disabilities, which represent groups that in some contexts may not have the legal capacity to form organizations, such as children (i.e., minors) with disabilities and individuals with intellectual disabilities. Some OPDs represent persons with all types of impairments, while others focus on a particular impairment, gender, or sectoral issue. They may represent people in a particular geographic area or those who belong to an international or national network. While OPDs can be direct responders, they also play a critical role in representing the perspectives and priorities of crisis-affected persons with disabilities throughout the humanitarian program cycle. In order to achieve an effective locally led response, their role must be recognized and supported.

Out-of-school children and young people: Children in the official primary school age range who are not enrolled in either primary or secondary schools are known as out-of-school children. Children and young people not enrolled in any formal or non formal education program.

P

Participation: Participation refers to a person's involvement in and influence of processes, decisions, and activities. It is a right extended to all and is the basis for working with communities and developing education programs. No group of people should be denied the opportunity to participate because they are hard to reach or difficult to work with. That said, participation is also voluntary, and people should be invited and encouraged to participate, rather than coerced or manipulated.

Participation in education may include a range of activities and approaches, starting with the removal of barriers to create a safe and inclusive environment for all learners so that their needs are met and that no child is left behind. It also means ensuring that all learners have the resources and support they need to actively engage with, analyze, or represent learning content, and to express themselves in an education setting. Active, meaningful participation in education also presumes that all learners' voices are heard and considered.

Participatory learning: An approach to teaching and learning which focuses on the learner. It encourages learning by doing things, using small groups, concrete materials, open questioning, and peer teaching. For example, learners use practical activities to understand mathematical concepts or work together to solve problems and ask and answer questions. Participatory learning is contrasted with teacher-focused methodologies, which are characterized by learners passively sitting at desks, answering closed questions, and copying from a blackboard. Participatory learning may also be used with teachers and education authorities to support them to analyze their needs, identify solutions, and develop and implement a plan of action. In these contexts, it may include community participation, coordination, and analysis.

Peacebuilding: Measures designed to 1) promote peaceful relations; 2) strengthen viable political, socio-economic, and cultural institutions capable of handling conflict; and 3) strengthen other mechanisms that will create or support the necessary conditions for sustained peace. Activities that aim explicitly to address the root causes of conflict and contribute to peace at large with the aim to work on conflict, seeking to reduce drivers of violent conflict and to contribute to the broader societal level peace.

Pedagogy: The strategies or styles of teaching and learning processes; the study of being a teacher. Pedagogy is the observable act of teaching and modeling values and attitudes that embodies educational theories, values, evidence, and justifications. For example, a child-friendly pedagogy using a rights-based curriculum aims at fostering not only core competencies but citizenship, non-discrimination, peace, and a participatory and enabling environment for learners to voice their own ideas and learn to listen to and respect different views.

Play: A spontaneous, voluntary, pleasurable, and flexible activity involving a combination of body, object, symbol use, and relationships. In contrast to games, play behavior is more disorganized, and is typically done for its own sake, i.e. the process is more important than any goals or endpoints. Recognized as a universal phenomenon, play is a legitimate right of childhood, as recognized by the United Nations Convention on the Rights of the Child. Play helps children develop pre-literacy skills, problem-solving skills, and concentration, while also generating social learning experiences and helping children to express possible stresses and problems.

Positive discipline: A long-term perspective on developing positive attitudes and behavior shared by both children and adults, notably teachers. It includes the development of self-discipline and mutual respect. Often initiated (or introduced through teacher training) in response to punitive discipline that instills fear and relies on physical or humiliating punishment. Strong school-community partnerships are needed to enable a real and sustained shift toward positive discipline.

Post-secondary education: see tertiary education.

Power: The ability to influence others and impose one's beliefs. All power is relational, and the different relationships either reinforce or disrupt one another. Power is not only an individual relationship but a cultural one, and power relationships are shifting constantly. Power can be used malignantly and intentionally, but need not be, and individuals within a culture may benefit from power of which they are unaware.

Wealth, race, citizenship, patriarchy, heterosexism, and education are a few key social mechanisms through which power operates. Although power is often conceptualized as power over other individuals or groups, other variations are power with (used in the context of building collective strength) and power within (which references an individual's internal strength).

Preparedness: Activities and measures taken in advance of a crisis to ensure an effective response to the impact of hazards, including issuing timely and effective early warnings and the temporary evacuation of people and property from threatened locations.

Prevention: Actions taken to avoid the adverse impacts of hazards and related disasters.

Primary data: Any data that is collected directly from its original source for the objective in question.

Professional development: A wide variety of specialized training, formal education, or advanced professional learning intended to help administrators, teachers, and other educators improve their professional knowledge, competence, skill, and effectiveness. In practice, professional development for educators encompasses an extremely broad range of topics and formats.

Protection: All activities aimed at ensuring the full and equal respect for the rights of all individuals, regardless of age, sex, gender, ethnicity, social or political affiliation, religious beliefs, or other status. It goes beyond the immediate life-saving activities that are often the focus during an emergency. Protection is in accordance with the letter and spirit of the relevant bodies of law, namely human rights law, international humanitarian law, and refugee law.

Protracted crisis: Protracted crisis situations are characterized by recurrent natural disasters and/or conflict, longevity of food crises, breakdown of livelihoods, and insufficient institutional capacity to react to the crises.

Psychosocial: The interaction between social aspects (such as interpersonal relationships, social connections, social norms, social roles, community life, and religious life) and psychological aspects (such as emotions, thoughts, behaviors, knowledge, and coping strategies) that contribute to overall wellbeing.

Psychosocial disabilities: Persons with psychosocial disabilities include those who have what is known in medical terms as "mental health conditions" and who face significant barriers to participating in society on an equal basis with others.

Q

Qualitative data: The attributes or properties that an object possesses, often in an effort to answer why or how. The properties are categorized into classes that may be assigned numeric values for analysis.

Quality education: Understanding of what "quality" means may vary between contexts, and different actors may have their own definitions. Broadly, quality education encompasses seven characteristics.

1. Rights-based: Quality education is accessible, equitable, protective, participatory, non-discriminatory, and inclusive of all people.
2. Contextualized and relevant: Education systems address the needs of the learners by using culturally and linguistically relevant learning materials.
3. Holistic development of learners: Quality education promotes cognitive development, social and emotional skills, mental health and psychosocial wellbeing, values of responsible citizenship, economic sustainability, and peacebuilding.
4. Teaching and learning: Teachers receive adequate compensation and relevant training so that they understand pedagogic content and have the knowledge and skills they need to support learners' holistic development.
5. Enabling resources: Quality education includes adequate and relevant resources for teaching and learning and fosters links between the resources available in the learning environment, home, and community to improve holistic learning outcomes.
6. Learning outcomes: Quality education allows learners to develop the necessary knowledge, skills, and competencies to meet certification requirements, progress through the education system, and access lifelong learning opportunities.
7. Learning continuity: Quality education provides sustained learning opportunities across the humanitarian-development-peacebuilding nexus.

Quantitative data: Expresses a certain quantity, amount, or range, often in an effort to answer how many or how often. Usually, there are measurement units associated with the data, such as meters, in the case of the height of a person.

R

Race: A social construct produced by the dominant group in society to exert power over different groups.

Racism: A power construct and a form of discrimination that is particularly complex and difficult to prove due to the evolving nature of prejudiced attitudes and discriminatory behavior in global minority countries. It manifests itself overtly and covertly, with structural racism occurring through subtle and subversive forms of differential treatment.

Rapid response mechanism: Operational, programmatic, and partnership models designed to increase the available capacity of humanitarian actors to respond to the needs of vulnerable populations quickly and efficiently. They establish assessment and response tools, response thresholds, pre-position supplies, and train response teams. Rapid response mechanisms are generally multi-sectoral and are often used by coordination mechanisms to provide a rapid injection of resources when necessary.

Recovery: The restoration and improvement of facilities, livelihoods, living conditions, or psychosocial well-being of affected communities, including efforts to reduce disaster risk factors.

Referral: The process of directing a child, young person, or family to another service provider because the assistance required is beyond the expertise or scope of work of the current service provider.

Refugee: According to the 1951 Refugee Convention, a refugee is someone who "owing to a well-founded fear of being persecuted for reasons of race, religion, nationality, membership of a particular social group or political opinion, is outside the country of their nationality, and is unable to, or owing to such fear, is unwilling to avail themselves of the protection of that country."

Relevant education: Learning opportunities that are appropriate for learners. Relevant education takes into account local traditions and institutions, positive cultural practices, belief systems, and the needs of the community. It prepares children for a positive future in society in the national and international context. Relevant education is an element of quality education and refers to what is learned, how it is learned, and how effective the learning is.

Remedial program: An additional targeted support, concurrent with regular classes, for students who require short-term content or skill support to succeed in regular formal programming.

Remote learning: A term that developed during COVID-19 school closures, remote learning is emergency and temporary distance learning. In countries with good internet infrastructure, remote learning essentially equaled online learning. In many others, it meant distance-based technologies, such as radio, TV, and phone-based support, with and without online learning.

Resilience: The capacity of a system, community, or individual potentially exposed to hazards to adapt. This adaptation means resisting or changing to reach and maintain an acceptable level of functioning and structure. Resilience depends on coping mechanisms and life skills such as problem-solving, the ability to seek support, motivation, optimism, faith, perseverance, and resourcefulness. Resilience occurs when protective factors that support wellbeing are stronger than risk factors that cause harm.

Resource mobilization: The process by which donors and sometimes the public are approached to request resources to respond to an emergency or other situation. Communication to this end is based on needs analysis and strategic planning processes and documents.

Right to education: International human rights law guarantees the right to education. The Universal Declaration on Human Rights, adopted in 1948, proclaims in its article 26: "everyone has the right to education." Since then, the right to education has been widely recognized and developed by a number of international normative instruments elaborated by the United Nations, including the International Covenant on Economic, Social and Cultural Rights, the Convention on the Rights of the Child, and the UNESCO Convention against Discrimination in Education. It has been reaffirmed in other treaties covering specific groups (women and girls, persons with disabilities, migrants, refugees, indigenous people, etc.) or contexts (education during armed conflicts). The 1951 Convention on the Status of Refugees, for example, guarantees a refugee's right to education as do various instruments on behalf of internally displaced persons (the Kampala Convention and the Cartagena Agreement). The right to education has been incorporated into various regional treaties and enshrined as a right in the vast majority of national constitutions.

Risk: The product of external threats such as natural hazards, HIV prevalence, gender-based violence, or armed attack and abduction, combined with individual vulnerabilities such as poverty, physical or mental disability, or membership in a vulnerable group.

Risk assessment: A methodology to determine the nature and extent of risk by analyzing potential hazards and evaluating existing conditions of vulnerability that could pose a potential threat or harm to people, property, livelihoods, and the environment on which they depend.

S

Safety: Freedom from physical or psychosocial harm.

School health services: Services provided by a health worker to students enrolled in primary or secondary education, either within school premises or in a health service situated outside the school.

School-related gender-based violence: Explicit acts or threats of physical, emotional, and sexual violence occurring in and around schools perpetrated as a result of unequal gender norms and power dynamics. It includes bullying, corporal punishment, verbal or sexual harassment, nonconsensual touching, sexual coercion, assault, and rape. Male and female teachers and students can be both victims and perpetrators.

Secondary data: Data collected by someone other than the user.

Secondary education: A program of two stages: lower and upper secondary. Lower secondary education is generally designed to continue the basic programs of the primary level, but the teaching is typically more subject-focused, requiring more specialized teachers for each subject area. The end of this level often coincides with the end of compulsory education. In upper secondary education, the final stage of secondary education in most countries, instruction is often organized even more along subject lines and teachers typically need a higher or more subject-specific qualification than at lower secondary.

Security: Protection from threat, danger, injury, or loss.

Sexual and reproductive health: Addresses the reproductive processes, functions, and systems at all stages of life, and is aimed at enabling men and women to have responsible, satisfying, and safe sex lives, as well as the capacity and freedom to plan if, when, and how often to have children.

Sexual exploitation and abuse: Forms of gender-based violence that have been widely reported in humanitarian situations. While sexual exploitation and abuse can be perpetuated by anyone, the term has been used in reference to sexual exploitation and abuse perpetrated by personnel of humanitarian organizations, including both civilian staff and uniformed peacekeeping personnel.

Shock: Sudden and potentially damaging hazard or other phenomenon, or moment at which a slow-onset process (a stress) passes its "tipping point" and becomes an extreme event.

Slow-onset disaster: A disaster that evolves gradually from incremental changes occurring over many years or from an increased frequency or intensity of recurring events. Slow-onset disasters relate to environmental degradation processes such as droughts and desertification, increased salinization, rising sea levels, or thawing of permafrost.

Social and emotional learning: The process through which individuals learn and apply a set of social, emotional, cognitive, and related skills, attitudes, behaviors, and values that help direct their thoughts, feelings, and actions in ways that enable them to succeed in school, work, and life. SEL has been defined in a variety of ways. The broad term has served as an umbrella for many sub-fields of psychology and human development, each with a particular focus (e.g., academic achievement, global citizenship) and has led to many types of community programs and educational interventions (e.g., bullying prevention, character education, peace education, life skills, social skills training, workforce development, 21st-century skills).

Social and emotional skills: Also known as transferable skills, 21st-century skills, soft skills, or life skills allow young people to become agile, adaptive learners and citizens equipped to navigate personal, academic, social, and economic challenges. Social and emotional skills include problem-solving, negotiation, managing emotions, empathy, and communication, among others.

Stakeholder: A person, group, or organization with interests in the decision-making and activities of a business, organization, or project. Stakeholders can be members of the organization they are interested in, or they can have no official affiliation. Stakeholders can have a direct or indirect influence on the activities or projects of an organization.

Stateless person: A person who is not considered as a national by any State under the operation of its law. In simple terms, this means that a stateless person does not have a nationality of any country. Some people are born stateless, but others become stateless.

Stress: A longer-term trend that undermines the potential of a given system and increases the vulnerability of actors within it.

Structural racism: A system in which public policies, institutional practices, cultural representations, and other norms work in various, often reinforcing ways to perpetuate racial group inequity. Structural racism identifies dimensions of our history and culture that have allowed privileges and disadvantages associated with different races to endure and evolve. Structural racism is not something that a few people or institutions choose to practice. Rather, it is a feature of the social, economic, and political systems in which we all exist.

Student or learner-centered learning: Student-centered learning is a synonym for a wide variety of educational strategies generally known as personalized learning or personalization (among many other possible terms). Educational decisions are made by considering what students need to know or what methods would be most effective in facilitating learning for individual students or groups of students. Student-centered learning typically refers to a proposed alternative to existing or more traditional approaches to schooling that some educators would view as being either teacher-centered or school-centered.

Student-teacher ratio: The average number of students per teacher at a given level of education, based on headcounts of both students and teachers.

Sudden-onset disaster: A disaster triggered by a hazardous event that emerges quickly or unexpectedly. Sudden-onset disasters may be climate-related (e.g., floods, cyclones, tornadoes, landslides, earthquakes, tsunamis, wildfires, or volcanic eruptions) or not (e.g., chemical explosion or critical infrastructure failure). Depending on their severity and the affected community's vulnerabilities and adaptive capacity, they may also result in temporary (or sometimes protracted) displacement.

Systems strengthening: To strengthen an education system means to align its governance, management, financing, and performance incentive mechanisms to produce learning for all. It means, first of all, recognizing the many providers, consumers, and stakeholders in education and the roles that these participants have in the system. Accountability relationships among them should be clear, coordinated, and consistent with their assigned functions in support of national education goals. Performance and learning outcomes should be monitored and measured so that a robust feedback cycle linking policy, financing, and results is established. Systems strengthening should be informed by an analysis of the political economy which considers the relationship between structures, institutions, and agents that influence education within a given context.

T

Teacher wellbeing: Encompasses how teachers feel and function in their jobs. It is context-specific and includes teachers' affections, attitudes, and evaluations of their work (see *wellbeing*).

Teachers and other education personnel: The term "teacher" generally refers to someone directly responsible for the learning of children, young people, and adults. They may be:

- Classroom teachers
- Early childhood or pre-school teachers
- Higher education faculty
- Special education teachers
- Subject specialists and vocational trainers
- Religious educators
- Head teachers
- Volunteers from the community

"Education personnel" refers to pedagogical, administrative, and support personnel involved in planning, delivering, monitoring, evaluating, and quality assurance of education and teaching practices at all levels. This includes school principals, ECD and tertiary personnel, deputies, advisors, supervisors, counselors, mentors, paraprofessionals, and classroom specialists and assistants, including those who support the learning of persons with disabilities. Many of these personnel will have been teachers.

Teaching and learning: There are diverse approaches to teaching which also implicitly reflect the approach to learning. The didactic approach mainly entails lecturing and is typically teacher-centered and content-oriented, i.e. teaching as transmission where the learners are considered to be the passive recipients of information transmitted. Teaching can also be seen as supporting the process of learners' knowledge construction and understanding, building on what is already known by the learner and involving a learner-centered approach, i.e. teaching as facilitation. Another approach emphasizes the development of learners' cognitive processes and awareness and control of thinking and learning.

Technical and vocational education and training: Designed mainly to provide learners with the practical skills, know-how, and understanding necessary for direct entry into a particular occupation or trade (or class of occupations or trades). Successful completion of such programs normally leads to a labor market-relevant vocational qualification recognized by the national competent authorities, e.g., Ministry of Education, employers' associations, etc.

Tertiary education: Tertiary education builds on secondary education, providing learning activities in specialized fields of education. It aims at learning at a high level of complexity and specialization. Tertiary education includes what is commonly understood as academic education but also includes advanced vocational or professional education. It comprises short-cycle tertiary education, Bachelor's or equivalent level, Master's or equivalent level, and doctoral or equivalent level, respectively. The content of programs at the tertiary level is more complex and advanced than in lower levels. The term "post-secondary education" is also widely used.

Transitional education plan: A national policy instrument, developed under the leadership and responsibility of state authorities (national or regional). In situations where longer-term planning or the implementation of an existing ESP is compromised by contextual uncertainties, a TEP enables the state and its partners (development, humanitarian, and civil society) to develop a structured plan that will maintain progress towards ensuring the right to education and longer-term educational goals.

TEPs are generally three-year plans. They seek to address immediate needs and reduce the risk of future crises. TEPs include a strong focus on strengthening system capacity, with the aim of developing capacities for the preparation of an ESP by the end of the TEP implementation period. TEPs do not necessarily cover the full education sector. They target a smaller number of priorities and generally include a range of selected priorities that support the transition from emergency responses to longer-term development. TEPs require less time to prepare (generally less than 12 months).

Triangulation: The use of more than one method or source of data in the study of a social phenomenon so that findings may be cross-checked.

V

Vulnerable groups: Segments of the population that are more susceptible to experiencing harm, discrimination, or disadvantage due to various factors such as their social, economic, geographic location, or physical circumstances. These groups may face increased risks, have limited access to resources or opportunities, and require specific support and protection to ensure their well-being and equal participation in society. Vulnerable groups can vary across different contexts, but some common examples include children, elderly, persons with disabilities, women and girls, ethnic and racial minorities, people who are LGBTQIA+, immigrants and migrants, refugees, displaced persons, etc. It is important to note that these groups are not mutually exclusive, and individuals can belong to multiple vulnerable groups simultaneously.

W

Wellbeing: The condition of holistic health and the process of achieving this condition. It refers to physical, emotional, social, and cognitive health. Wellbeing includes what is good for a person: participating in a meaningful social role; feeling happy and hopeful; living according to good values, as locally defined; having positive social relations and a supportive environment; coping with challenges using positive life skills; having security, protection, and access to quality services. Important aspects of wellbeing include: biological, material, social, spiritual, cultural, emotional, and mental (see cognitive).

Y

Young people: The term 'young people' is a fluid concept with no fixed definition. It encompasses concepts such as 'youth' and 'adolescents'. For instance, the UN defines youth as persons aged 15 to 24 years, but in some contexts, this age can range up to 35. Within a country or culture, there can be different ages at which an individual is considered to be mature enough to be entrusted by society with certain tasks. In emergency situations, young people have needs that are different from those of younger children and adults. "Young people" refers to those in a period of progression towards independent responsibility. Definitions vary from one context to another depending on socio-cultural, institutional, economic, and political factors.

ANNEX 2: INDEX

ANNEX 3: RELEVANT LEGAL INSTRUMENTS

International legal instruments, soft law, and global frameworks underpinning the INEE MS

International legal instruments and related soft law

Convention Relating to the Status of Stateless Persons (1954)

Convention Relating to the Status of Refugees (1951) (Articles 3, 22)

International Covenant on Civil and Political Rights (1966) (Article 2)

International Covenant on Economic, Social and Cultural Rights (1966) (Articles 2, 13, 14)

International Convention on the Elimination of all Forms of Racial Discrimination (1969) (Articles 5, 7)

Convention on the Elimination of All Forms of Discrimination against Women (1979) (Article 10)

Rome Statute of the International Criminal Court (1998) (Article 8(2)(b)(ix) and 8(2)(e)(iv))

Guiding Principles on Internal Displacement (non-binding) (1998) (Paragraph 23)

UNESCO Universal Declaration on Cultural Diversity (2001) (Article 5)

Convention on the Rights of Persons with Disabilities (2006) (Article 24)

United Nations Declaration on the Rights of Indigenous Peoples (2007) (Article 14)

United Nations General Assembly Resolution on the Right to Education in Emergency Situations (2010)

United Nations Security Council Resolution 2601 - the protection of education in armed conflict (2021)

Fourth Geneva Convention (1949) (Articles 3, 24, 50) and Additional Protocol II (1977) (Article 4.3 (a))

Universal Declaration of Human Rights (1948) (Articles 2, 26)

Convention on the Rights of the Child (1989) (Articles 2, 22, 28, 29, 30, 38, 39)

Global frameworks and soft law

Code of Conduct for the International Red Cross and Red Crescent Movement and Non-Governmental Organizations (NGOs) in Disaster Relief

Comprehensive School Safety Framework

Core Humanitarian Standard on Quality and Accountability

Education 2030: Incheon Declaration and Framework for Action

Global Compact for Safe, Orderly and Regular Migration (2018)

Global Compact on Refugees (2018)

Global Convention on the Recognition of Qualifications concerning Higher Education (2023)

New York Declaration for Refugees and Migrants (2016)

New Ways of Working (2017)

Protection Principles of the UN High Commissioner for Refugees

Safe Schools Declaration (2015)

Sendai Framework for Disaster Risk Reduction (2015)

Sphere Humanitarian Charter

The Grand Bargain (2016)

The 2030 Agenda for Sustainable Development (2015) (Sustainable Development Goal 4)